THE HEA

Dr. Toby Musgrave is a horticulturist and garden historian, and author of a number of books including the best-selling *The Plant Hunters*, *An Empire of Plants*, *The Seven Deadly Sins of Gardening*, *Courtyard Gardens* and *Cottage Gardens*. Presenter of the DVD *Your First Garden Made Easy*, Toby designs gardens around the world and lectures widely on garden history and garden design. For more information visit www.TobyMusgrave.com

THE HEAD GARDENERS

Forgotten Heroes of Horticulture

TOBY MUSGRAVE

*Hortis qui praesunt, vos nunc priscosque ministros
rite salutamus: floreat omne genus.*

DR ARMAND D'ANGOUR 2007

to Vibeke
for everything
my love and thanks

———◆———

First published 2007 by Aurum Press Limited
7 Greenland Street
London NW1 0ND
www.aurumpress.co.uk

This paperback edition first published in 2009 by Aurum Press

A catalogue record for this book is available from the British Library.

ISBN   978 1 84513 411 2

3   5   7   9   10   8   6   4   2
2009   2011   2013   2012   2010

Designed in Adobe Caslon by Peter Ward
Typeset by Saxon Graphics, Derby
Printed and bound in the UK by CPI Bookmarque, Croydon, CR0 4TD

CONTENTS

Acknowledgements   vi
Introduction   vii

Chapter 1 – In the Beginning   1

Chapter 2 – The Eighteenth Century   23

Chapter 3 – Education and Apprenticeship   52

Chapter 4 – The Practical Working Life of a Trainee   69

Chapter 5 – The Head Gardener   90

Chapter 6 – The Head Gardeners' Contributions   107

Chapter 7 – Paxton of Chatsworth   151

Chapter 8 – Barnes of Bicton   184

Epilogue   216
Appendix A   220
Bibliography   230
Notes   233
Index   243

ACKNOWLEDGEMENTS

I am grateful for the permission of Her Majesty Queen Elizabeth II to make use of the material from the Royal Archives at Windsor Castle.

My thanks to all who have helped in the production of this tome. Especially to Dr Armand D'Angour for taking the time and interest to compose such an appropriate elegiac couplet, Chris Jones for her hospitality and conviviality, Dr Brent Elliott and the staff of the Lindley Library, the staff of the Rare Books Room at the University of Cambridge Library, and Penrhyn Castle, National Trust for kind permission to reproduce the oral archive of Norman Thomas. Thanks also to Sarah Dalkin and all at Aurum Press. Of course to Vibeke and Tasso. And last, but not least, to all head gardeners past and present who have made and continue to make gardens such a beautiful and pleasurable part of life.

INTRODUCTION

Adam could be called the first head gardener, for the practice of making gardens both as a form of art and for the production of edible crops is as old as civilisation itself. How far back gardening can be traced in England is, however, a matter of conjecture. Certainly the Romans brought to these shores both gardening skills and new plants, including varieties of rose, the vine and the sweet chestnut (*Castanea sativa*). The craft of horticulture was subsequently preserved behind the walls of monastic establishments during the Dark Ages before later invaders, the Normans, brought more new plants and more new ideas. A glance through any book on the subject of British garden history reveals that as successive centuries passed, and garden fashions came and went, so hundreds of great gardens were made by Lord this, Earl that, or Duke the other. These wealthy noblemen, and later, the socially aspirant *nouveaux riches* certainly footed the bills, but the physical creation and practical management of grand ornamental grounds and bounteous kitchen gardens required a large labour force overseen by a skilled and expert head gardener.

CHANGING ROLES OF THE GARDENER

It is the Pipe Rolls (or royal accounts) from the reigns of Henry III, and subsequently Edward I, that contain the first named English gardener – one Edmund the Gardener, who received 2½ pence per day for his work at Windsor Castle (Berkshire) between 1256 and 1277. Edmund's epithet gives his profession but tells little of what he actually did; indeed for several hundred years after the Norman Conquest, the word 'gardener' was widely used as a general term. Before 1606 and the Royal Charter that established the Company of Gardeners, a gardener could be anyone 'of various skills and often diverse social standing',[1] while the term itself encompassed 'botanist, florist, forester, fruiter, fruit grower, garden implement dealer, green grocer, herbalist, horticulturist, sundriesman, landscape gardener, market gardener, nurseryman, plant merchant, seedsman and sower'.[2]

In the following three centuries, however, the horticulture industry evolved, diversified and became more sophisticated; so that by the turn of the nineteenth century there were demarcated but inter-related specialisms. The market gardener grew edible crops for market, while the landscape gardener designed gardens. Orchardmen produced and sold fruit trees, seedsmen sold seed, and florists raised and sold 'new varieties of a limited range of bulbs and fibrous-rooted plants, which became known as Florists' Flowers'.[3] Nurserymen supplied a wider range of ornamental plants, be they run of the mill varieties or more sought-after items such as large specimens or rare plants from abroad. And the master or head gardener was a man charged with the responsibility of managing, maintaining and developing both the ornamental and productive gardens associated with a large country house estate.

However, one aspect of the head gardener's story that changes little down the centuries is the paucity of information about the men themselves. Not surprisingly, the closer we come to the modern day, the more information was generated and has survived. But for the largest part of the past millennium or so, the head gardener remains an unsung and elusive hero – his name and something of his works may have survived, but little about the man himself.

What is a matter of record is that the head gardener emerged as a man of influence within the spheres of horticulture and botany during the seventeenth and, more notably, the eighteenth century. Certain head gardeners did become famous – but often for another reason: in the eighteenth century, for example, 'Capability' Brown as a landscape designer, Philip Miller an author, and James Gordon a nurseryman. But it was in the nineteenth century that the head gardener's star rose to its zenith, a position it held until the outbreak of the First World War. The stereotype of a head gardener of this period is a ferocious-looking, conspicuously bewhiskered chap, sporting a bowler hat, waistcoat and long apron; his fearsome demeanour consistent with his position as autonomous ruler of a large domain who terrorised his staff and employer alike. The engravings and, later, the photographs, of head gardeners of this time do nothing to belie this myth; nor does the behaviour of some notorious miscreants. In spite of their formidable appearance, however, the vast majority of head gardeners were honest men who worked exceedingly hard for a poor wage. Thus another truism that has remained constant down the centuries is that head gardeners do not so much have a job as a vocation – a vocation which is undertaken for the love of the work and certainly not for the financial reward! The names of many of the nineteenth century's head gardeners are a matter of record, but with the possible exception of Sir Joseph Paxton of Chatsworth (Derbyshire) have been forgotten. In many instances, their gardens are still extant, albeit shadows of their former glories – Battersea Park (London), Belvoir (Leicestershire), Bicton Park (Devon), Cliveden (Buckinghamshire), Elvaston Castle (Derbyshire) and Shrubland Park (Suffolk) to name but half-a-dozen. But even though head gardeners of some of the century's finest gardens were 'stars' within their gardening world, who today remembers John Gibson, William Ingram, James Barnes, John Fleming, William Barron and Donald Beaton, or what they achieved?

SKILLS AND CHARACTERISTICS REQUIRED

In an age without formal horticultural education, and although 'only' a servant, the head gardener had to be intelligent, adaptable and ingenious, and be possessed of superb managerial skills and honed horticultural talent. He achieved his position by successfully demonstrating the resilience and aptitude necessary to endure a long and rigorous apprenticeship. Once appointed, he continued to master all new developments as the science of horticulture and art of garden-making moved forward apace. And if he wished to climb to a position of eminence, he had to help drive that progress. Such work was in addition to the daily management of a domain as large as its responsibilities were complex, for the head gardener was tasked to make gardens that were never anything less than perfect. The formal gardens, the ornamental grounds and the conservatory were a 'shop window' for demonstrating his employer's refinement, taste and wealth. As such, they had to be manicured and flawless, filled with rare and exotic plants, and their scale as attention-grabbing as their complexity. No less was demanded from kitchen gardens, for serving the earliest asparagus or the most perfect pineapple at the dining table was another opportunity for one-upmanship. To meet the diversity of demands head gardeners worked at the cutting edge of horticulture, but in spite of what was expected from them, head gardeners were surprisingly poorly paid and under-appreciated. Yet it was these professionals who were the vanguard of the horticultural advances that transformed gardens and gardening who made the nineteenth century the golden age of gardening, and whose influence is still felt today.

It was head gardeners who revolutionised garden fashions. Joseph Paxton with his harmonious co-existence of art and nature at Chatsworth, John Fleming and John Gibson with their new systems of bedding, and Edward Kemp whose *How to Lay Out a Small Garden* (1850) revolutionised suburban villa gardens. It was head gardeners who played a fundamental role in determining what was grown. Controlled hybridisation programmes in private gardens resulted in hundreds of new plants types, many of which became commercially important, be they dessert fruits (Thomas Foster's Seedling grapes), vegetables (Robert Fenn's Jersey Royal potato), or flowers (Peter Grieve's variegated-leaved pelargoniums). It was head gardeners, through their competitive aspirations to win at the great Horticultural Shows, who continually pushed forward the boundaries of plant culture and cultivation. George Johnston pioneered grape and fruit cultivation, winning over £300 in prize money between 1868 and 1875, and the development of the chrysanthemum owed much to Edwin Molyneux, who exhibited and won widely in the 1880s. It was head gardeners whose experiences and horticultural expertise helped expand commercial horticultural industries such as nurseries, fruit farming and market gardening. Indeed, it was a head gardener, John Wills, who founded the entirely new trade of floristry and flower decoration. It was head gardeners who made technical advances that had wider ramifications. Paxton revolutionised glasshouse architecture and set a fashion with 'Hothouses for the Million', while William Barron developed a technique for transplanting mature trees and thus created the first 'instant gardens'. And it was head gardeners who passed on their philosophy and techniques to a much wider audience through books and the new phenomenon of the popular, weekly gardening magazine which influenced the shape and content of gardens at every social level.

The education and apprenticeship, life and work, and contributions of the nineteenth-century head gardener are examined in detail in subsequent chapters, together with case studies featuring two of the most significant gardeners of the era – Sir Joseph Paxton and James Barnes. But it is always wise to start a story at the beginning, and so the first two chapters set the scene and reveal how the world and role of the head gardener evolved in the years to the nineteenth century.

CHAPTER I

In the Beginning

From mediæval times until the twentieth century, as with most other crafts, the education of a head gardener was a matter of an apprenticeship and working one's way up through the ranks. Practical gardening skills were passed on from the master by demonstration, emulation and word-of-mouth. The level of literacy amongst gardeners in the years before the nineteenth century when a mastery of the three Rs became a prerequisite to an apprenticeship must be a matter of speculation. Some or most master gardeners would perforce have been literate in order to maintain records and accounts, and from the eighteenth century some apprentices must also have been literate as publishers began to print books targeted specifically at this readership. However, in earlier centuries there were no books. Indeed, the first British gardening book, the anonymous *The crafte of graftynge & plantynge of trees* was published by the press of Wynkyn de Worde in *c*.1520. By 1550, if the various editions are also counted, some twenty works had appeared.[1] However, it is Thomas Hill's *The profitable arte of gardening* (1568) that is considered to be the first general gardening book to be published in England.[2] Hill subsequently wrote a second gardening manual – *The Gardeners Labyrinth* (1577) and both tomes provided practical information about the art and craft of gardening and garden-making. Given the cost of books at the time, it is reasonable to assume that Hill's readership would not have been the head gardener but the garden owner. The books would have been an expensive but useful reference source and afforded the employer the knowledge to communicate with his head gardener from an informed standpoint.

In some cases little has changed in over 400 years. Today's gardener would surely agree with Hill in his first chapter of *The Gardeners Labyrinth* entitled 'The Art of Gardening' that:

> Seeing a fruitfull and pleasant Garden, can not be had without good skill
> and diligent minde of the Gardener on matter of the ground, neither can

1

The ſecond part of the Gar⸗
deners Labyrinth, vttering ſuche skilfull
experiences and vvorthy ſecretes, about the parti
cular ſowing and remouyng of the moſt Kitchin
herbes, with the wittie ordering of other daynſie
Herbes, deleſtable flowers, pleaſant fruites, and fyne rootes, as the
like hath not heeretofore bin vttered of any. Beſides the
Phiſicke benefites of each herbe annexed, with
the commoditie of waters diſtilled out
of them, ryghte neceſſarye to
be knowen.

The second part of The Gardeners Labyrinth, *published in 1577 by Thomas Hill.*
While most information within the covers of this book focused on the productive
gardens, from an early time gardens were clearly also a place of beauty and relaxation.

profit arise by Gardening, without cost and charges therein bestowed:
neither perfectly can it be attained without Art, instructing the due seasons
of the yeare:[3]

It may be that Hill himself was a master gardener, for *The Gardeners Laby-*
rinth was published under the pseudonym of Didymus Mountain. Certainly,

a Richard Mounteyn was paid £2 5s 6d at Christmas 1545 as keeper of King Henry VIII's garden at St James'; and a Mountain Jennings was later chief gardener to the first Earl of Salisbury at Hatfield House (Hertfordshire). Or did Hill, by 190 years, pre-date the clever marketing technique used to popularise John Abercrombie's *Every Man his own Gardener* (1767) and paid a respected 'name' to front an unknown author (see pages 48–9)?

EARLY PRODUCTIVE GARDENS

Early gardening books provide a direct insight into gardening of the time, and not surprisingly their contents were heavily slewed towards the edible garden. The kitchen or productive garden has always been enclosed in order to prevent theft (both animal and human) and to provide a sheltered environment in which to cultivate. The form of enclosure could be a thick hedge, probably of prickly quickthorn (*Crataegus monogyna*), or preferably a wall. The latter not only offered a greater level of security and protection but also an additional growing surface against which to train fruit trees. In order that the wall-trained fruit received the most heat, brick walls were preferred because brick absorbs, and subsequently radiates out, solar heat more efficiently than stone. Indeed, many of the new varieties of top fruit obtained from France and the Low Countries by the likes of Richard Harris and John Tradescant the Elder in the sixteenth and seventeenth centuries required the additional shelter to protect their blossom from late frosts and the extra warmth to ripen their fruit. To maximise the cropping area, fruit trees were trained and shaped – fans for almonds, apricots, morello cherries, nectarines and peaches, and espaliers for the more vigorous fruits such as apples, certain cherries, pears and plums. From the seventeenth century onwards, the latter were often grafted on to dwarfing root stock to reduce their height.

OPEN GROUND LAYOUT

The central space enclosed by the walls given over to raising crops and flowers was known as the 'open ground'. Of square or rectangular shape, it was divided by access paths into two, four, six or eight 'quarters', each of which was then subdivided. In the Middle Ages, both utilitarian monastic and ornamental Norman gardens favoured raised beds in which to grow plants, and so by the time Hill came to describe the system in his *The Gardeners Labyrinth*, it was a centuries' old practice. However, his description reveals to what point the technique had evolved, and more importantly how the garden was laid out. Hill recommended that the borders below the wall or hedge be planted with herbs or flowers, while the open ground be divided into quarters by paths 3–4ft (0.91–1.22m) wide and surfaced with hard-packed sand or gravel. Such loose materials were hard-wearing and reflected the heat but gravel, especially, became mucky. Within the quarters the beds were to be up to 12ft (3.65m) long and at most 5ft (1.52m) wide – narrow enough to be cultivated from both sides without walking on them – and raised 1 to 2ft (0.30 to 0.61m). To allow access and aid drainage, the individual raised beds were separated by shallow trenches 1ft (0.30m) wide, while the trenches between the different sections within a quarter were 3½ft (1.06m) wide.

The quarters containing vegetables, Hill suggested, should be enclosed by a low wooden post and rail fence and surrounded by narrow flowerbeds planted with flowering favourites such as various types of *Dianthus* spp. (sweet William, carnation and pink), *Primula* spp. (cowslips and primroses), columbines, hollyhocks, iris and peonies. Within the beds were grown what Hill called 'herbes, rootes and salletts', not in rows but as a broadcast mix of seeds so that the flowers, medicinal herbs and vegetables all grew together in happy abandon. Thus, the enclosed, late-sixteenth-century gardens were multi-skilling. They were places of recreation as well as cultivation, of utility as much as beauty, and as such ornamented variously with bowers, arbours, seats, trellis-covered walks and raised beds formed into geometric patterns.

WHAT WAS GROWN

Growing edibles and medicinal plants is as old as gardening. Advice on cultivation makes up much of the contents of Cato the Elder's sole-surviving intact work, *De Agri Cultura* (*c*.160 BC), and later, such crops were essential to monastic self-sufficiency. From the time of the Norman Conquest until the sixteenth century, growing fruits, vegetables and herbs fell into the category of husbandry; that is to say provisioning the household all year round, a subject that also embraced growing cereals and field crops, planting orchards, the maintenance of pasture and the raising of animals. This was the subject of one of the most popular books of the sixteenth century – Thomas Tusser's (1524?–1580) *Five hundred pointes of good husbandrie* (1573).

The evolution of the productive garden was tied closely with what was available to grow. John Harvey in his authoritative *Mediæval Gardens* (1981) provides a revealing summary of plant introductions in the years up to the seventeenth century. From early sources it appears that in *c.* 800 there were approximately 100 taxa (a taxonomic category, as a species or genus) in cultivation, of which most were domesticated natives or early introductions by the Romans and exchanges between monastic houses. Over the next six centuries this number slowly rose to approximately 250 taxa. It was the Norman Conquest that stimulated the trickle of new plant arrivals. By the start of the thirteenth century borage was here, and by mid-century it was joined by the almond and lavender. Known to Ibn Bassal in Spain by 1080, the cabbage was mentioned as growing in the garden at Lambeth Palace in London in 1322, as were colewort, cucumbers and the gourd (*Lagenaria vulgaris*). In 1341 a reference is made to eating broad beans green, rather than as a field crop. Balm, clary, liquorice and mandrake were also all probably fourteenth-century arrivals, and certainly saffron was being cultivated soon after the mid-century.

In the fifteenth century new arrivals began coming from France including celery, red (orange) carrots, and cauliflower (although it was not seriously cultivated until the seventeenth century). Other fifteenth-century arrivals were dock patience or monk's rhubarb, basil, costmary, fenugreek and true spinach; and at the end of the century, the pea, which like the bean had been grown as a field crop, was improved by the gardener of the Hospital of St Mary of Roncesvalles at Charing Cross in London who produced the Rounceval pea whose fame lasted several centuries. But isolated in northern Europe far away from the excitements of the Renaissance, it took time for new plants to make their way to these shores, and some introductions came surprisingly late. The globe artichoke was being grown by Filippo Strozzi in the Florentine gardens of Villa Paradiso in 1460, but it did not cross the Channel until after 1500; similarly it was the sixteenth century before the parsnip, asparagus, the kidney bean, true endive and hops were first widely grown. Cultivation of the latter was stimulated by the shift in brewing from ale to beer. The earliest evidence of head lettuce is 1543.

Geoffrey Chaucer (*c.*1343–1400) gives an insight into the fruits grown, calling 'homely' or well-known, apple, bullace, cherry, hazel, medlar, peach, pear, plum, quince and service. A monk of St Albans writing about 1382 names in addition: blackberry, crab apples, gooseberry, mulberry, sloe, strawberry and walnut. It is also possible that the fig was here by the mid-fourteenth century, and legend has it Thomas à Becket planted the first fig at Tarring (Sussex) on his return from Rome in the middle of the twelfth century.

HOTBEDS

The soil in the open ground, exactly because it was open to the elements, warmed up and cooled down with the seasons. Thus it could not be expected to be productive in the winter months. However, it was discovered as early as Roman times that hardy crops can be 'forced' into harvest out of their natural season, and tender crops grown in cold climates, if they are provided with supplementary heat. The apparatus used to make the kitchen garden productive for a longer part of the year was the hotbed, which relied on the heat given off during the natural decomposition of manure.

Although both the Romans and the Moors in tenth-century Spain used hotbeds, it was our friend Hill who first suggested their use in an English gardening book, although it is probable that their use had been widespread for centuries. Hotbeds were usually created in an area screened off from the rest of the walled garden, and which in subsequent centuries became known as the frame yard. This was done for aesthetic and olfactory reasons – the creation and maintenance of hotbeds with their necessary dung-heaps, were not the garden's most attractive nor its most sweetly scented feature! In 1706 London and Wise described the ideal hotbed in *The retir'd gard'ner* – 4ft (1.22m) high, the same breadth and composed of horse manure covered with 8 or 9in (20.32 to 22.86cm) of mould. After about eight days it would have generated enough heat for planting, and when necessary was re-heated with fresh dung – although this was a delicate job if the plants growing in the hotbed were not to be damaged. A quarter-of-a-century later, Philip Miller, in his famous *The gardener's dictionary* (see page 31) highlighted the importance of hotbeds:

> Hot-beds are of general use in these Northern Parts of Europe, without which we could not enjoy so many of the Products of warmer Climes as

we do now; nor could we have the Tables furnished with the several Products of the Garden, during the Winter and Spring months, as they are at present in most parts of England, better than in any other Country in Europe; for altho' we cannot boast of the Clemency of our Climate, yet England is better furnished with all Sorts of esculent Plants for the Table, much earlier in the Season, and in greater Quantities, than any of our Neighbours; which is owing to our skill in Hot-beds.

Miller goes on to list some of the out-of-season crops that grew well on hotbeds. In January it was possible to harvest asparagus planted the previous autumn and a wide range of salad herbs – burnet, chervil, coriander, various types of cress, radish, mint, mustard, rape, tarragon, turnips. More salad crops and aromatic and pot-herbs including hyssop, lavender, marjoram, rosemary, Swiss chard, thyme and winter savory in February. And in March, a second crop of asparagus, cucumbers, kidney beans, peas and purslane, together with the usual salads and herbs. Later in the seventeenth century John Evelyn used hotbeds to grow tender exotics such as canna (*Canna Indica*), the Marvel of Peru (*Mirabilis jalapa*) and tuberose (*Polianthes tuberosa*).[4]

EARLY HEAD GARDENERS

As is the case with the name of Edmund the Gardener, it is surviving royal household accounts which provide much of the best early information about gardeners. The accounts of the king who was on the throne while the business of horticultural publishing was in its infancy – Henry VIII (1491–1547) – offer another glimpse into the realm of royal gardening from the perspective of those who did the work. Sadly it is only a glimpse because the details are scarce and patchy, and offer little if anything in the way of information about the men themselves, their lives or jobs.

Henry was a particularly enthusiastic enjoyer of gardens, an avid gardenmaker and passionate consumer of home-grown fruit and vegetables. Each of his royal gardens had its own head gardener. As well as the aforementioned Richard Mounteyn, both Robert Pury at Wanstead (Essex) and William Rutter at Windsor (Berkshire) were paid £4 per annum. For the manor of Chelsea in *c.*1543 'Henry Russell of Westminster, gardener' was paid 13s 4d for '2 banks of Rosemary by him brought to be set within the

King's Garden' and 26s 8d for six borders of lavender together with 3 loads of 'Calesse' sand for the great bowling alley.[5] Jasper, the gardener at Beaulieu (New Hall in Essex), was deemed a particularly skilled gardener with a talent for supplying the unusual. For not only was his salary of £12 3s 4d (or 8d a day) plus livery and housing three times that of Pury and Rutter, but he also received occasional, additional rewards for special services such as bringing artichokes, cucumbers and strawberries and various herbs to the king. Thus by the mid-sixteenth century gardeners could be specialists. Another such was John Lovell, who began his career at Greenwich, and by 1528 had risen to gardener at Richmond (Surrey) where he was responsible for supplying the King's table with fruit and nuts including damsons, filberts, grapes and pears, as well as flowers and 'sweet waters' (distillations). Henry even had a 'fruiterer', Richard Harris, who in 1533 introduced from France and the Low Countries numerous grafts of fruit trees, including many new Pippins (types of apple).[6]

In terms of who actually designed Henry's gardens, there is no doubt that the monarch himself took an active role in the process, but he also made use of the services of an expert. Even up until a week before his death Henry was making changes and improvements to his gardens, for on 21 January 1547 he authorised payment of £20 to Jehan Le Leu, a priest, who was to bring 'trees and sets of sundry kinds out of the realm of France'. The anglicised name of this priest-gardener was John Wolf, who is supposed to have introduced the apricot to England, probably in 1542. However, as with so many head gardeners down the years, even if their names are known, there is little if anything known about the man. And the word 'man' is used advisedly, for while women certainly did work in gardens – the fourteenth-century rolls of Ely Cathedral in Cambridgeshire list payments to women for weeding and digging vines, and sixteenth-century account books name 'weeder women' employed in the Privy Garden at Hampton Court Palace in Richmond-upon-Thames and at Hardwick Hall (Derbyshire) – it was not until 1891 that Swanley Horticultural College (Kent) became the first institution in England to offer women the opportunity to study for a formal horticultural education.

From what little is known about Wolf, he was called variously 'planter of grafts', 'maker and devisour [*sic*] of the King's arbours' and *confector viridariorum* (layer-out of gardens),[7] it appears he was Henry's head-gardener-in-chief. A skilled horticulturist and procurer of new plants, he was well thought of by the king, who in March 1538 granted him an annuity for life of 20 marks (£13 6s 8d). Much later in life Wolf published a translation from French of the snappily entitled *A short instruction veric* [sic] *profitable and necessarie for all those who delight in gardening, to know the time and season when it is good to sow and replant all manner of seedes* (1591), followed three years later by *The orchard, and garden: containing certyaine necessarie, secret, and ordinarie knowledge in grafting and garden.*

It is likely that Wolf designed Henry's new gardens at the Palace of Whitehall in London in the first half of the 1540s, and prior to that, and more significantly, Henry's first and greatest garden, at Hampton Court Palace, which was commenced in the early 1530s. The cost here was enormous – between 1538 and 1545 alone Henry spent £16,686 on the garden, the finances coming from the profits derived from the Dissolution of the Monasteries which began in 1536. And the garden was all about making a dynastic statement of regal power. Behinds its walls, the Privy Garden was laid out with walks passing between and around eight large, square grass plats or lawns, each defined by wooden railings painted in Henry's colours of green and white. Ornament was in the form of complicated topiary, twenty sundials and King's Beasts – carved heraldic emblems raised on posts. The self-explanatory Mount, its slopes planted with ornamentals, was crowned by a large banqueting house reached by a path that wound its way up the slope. And last but not least was the series of pond gardens, also ornamented with King's Beasts.

Henry's daughter, Elizabeth I (1533–1603), was canny enough to spare herself the expense of creating royal gardens for her pleasure by 'encouraging' her nobles to do so for her, and then 'rewarding' them with a hugely costly stay during one of her progresses. She also inherited her father's love of fruit, being particularly partial to cherries – so much so that her noblemen went to great lengths to get the fruit to ripen out of season. Sir Frances Carew of Beddington Park in what is now the London Borough of Sutton even managed to delay ripening by almost two months to coincide with her visit in August 1599. This retardation he achieved by covering the trees while the fruit was unripe with light matting or damp canvas. However, without royal stimulus, ornamental garden-making stagnated, particularly when compared to what was happening in Italy, where the great Renaissance gardens such as Villa d'Este (1550–80) and Villa Lante (1573–90) were being created.

THE SEVENTEENTH CENTURY

The seventeenth century was a very dynamic and volatile one, full of extremes. It began on a peaceful note in 1604, when a year after his accession James I (1566–1625) negotiated the Treaty of London. This put an end to the twenty-year-long Anglo-Spanish war, and in the subsequent peace, the first permanent English settlement was established in what would become America at Jamestown, Virginia in 1607. Thus began the first phase of great colonial expansion, and as the century progressed, the eastern colonies were developed, parts of Canada's Atlantic provinces acquired, and a number of Caribbean islands, including St Kitts, Barbados and Jamaica, colonised.

The century also saw great disruption and strife wrought by civil war and regicide; but such events must be set against great advances in the fields of scientific discovery and artistic attainment. William Harvey (1578–1657) revolutionised medicine when he proposed his hypothesis concerning the circulation of blood in 1616; Robert Boyle (1627–91) advanced the sciences of chemistry and physics and is remembered for Boyle's Law ($PV=k$); and Robert Hooke (1635–1703), a polymath, who as well as being a friend of Boyle and Sir Christopher Wren, formulated Hooke's Law of Elasticity ($F= -kx$) and through his studies of microscopy, coined the term 'cell'. In the field of the arts, architecture was stunned by the works of Wren (1632–1723), who designed and built the Sheldonian Theatre in Oxford, St Paul's Cathedral in London and Hampton Court Palace, to name but three. The wood carvings of Grinling Gibbons (1648–1721) were without compare anywhere in Europe. And ornamental garden design advanced dramatically in response to stimuli from the Renaissance and the Baroque.

James was a great gardening monarch and on 18 September 1606 he established gardening as a recognised profession when he incorporated by Royal Charter of 'The Master, Warden, Assistants and Commonality of the Company of Gardeners of London'. The Worshipful Company of Gardeners of London, which had begun life as a mediæval crafts guild and had been first mentioned in the City Corporation records in 1345, now had a Charter that defined the operations it controlled. To whit: 'the trade, crafte or mysterie of Gardening, planting, grafting, setting, sowing, cutting, arboring, rocking, mounting, covering, fencing and removing of plantes, herbes, seedes, fruites, trees, stocks, setts, and of contriving the conveyances to the same'.[8] One of the Guild's first tasks was the instigation of a seven-year apprenticeship.

At the time of James's accession, English garden design lagged far behind continental Europe in terms of artistic achievement. But now, with a generally peaceful Europe, there was an influx of new ideas for the first time in seventy-five years. James was a great patron of the arts, but in the vanguard of the garden revolution, and marking the first flush of the English Renaissance garden, were three gardens, two made by his wife, Anne of Denmark at Somerset House and Greenwich Palace (both in London and both *c.*1609), and the third by their son, Henry, Prince of Wales at Richmond Palace (1610–12). In all cases the designer was the Frenchman, Salomon de Caus *(c.*1576–1626), a hydraulic engineer who had visited and studied the great Renaissance gardens of Italy and brought their ethos to England. Subsequently, as the fortunes of the House of Stuart waxed and waned, so garden fashions were successively influenced by France under both Charles the first and the second, and, following the Glorious Revolution of 1688 that brought William III and Mary to the throne, by Holland.

NEW PLANTS

One of the new challenges faced by head gardeners of the time was the successful cultivation of the new plants arriving from the colonies, and in particular, those which did not find the British winter clement. A few new ornamental plant introductions had arrived on these shores in the sixteenth century, brought back directly from the New World by adventurers, or arriving here via France and Spain. Examples include *Tagetes erecta* and *Tropaeolum minus* (1535), *Yucca gloriosa* (*c.*1550), *Mirabilis jalapa*, *Canna indica* and *Passiflora incarna* (*c.*1568) and *Tagetes patula* (1572). Even the potato, a native of Mexico, which arrived in 1586 was initially grown as an ornamental. These exotics were complemented by other new arrivals from the Old World, as plants, long cultivated with great skill in Persia and Europe, gradually made their way across the Channel. Examples of these arrivals include *Eranthis hyemalis* (*c.*1576), *Tulipa gesneriana* (1577), *Fritillaria imperialis* (*c.*1580), *Lilium martagon* (1596) and *Cyclamen hederifolium* (1597). Old World arrivals continued throughout the seventeenth century – for example *Gladiolus imbricatus* (1604), *Helleborus niger*

11

(1629), *Cedrus libani* (*c*.1630), *Rhododendron hirsutu*m (1656), *Hypericum calycinum* (1676) and *Lathyrus odoratus* (1699). But, as Britannia began her ascendancy to rule the waves, so there was an ever-greater influx of new plants from further afield. New lands yielded up new and exciting plants – and in particular from the colonies in North America and South Africa. For example *Zingiber officinale* (1605), *Nicotiana tobacum* (*c*.1613), *Ipomoea purpurea* (1621), *Agapanthus africanus* and *Morus rubra* (1629), *Mimosa pudica* (1637), *Nerine sarniensis* (1659), *Yucca filamentosa* (1675) and *Quercus coccinea* (1691). And towards the end of the century, the ornamental plants of the West Indies were brought to the connoisseur's notice by two publications by Dr (later) Sir Hans Sloane (1660–1753) – *Catalogus plantarum quæ in insula Jamaica sponte proveniunt* (1696) and detailed *Voyage to the Islands of Madeira, Barbados, Nieves, St Christophers and Jamaica between 1687–89* (2 vols, 1707 and 1725).[9]

THE TRADESCANTS AND HATFIELD HOUSE

Rare horticultural treasures and novelties of any provenance were avidly sought and collected by those garden owners wealthy enough to afford such status symbols. One of the most fervent gatherers was Sir Robert Cecil (1563–1612), Secretary of State to both Elizabeth I and James I, who raised him to first Earl of Salisbury in 1605. Two years later James I 'persuaded' Cecil to exchange his mansion and fine gardens of Theobalds near Cheshunt (Hertfordshire), which James loved so much, for nearby Hatfield House plus an additional seventeen manors in twelve counties. Building a new house and gardens in the latest style, Cecil also wanted his garden to be filled with an extensive collection of horticultural rarities.

Cecil's position within government and his closeness to the King meant that those who sought his favour were wont to gift him plants. Marie de Medici (wife of King Henri IV of France), for example, sent 500 fruit trees together with two gardeners to plant them, while Madame de la Broderie (wife of the French ambassador) donated 30,000 vines for the vineyard. However, many of Cecil's treasures were procured for him by his head gardener, John Tradescant the Elder (*c*.1570–1638), about whom much has been written.

Tradescant began at Hatfield in 1610 and an indication of how crucial Cecil saw him to the success of his enterprise was the high salary paid him

– £50 per annum. Tradescant travelled widely to fill Cecil's garden. In the autumn of 1610 he visited the Low Countries and France, obtaining fruit trees including cherries, quince, medlars, Provins roses and flowers. In Haarlem, for example, he purchased 800 tulip bulbs for 10s. per hundred, as well as arbor-vitae (*Thuja occidentalis*), which had come from the French colonies in Canada as early as 1536. From Leiden, came new varieties of gillyflowers (*Dianthus caryophyllus*) and 'fortye frittelaries' at 3d. each.

Sadly, Cecil did not live to see his dream garden realised, and after working for his heir for a couple of years, Tradescant moved on to be head gardener to Edward Lord Wotton at Canterbury (Kent) from about 1615 until 1623. During this time he travelled with Sir Dudley Digges to Russia in 1618, and in 1620–1 sailed on HMS *Mercury* as part of a fleet sent to the Mediterranean to worry the Barbary pirates. The former expedition yielded hellebores, European larch (*Larix decidua*), a purple crane's-bill and *Rosa acicularis*, 'the wild bryer of Muscovia'. On the latter trip he found a particularly fine variety of apricot, a purple clover (*Trifolium* spp.) and a *Cistus*. Becoming an 'adventurer' of the Virginia Company in 1617 also opened up the opportunity to acquire plants from the new colonies in Virginia. Tradescant's introductions from North America include the spiderwort (*Tradescantia virginiana*), Virginia creeper (*Parthenocissus quinquefolia*) and stag's horn sumach (*Rhus typhina*).

Next, Tradescant moved to Newhall (Essex) where he richly filled the garden for his new employer, the royal favourite, Lord Buckingham; and following Buckingham's assassination in 1630 he was appointed Keeper of the royal gardens to Queen Henrietta Maria at Oatlands (Surrey) on a substantial salary of £100 per annum. This post he held until his death in 1638 when it passed to his son, John the Younger (*bap.*1608–62). Both father and son developed their garden in South Lambeth, London, gathering together a notable collection of rare and unusual plants (as well as the Ark, a museum of curiosities, purchased on the death of the younger Tradescant by Elias Ashmole and which formed part of what became the Ashmolean Museum in Oxford). There is some suggestion, too, that the elder Tradescant also functioned as a garden consultant to various aristocrats associated with the court, and in 1636 advised on the laying out of the new Botanic Garden at Oxford. England's first, its inception was the brainchild of the Earl of Danby who had founded it in 1621.

ROYALTY RETURNS

Following the Commonwealth (1649–60), when ornamental gardens were considered by the Puritans to be far too frivolous, the return of Charles II (1630–85) in 1660 breathed new life into gardening. Charles, who had spent part of his exile in France, brought back with him many fashionable French ideas, and two gardeners. The Calendar of State papers reveal that in June 1661 a warrant was issued 'to pay to Andrew and Gabriel Mollet £240 yearly, for wages as the King's gardeners, and for them to have the lodgings in St James's Park belonging to the gardeners'. This was, in fact, a return visit for the elder brother, André, who had designed gardens at St James's Palace (*c.*1630) and Wimbledon House (1642) for Queen Henrietta Maria (1609–69), the French wife of Charles I (1600–48).

For Henrietta Maria's son, André designed a new formal garden in the French Renaissance style. Of this approach Mollet was an adept practitioner, and may have contributed to it the effect called a *patte d'oeil* or 'goose-foot' – three radiating avenues extending from the central point on a façade, such as can still be seen at Hampton Court Palace. However, the doyen of the French style was André le Nôtre (1613–1700), epitomised by his gardens at Vaux-le-Vicomte which he created for King Louis XIV's finance minister, Nicolas Fouquet, between 1658 and 1661 and subsequently, from 1661, at Versailles for the King himself. With its intense formality, symmetry and balance, the French formal garden was a very definite statement of man's dominance over nature. Based around a main axis, elaborate and intricate *parterres de broderie* – literally embroideries on the ground, the pattern picked out with low-clipped hedges of box and ground coverings of coloured earths, with often an edging of turf – were laid out on a terrace beneath the house windows and ornamented with numerous exotic fountains and statuary; beyond was the areas of tamed woodland through which were driven straight *allées* or walks lined with clipped hedges or trees dividing the area into a regular grid pattern filled with groves of trees or *bosquets*, augmented with fountains, sculpture, statues and buildings; and beyond all this, the extensive *allée*-pierced wilderness of trees.

Charles' new garden was to be made on the flat land abutting the River Thames at Hampton Court Palace, and with it he wished to welcome his Spanish bride, Catherine of Braganza. Work on digging the Long Water took place through the winter of 1661–2 at a cost of £1,446, and although Catherine's reaction to the new garden is not known, within a month or so of her arrival John Evelyn visited on 9 June 1662 and noted in his diary that:

> The Park formerly a flat, naked piece of Ground, now planted with sweete rows of lime-trees, and the Canale for water now neere perfected: also the hare park: In the Garden is a rich & noble fountaine, of Syrens & statues etc: cast in copper by Fanelli, but no plenty of water: the Cradle Walk of horne-beame in the Garden, is for the perplexed twining of the Trees, very observable &c: Another parterr there is which they call Paradise in which a pretty banqueting house, set over a Cave or Cellar; all these Gardens might be exceedingly improved, as being too narrow, for such a Palace.

André Mollet was also the author of *Le Jardin de plaisir* (1651 in Sweden) translated as *The garden of pleasure* (1680) which contained eleven chapters discussing the various types of flowers, herbs and fruits suitable for 'a garden of pleasure', and offered many plates of designs for gardens in the French Renaissance style. The book may have been influential in informing an élite English readership about such intricacies, but it is also a very rare book, so how wide its readership in fact was, can only be guessed at. Certainly, outside royal gardens, the *parterre de broderie* was in fact quite scarce. Some noblemen's gardens, such as those of the Earl of Chesterfield at Bretby (Derbyshire, from 1669), were filled with a formal arrangement of parterres, labyrinths, wildernesses, avenues, fountains, canals, grottoes, aviaries and summerhouses and which emulated Versailles in their complexity and beauty, if not their scale. But on the whole, the combination of England's undulating topography and the English reserve precluded vast linear displays and tempered the flamboyant French style.

Sadly, Gabriel died in 1663 and in an undated petition, probably from the same year, André is referred to as 'Chief gardener in St. James's park'. However, he did not enjoy his new post for long, for on 8 February 1666, came an 'Order for a warrant to pay to John Rose, appointed Keeper of St. James's garden, in place of Andrew and Gabriel Mollet, deceased, £240 a year for wages, for keeping the said garden'. With the Plague rampant during the 1660s it may be that this disease was the cause of the brothers' early demise.[10]

John Rose (1622–77) was born at Amesbury (Wiltshire), the younger son of a yeoman farmer, and probably served his apprenticeship at Amesbury House, the seat of Sir William Seymour, later the Duke of Hertford

This pattern for a parterre de broderie from the English version of André Mollet's The garden of pleasure *(1670) reveals just how complex their design could be – and how much work would be required to keep them in peak condition.*

and the second Duke of Somerset. Moving to London, Rose, according to the author and garden designer Stephen Switzer (*bap* 1682–1745), worked as 'first gardener to the Lord Essex at Essex-house in the Strand'. It was Essex who sent Rose to France for the first time, probably early in the 1640s – a visit that turned out to be very fortuitous, for Rose saw the work of, and may have studied with André Le Nôtre, who was then in his mid-twenties, or under his father Jean (*d.*1655) who was in charge of the parterres at the *grand jardin* of the Tuileries and designer of parterres for all the royal gardens. This experience subsequently placed him in a perfect position to be of assistance to the francophile king. On 14 October 1661 Rose was initially appointed the king's gardener at St James's under Mollet. And it is Rose, who according to Stephen Switzer, was 'esteemed to be the best of his profession in those days' who is supposed to be the figure presenting the first pineapple grown in this country to the king in the famous painting attributed to Hendrik Danckerts (see page 203).

Formal garden design remained the fashion throughout the thirteen-year reign of William III (1650–1702) and Mary II (1662–94) which ended in 1702 with the accession of Queen Anne. But the all-out French style was tempered with ideas such as smaller, more intimate scale, the use of 'clipped greens' (topiary) and wider use of flowers, brought by the royal couple from Holland. Mary also brought her tropical plant collection of exotics from the East Indies. The transfer took place in 1699, and the collection was housed in three purpose-built hothouses, each 55ft (16.76m) long, erected at Hampton Court Palace. The collection, according to the third Christopher Hatton of Kirby Hall (Northamptonshire), contained 'about 400 rare Indian plantes wch. [*sic*] were never seen in England'. Mary now began to expand her collection, dispatching her own plant collectors to the Canary Islands and Virginia, and obtaining seed from the Cape (South Africa), East India and Barbados. Mary not only gave making such collections the royal seal of approval, but she was so passionate about plants that in late 1690 or early 1691 she appointed Dr Leonard Plukenet as her personal botanist on a salary of £200 per annum.

This was the same salary paid to George London (*d*.1714) who in 1688 had been appointed Master Gardener and Deputy Superintendent of the Royal Gardens by William Bentinck, King William's great friend whom he had made both the first Earl of Portland and Superintendent of the Royal Gardens. London had proved his royal allegiance by assisting his previous employer, Henry Compton (1632–1713), Bishop of London, in getting Princess Anne (Mary's sister) out of London and away from any danger during the turbulent times between William landing and her father, James II, leaving England. However, when Anne ascended the throne, she showed her gratitude by sacking London and replacing him with his friend and business partner Henry Wise (1653–1738)! On the Queen's explicit instructions – she both detested her dead brother-in-law and hated the smell of box – Wise was ordered to rip out most of what William and Mary had planted at Hampton Court Palace.

London had been apprenticed to John Rose sometime in the period from 1661 to 1667, and Rose, recognising London's talents and perhaps remembering his visit sponsored by the Earl of Essex, sent London to France to study the gardens. Another great influence on London was Bishop Compton, who according to Switzer, was his 'Great Encourager', employing him in 1675 as head gardener at Fulham Palace in London. Compton was one of the great horticulturists and collectors of his day, and a very generous man, giving wide access to his garden, and giving away many plants. Again, according to Switzer:

> This Reverend Father was one of the first that encouraged the
> importation, raising, and increase of exoticks, in which he was the most

curious man in that time, or perhaps will be in any age; and by the
recommendation of chaplains into foreign parts, had like-wise greater
advantages of improving it than any other gentleman could. He had
above 1000 species of exotick plants in his stoves and gardens, in which
last place he had endenizon'd a great many that have been formerly
thought too tender for this cold climate. There were few days in the year,
till towards the latter part of his life, but he was actually in his garden
ordering and directing the removal and replacing of his trees and plants.
A virtuous and laudable pattern, and a person by whom gard'ning has
not a little been recommended to the world.[11]

LONDON AND WISE – THE BROMPTON PARK NURSERY

Head gardeners have never made their fortunes being 'just' head gardeners,
and one well-trodden path to financial improvement was to leave one's
position and move into trade. The most successful exponents of this transition were London and Wise who, from 1690 until Wise's retirement in
1717, made the Brompton Park Nursery in London peerless (the site of
the nursery is now under the Natural History and Victoria and Albert
Museums in Kensington). The nursery had been established in 1681 when
London, who was also head gardener to the Earl of Arlington near St
James's Park, and 'two gardens in Bedfordshire, both new' which he had
most likely designed,[12] joined forces with three other head gardeners: Roger
Looker (*d.*1685), gardener to Queen Catherine (wife of Charles II) as well
as another eight great gardens under his management including Hatfield
House; Moses Cook or Cooke (*d.*1715), gardener to the Earl of Essex at
both Hadham Hall and his new creation at Cassiobury (both Hertfordshire), and the author of the excellent work published in 1676 on *The
manner of raising, ordering, and improving forrest-trees*; and John Field
(*d.*1687), gardener to William Russell, the fifth Earl of Bedford, at Woburn
Abbey (Bedfordshire).[13] Two years after the demise of Field, Cook sold his
share to Wise, about whose early life surprisingly little is known, although
he may also have been an apprentice of John Rose. In 1690 London and
Wise became partners and together they made the 100 acres (40.47ha) of
Brompton Park Nursery as financially successful as it was famous. In some
ways, the pair were as one, not unlike Sir John Vanbrugh and Nicholas
Hawksmoor, with London in the field and Wise mostly administering the

nursery, although Wise did work on garden projects, indeed, he worked with Vanbrugh at Blenheim Palace (Oxfordshire) from 1705, overseeing the creation of the new garden. Also an expert on fruit cultivation, in 1708 Wise drew up an exhaustive list of the fruit grown at Blenheim Palace, Hampton Court Palace and Windsor Castle.

Good organisation, innate talent and a superb network of contacts made the nursery highly productive and efficient. Within four years of its inception, for example, it was able to send to Woburn Abbey in a single order 200 apple trees, 100 gooseberries, 100 currants, 50 pears together with mulberries, peaches and nectarines. And for one improvement Windsor Castle were sent 41,150 whitethorn for hedges, hundreds of fruit trees and vines, and 238 spruces clipped into pyramids, each 9ft (2.74m) tall. As well as the 'very brave and noble assembly of the flowery and other trees…evergreens and shrubs' noted by John Evelyn, the nursery also sold vegetables, herbs, fruit trees and flowers. And although the core business was likely to have been trees and shrubs of the more common varieties, rare exotics were also available. The nursery's ability to import and grow exotics probably derived from London's association with Bishop Compton; and cultural skills were so honed that the king over-wintered his 'greens' from Kensington Palace in the nursery's long greenhouse, the front of which was glass and wood and the remainder of which was brick. By 1694 the nursery employed twenty men and two women, each earning 4 shillings a week, and was more than able to deal with the great demand for trees, shrubs and plants that it received from all over the country. Two years later lists of trees, shrubs and exotics grown at the nursery took up a full ten pages in T. Langford's *Plain and full instructions to raise all sorts of fruit-trees that prosper in England*, and in 1705 it was calculated by topographer John Bowack in his *The antiquities of Middlesex* that the stock of the nursery was valued at over £40,000.

The nursery also supplied plants to the other division of the business – garden design. London and, later, Wise set garden fashions for twenty-five years. Working in a style that drew predominantly from the French, but included aspects of the Dutch formal styles, they laid out parterres, canals and elaborate water works, fruit gardens, 'clipped greens', tender evergreens such at citrus, planted wildernesses and avenues – all on a grand scale. Of their activities, Switzer, who had been apprenticed to London in 1699, wrote in his *The Nobleman, Gentleman, and Gardener's Recreation* (1715) 'The planting and raising of all sorts of trees is so much due to this undertaking that 'twill be hard for any of posterity to lay their hands on a tree in any of these kingdoms that have not been a part of their care'. Of London himself, he exclaimed that:

> It will perhaps be hardly believed, in Time to come, that this one Person actually saw and gave Directions, once or twice a Year, in most of the Noblemens and Gentlemens Gardens in England. And since it was common for him to ride 50 or 60 Miles in a Day, he made his Northern Circuit in five or six Weeks, and sometimes less; and his Western in as little Time: As for the South and East, they were but three or four Days Work for him; most times twice a Year visiting all the Country-Seats, conversing with Gentlemen, and forwarding the Business of Gard'ning in such a degree as is almost impossible to describe.

The Brompton Park Nursery's first commission from 1683 was Longleat (Wiltshire) for Lord Weymouth. With each of the four original partners taking month-long stints overseeing the works, the garden, which was subsequently swept away by 'Capability' Brown in 1757, cost an estimated £30,000. Amongst their numerous subsequent commissions were: Woburn Abbey (1683); Chatsworth (1688) where the West Parterre measured 245 by 187ft (74.68 by 57m) and cost £120 and the Great Parterre was a whopping 473 by 227ft (144.17 by 69.19m); Castle Howard (North Yorkshire, 1698); Melbourne Hall (Derbyshire, 1704); Blenheim Palace (1705); and, of course, the royal gardens: Windsor Castle (1683), Hampton Court Palace (1699) and Kensington Palace (1704). Of the royal commissions, the gardens at Hampton Court Palace were the most notable, and the Privy Garden alone required that Wise lower the whole area by a depth of 10ft (3.05m) in order to provide an appropriate foreground to Wren's new wing. In total, about 75 per cent of the £83,000 spent on the royal gardens between 1689 and 1695 is attributable to Hampton Court Palace. However, the very intricate Great Fountain Garden, filled with *parterres de broderie* and laid out under the east front facing the Long Water (from 1689), was designed by a Huguenot, Daniel Marot, who had already worked on William's garden at Het Loo in Holland.

London and Wise also published two books. The first was a translation from the French of *Instructions pour les jardins fruitiers et potagers* by Jean de La Quintinie (1626–88), who was chief director of all of King Louis XIV's gardens. Entitled *The compleat gard'ner...Made English by John Evelyn*

Four plates from The French gardiner *(1658) translated by John Evelyn showing various garden-related scenes, including a parterre, a simple arrangement of raised beds, and women preserving fruits in the kitchen.*

(1693), and although attributed to Evelyn, it is likely that the majority of the translation was the work of London. Certainly he and Wise were responsible for the less-expensive, abridged version (1699).[14] Their second title, *The retir'd gard'ner* (1706) was also a translation, abridgement and adaptation – this time of two French works, François Gentil's *Le jardinier solitaire* and Louis Liger's *Le jardinière fleuriste et historiographe*. The book takes an interesting format of a conversation, or perhaps more aptly, an interrogation of a Gardener by a Gentleman. The latter puts a series of questions to the former, who answers at length. In the chapter entitled 'New Reflections on the Culture of Trees', for example, the Gent asks 'Pray tell me what's the Origine of Sap?' to which the Gardener replies 'I shall take pleasure in satisfying your Request, and letting you know my Opinion of the Matter', before launching into a detailed account which, perhaps more by luck than science, turns out to be a remarkably accurate description. It is explained that sap 'proceeds from the Salt of the Earth' which 'dissolves and mixes itself with all parts of the Earth' and 'communicate themselves afterwards to the Roots of Trees, which are nourished by them'. The book also contains directions for making different types of parterres, which were about to crash from fashion, with illustrations very similar to those in Mollet's *The garden of pleasure*.

However, times and fashions change. War with France in the late seventeenth century saw things French fall from fashion, and as the eighteenth century dawned, there came with it a reawakening and new interpretation of nature. Inspired by a rediscovery of the classics and the Grand Tour taken by every young man of education and means, nature came to influence garden fashions throughout the 1700s.

CHAPTER 2

The Eighteenth Century

INTRODUCTION

The eighteenth century, in particular the second half of it, was a boom time for Britain and not just England, for the Acts of Union of 1706 and 1707 that came into effect on 1 May 1707 created the Kingdom of Great Britain. The empire was growing – Clive's victory at the Battle of Plassey in 1757 signalled the start of British rule in India; Captain James Cook claimed the new lands of Australia and New Zealand during his epic voyage (1768–71); and elsewhere the army and navy was acquiring colonies from other European powers such as Spain and France. Yet Britain also suffered the shock of the American War of Independence and the ignominy of losing its thirteen American colonies in the early 1780s. Trade was ever-increasing on a global scale, especially and somewhat ironically with the new nation of America. And with the advances in technology and manufacturing that heralded the dawn of the machine age, Britain was now on the path to the position of global supremacy that it achieved in the mid-nineteenth century.

At a national level Britain remained predominantly a rural country. However, agricultural techniques had improved so radically that an industry, which at the start of the century had not changed much since mediæval times, by its close was efficient, organised and productive. The advances owed much to the pernicious Enclosure Acts which empowered existing landowners to greedily acquire more land by taking what had, until then, been Common Land. Enclosure created larger fields and easier-to-manage field systems, simultaneously facilitating the implementation of technological and cultivation advances such as drainage, the use of fertilisers, Charles 'Turnip' Townsend's four-field crop-rotation system and the use of machinery such as Jethro Tull's seed drill. Arable farming also benefited from breeding programmes that created improved breeds of sheep and cattle. Between 1710 and 1795 the average weight of an ox at Smithfield

Market, the main meat market for England, rose from 370lb/167.8kg to 800lb/362.88kg. Most successful in this field was Robert Bakewell of Dishley (Leicestershire), who developed strains with high-quality, high-fat content meat.

Thus as farming yields, rents and incomes all rose, so land remained the main wealth-producing powerhouse. It also provided its owners with social prestige and political power, but ownership was pretty much a 'closed shop', changing hands between landed families through inter-marriage and/or inheritance. With skill, however, one could 'buy into' at least landed gentry by taking a name- and fortune-making route through a military career, trade or banking. But it had to be a substantial fortune, for according to Turner:

> At least five or six thousand pounds a year was required to support a great house, to allow for the expenses of the London season and to enable the owner to patronise the arts. More comfortably it required £10,000 a year, and the relative value of this can be appreciated when we learn that the labourers who worked on ['Capability'] Brown's improvements at Castle Ashby (1761) earned only eight pence per day. To raise £10,000 a year from rents between ten and twenty thousand acres of land was needed, depending on the quality of the ground and its location. From this we can calculate that the land owned by the 400 wealthiest and most powerful families amounted to about a fifth of the cultivated area of the country.[1]

As fashions changed and nature was rediscovered, so it was these rich land-owners, generally an educated, leisured and enlightened class (although not all were so – the Earl of Lincoln had an apprentice boy beaten to death for daring to stare at him), who began to purchase both extensive and expensive designed landscapes. The fashion for landscapes took hold relatively slowly. The formal creations of London and Wise continued to dominate garden design into the second decade of the century, but with the retirement of Wise in 1717, one of London's apprentices, Stephen Switzer, now took up the baton of garden design. He, however, began to run on a different track. After completing his apprenticeship, Switzer remained at Brompton Park Nursery and became involved in the garden-making business, assisting London at Castle Howard (Yorkshire) and Kensington Palace, and Wise at Blenheim Palace. Then, establishing his own business as a landscape designer, he worked first for the Bertie family, transforming Grimsthorpe (Lincolnshire). Here Switzer simplified the formality of the French style, and in the process, became a herald of the return to nature that would come to dominate eighteenth-century landscape design.

Switzer published his ideas, principles and theories first as *The Nobleman, Gentleman, and Gardener's Recreation* (1715), a tome which he subsequently expanded to the three volumes of *Ichnographia Rustica* (1718). Six years later he set up as a seedsman in Westminster Hall in London, but continued to write, publishing throughout the 1720s a series of informative books, notably *Practical fruit-gardener* (1724) and *Practical kitchen gardiner* (1727) and pamphlets concerning many issues of landscape design, fruit and vegetable cultivation, and agricultural improvement. As subsequent designers – especially Charles Bridgeman and William Kent – further loosened the bounds of formality, so nature was welcomed in. At a practical level, not only were landscapes far less expensive to maintain than their fiddly, formal counterparts of the previous century, but they could be used to make money – animals could be grazed and, as the sylvan idylls with their forests matured, they yielded timber.

PRODUCTIVE GARDENS

The Prince Regent (later George IV, 1762–1830) was especially interested in good food, to the extent that he engaged, at great expense, the famous French chef, Antonin Carême. As recipes and menus became more exotic and exciting, so the head gardener was required to produce a wider range of crops and to produce them out-of-season. At the same time entertaining or hosting became more popular, so increasing quantities were required to supply the dining table of the country house and during the season, the town house, too. Particularly popular were asparagus, mushrooms, broccoli and globe artichokes, and the most fashionable fruits were grapes, melons and, above all, pineapples.

Consequently, the kitchen garden increased in area, dependent on the size of the household. At the upper end of the scale were large establishments such as Blenheim Palace, where the walled garden built by Wise encloses 12 acres (4.85ha). However, smaller establishments did not need to be so grand. The Gentleman inquisitor in London and Wise's *The Retir'd Gard'ner* (1706) is establishing a modest country estate, and when asked how big the productive garden should be, the Gardener replies that he recommends the fruit and kitchen garden be 4 acres (1.62ha) in extent, divided into eight 'quarters' each 94ft (28.65m) long by 58ft (17.68m) wide, set about a central dipping pool for water.

Paths from 2 to 7ft (0.61 to 2.13m) wide divided the beds, and the whole garden was surrounded by a 3ft (0.91m)-wide border edged with

The frontispiece of The gentleman and gardeners kalendar *(1718) by Richard Bradley shows citrus trees in tubs and various forms of protected cropping including bell jars, cloches and a wooden-framed screen for wall-trained fruit trees.*

aromatic herbs:[2] Four decades or so later, Henry Stevenson (1683?–1748) in the second edition of his *The Gentleman Gard'ner's Director* (1744) opines that for a family of seven or eight, a kitchen garden enclosed by walls 11 to 12ft (3.35 to 3.66m) high 'requires the Bigness of half an Acre, or 80 Perches [0.6ha]. With borders beneath the tree-planted walls 8 to 9ft [2.44 to 2.72m] broad, and the open ground divided into squares or rectangles and separated by paths of sand, not gravel, which became too dirty when run over by wheelbarrows.'[3] Later in the century, the French author Jean-Baptiste de La Quintinie recommended the quarters be 90 to 120ft (27.43 to 36.58m) by 40 to 45ft (12.19 to 13.72m), with main walks a minimum of 6 to 7ft (1.83 to 2.13m) wide, with the service paths of 2ft (0.61m).

Location

Prior to the eighteenth century the kitchen garden had been placed near the house for convenience, ideally located with a south-facing aspect, on rich, well-drained soil and with an ample water supply. When London began improvements to the gardens at Bretby (Derbyshire) in 1699 for the Earl of Chesterfield, he placed the orchard and kitchen garden, hidden by their walls, to the east and west of the main approach drive. To the north of the house were the extensive formal gardens designed in the French style, and which included a seven-bay pedimented ornamental greenhouse. But the naturalistic landscape style demanded an uninterrupted vista, and this required that walled kitchen gardens be hidden at a distance from the house, sometimes up to a mile (1.6km) away. Another practical reason for putting distance between the house and the kitchen garden was the smell – an awful lot of dung was used!

Open ground

In the second half of the seventeenth century the raised bed-and-shallow trench system sown with a mix of seeds gave way to a new innovation. Inspired by the seed drill, gardeners began to sow large areas of the quarters with seeds of a single crop in rows or, as they were then known, 'trayles' or 'drills'. The borders below the walls were also used differently. In addition to the fruit trees, and so as not to interfere with their roots, shallow-rooted crops were sown, the choice dictated by the wall's aspect – salads and late strawberries for north-facing, legumes in the south- and east–facing, and in the west-facing, summer planting to overwinter and be transplanted into south-facing beds next spring. This more organised and efficient system became the norm, but because the kitchen garden still retained a place on any garden tour, it had to look attractive. The quarters were often laid out symmetrically and edged with borders of sweetly scented flowers and herbs to nullify some of the more 'earthy' smells. Where soil in the beds required retaining, this continued to be done with wooden planks, large stones or low-cut hedges. Box was universally championed, but other suggestions included lavender, hyssop, juniper and even yew. The main paths were also ornamented with topiaried fruit trees, and the English innovation, the contre-espalier or free-standing espalier. Elsewhere, garden ornaments such as bowers, beehives, aviaries, dovecots, topiary, sundials and fruit walks also appeared.

What was grown

As has been referred to, one of the reasons for the increased size of the kitchen garden was the range of crops raised. The tree fruits grown outside remained the favourites – apple, apricot, cherry, peach and pear, and as we shall see these were supplemented by those grown under glass. In the open ground, even the relatively small 1.5 acre (0.61ha) kitchen garden recommended by Henry Stevenson, grew a remarkable range of vegetables and herbs. For 'Kitchen-stuff' he allots the following – one perch being an area of 1/160th of an acre or 272.23sq ft (25.29m^2).

	Perches[4]
For the Hot-bed Quarter, on which are Planted, Melons, Cucumbers &c.	4
For Pickling Cucumbers	2
For Salading	8
For Horse-Radish, Skerrots, and Shallots	1
For Pot-Herbs, viz. Mint, Sage, Penny-Royal, Hyssop, Savoury, Marjoram, Burnet, Clary, Parsley, Thyme, Sorrel, Rosemary, Borage, Angelica, &c.	4
For Asparagus	3
For raising it on Hot beds	2
For Artichoaks, Spinage, and Radishes	2
For Rasps, 10 Rows	2

For Beans	4
Strawberries	1
For Peas	8
For Kidney-beans	2
For Colliflowers, which after may be used for Blanching Cellery	2
For Cabbages	3
For Brocoli and Savoy Plants	4
For Carrots	3
For Parsnips	2
For Potatoes	3
For Onions	3
For Summer Turneps	2
For Accidental Things and Alleys	20

The last entry may include Gooseberries and Curran-trees'

A comparison between this list and the proposals made by London and Wise does not reveal anything surprising, just an additional 14 crops: beets (red, white and Roman), chicory, colewort, endive (plain and curled), fennel (Italian), garlic, leeks (London and French), rocambole (a type of leek), salsify and scorzonera. But London and Wise do offer a little more detail about the varieties grown: English, Dutch and Russian cabbages; yellow, orange and red carrots; large, small, white, and speckled kidney beans; black, white, London and Spanish radishes; Dutch and yellow savoy; black and white spinach; long and round turnips; and Strasbourgh (*sic*), London, white Spanish and black Spanish onions. But by far the most varied vegetable was the pea, of which they list twenty-one varieties (Edward's early, Flanders early, Green's early, Barnes hotspur, sandwich and Reading peas, grey, blue, green and white rouncivals, large, small and dwarf sugar peas, egg peas, Dutch admiral's peas, crown or rose peas, hotspur, gosport, Spanish and Windsor).[5]

For the eight Perches of 'Salading' Stevenson recommends some thirty-six crops to be grown in Salad Beds: balm, belgrade, burnet, cellery, chervil, cives, corn Salad, cresses, endive, hartsthorn, lettuce (Roman, cosse, silesian, cabbage and lop), mints, mustard (leaves), *Nasturtium* (buds and flowers), onions, parsley, purslane, rampions, radish (leaves), rocket, sampier, sage (red), scurvy-grass, shallots, sorrel (French and Greenland), spinage, succory, sweet-fennel, tarragon, turnep (leaves) and trip-Madam. There would have also been beds of aromatic and pot herbs, most of which were by now familiar favourites.[6]

HEAD GARDENERS

The eighteenth century was one of frenetic horticultural activity, even so one man stands head-and-shoulders above the rest as the century's most accomplished and influential head gardener – Philip Miller (1691–1771). In 1673 the Chelsea Physic Garden was founded by the Worshipful Society of Apothecaries of London for 'herborising expeditions'[7] for the purpose of training apprentices in plant identification and use. In 1722 and after a period of difficulties, the garden was rescued by Sir Hans Sloane, who had purchased the Manor of Chelsea from Charles Cheyne in 1712. Sloane offered the 4-acre (1.62ha) site to the Society in perpetuity at a lease of £5 a year and on the proviso that annually, fifty new herbarium specimens from plants grown in the Physic Garden were submitted to the Royal Society.

It was Patrick Blair, a Scottish doctor and author of *Botanik Essays* (1720), who recommended Miller to Sloane as the ideal head gardener to turn around the fortunes of the Chelsea Physic Garden. Given a good education and training by his father who was a nobleman's gardener in Bromley (Kent) and later a market gardener at Deptford near London, Miller travelled through England, Holland and Flanders before establishing his own nursery specialising in ornamental trees and shrubs in St George's Fields in Southwark (now in south London). He took up the post in 1722, and quickly proved his worth as a knowledgeable botanist and skilled horticulturist. During his forty-eight-year watch, he gathered together the most diverse collection of plants (many of which were 'outlandish') in any botanic or physic garden in Europe, and developed the garden's reputation to a position of second to none in Europe. Miller achieved this not just because he was a skilled gardener and travelled widely to collect plants, but because he also developed a wide and far-reaching network of friends and contacts with whom he corresponded and who supplied him with new plants (many on a swap basis). Amongst Miller's many friends, he counted John Rae, Joseph Banks, Hans Sloane, Peter Collinson and even Alexander Pope. He also corresponded with Carl Linnæus, the Swedish botanist, physician and zoologist whom he first met in 1736 when Linnæus was gardener to George Clifford (a Dutch merchant of English extraction) and was sent to Miller to ask for certain plants. Nine years earlier, Clifford had given Miller a number of plants new to him, including the strawberry (*Fragaria chileonsis*) when he visited Holland, and now he was claiming his dues. Other donors included John Bartram in the colonies, Herman Boerhaave, the director of the famous Dutch botanic garden in Leiden from 1709, and the botanist William Houstoun (or Houston) who sent seed from his expeditions to Mexico and the West Indies (1730–31). Indeed, so good was Miller at acquiring and growing new plants that during his tenure he quintupled the number of plants grown in the garden.

Miller was also a prolific author, and he dedicated his most famous work *The gardener's dictionary* (1731) to Sloane. From the outset, Miller intended his dictionary to be a practical manual. As he made clear on his title page, it contained 'the methods of cultivating and improving the kitchen, fruit and flower garden as also the physick garden, wilderness, conservatory and vineyard, according to the practice of the most experienc'd gardens of the present age'. Miller also provided detailed botanical information, giving descriptions of all the plants in cultivation, together with instructions on how to grow them. He also included 'the history of the plants, the characters of each genus, and the names of all the particular species, in Latin and English, and an explanation of all the terms used in botany and gardening'. In his Preface to the eighth edition (1768) Miller noted that the number of plants now in cultivation in Britain was more than double what it was when the first edition came out some thirty-seven years earlier – many had to be named before they could be included.

Miller's was the first comprehensive garden dictionary published in English. Unfortunately with a subscription costing either £1 5s for the small edition or £1 15s for the large one, what is arguably the most influential gardening book of the century was not within the reach of the head gardener. As revealed by the list of some 400 subscribers, the readership was clearly targeted at the gentry, clergy, academics, other Fellows of the Royal Society and a few leading nurserymen. But the fact that by 1768 the dictionary had been published in eight editions, and had been translated into German, French and Dutch, also shows how much demand there was for the information held within the covers. Always a practical man, Miller realised the price was beyond a gardener's means and in 1735 an abridged version focusing on plants, their culture and cultivation was printed for the gardener at a reduced, but still quite substantial, 18s.

Despite his numerous achievements Miller was not appreciated in the way he deserved to be by the Garden Committee of the Society of Apothecaries. In an unseemly show of ingratitude, Miller was accused of

The frontispiece of what is probably the most important gardening book of the eighteenth century, Philip Miller's The gardener's dictionary *(1731). The garden style is formal French, with, on the left side, an orangery in front of which are citrus planted in square tubs.*

presumption and decades of overstepping the mark in his dealings with the Society, and he was forced to take leave of the garden on 6 February 1771.[8] However, let us leave his eulogy to John Rogers who met Miller and wrote of him in *The Vegetable Cultivator* (1839) that 'Medicine, botany, agriculture and manufactures are all indebted to him' and that his dictionary was 'as the first bright beam of gardening issuing from the dark cloud of ignorance in which it had previously been enveloped; but having once broken through, it had continued to shine with increasing splendour for the last century. It may be almost said to have laid the foundation of the horticultural taste and knowledge in Europe.'

The legacy of Philip Miller was undoubtedly his publications, but it also lived on through one of his protégés from the Physic Garden. William Aiton (1731–93) was born at Boghall (Lanarkshire), the son of a farmer. He moved south to England in 1754, and in 1755 became assistant to Miller. He was clearly a talented horticulturist, because, four years later, when John Haverfield, head gardener to Augusta, dowager Princess of Wales (widow of Prince Frederick and mother of George III) asked Miller to recommend someone 'to form and arrange a botanical garden at Kew', Miller had no hesitation in giving Aiton's name. The botanical garden that Aiton gardened until his death, and for which he received an annual salary of £120 by 1770, covered about 10 acres (4.05ha) and was a part of Augusta's larger garden at Kew. Following the death of his mother in 1772, George III (1738–1820) united Kew with the neighbouring royal residence of Richmond, although Love Lane physically separated the gardens until 1802 – today its line is marked by the Broad Walk. Aiton, with assistance from Sir Joseph Banks (1743–1820), continued to develop the botanic garden, and upon the retirement of Haverfield in 1783, added the pleasure grounds and productive garden to his responsibilities, becoming the first superintendent of Kew per se. In 1789 Aiton, with help from Banks' assistants, Daniel Solander and Jonas Dryander, published the three volumes of *Hortus Kewensis*. More than sixteen years in the preparation, this was a catalogue of some 5,500 taxa growing at Kew, with details of whence they came and when. Indeed, between them, Aiton and Banks developed Kew's European-wide reputation for excellence, and were responsible for introducing most of the 7,000 new taxa that arrived in Britain during George III's reign.

THE GREENHOUSE

Given a fillip by Queen Mary (see page 17), collecting tender exotic plants had become popular by the turn of the eighteenth century, and indeed throughout the century, the cultivation of both sub-tropical and tropical plants became better understood and more successful as glasshouse technology improved. Indeed, the evolution of the glasshouse or greenhouse sprang from a desire at the time of the Italian Renaissance to cultivate tender citrus trees. Grown in large, ornate terracotta pots, and with their shapely form, attractive evergreen leaves, sweetly scented flowers and coloured fruits, citrus were *the* exotic to have and grow before tender species began to arrive from the New World and the West and East Indies. In Italy the pots and their valuable incumbents were moved into a dry cave or a temporary wooden shack in order to provide protection from winter frosts. In Northern Europe, though, citrus were treated with more dignity, and thus evolved the *orangerie* and the greenhouse.

The honour of growing the first orange trees in England goes to Sir Francis Carew of Beddington Park. Legend has it that the trees were raised from pips given to Carew by Sir Walter Raleigh in about 1560. Certainly the trees were mature by 1580 and still producing a copious crop over a century later – in 1690 the harvest was more than 10,000 fruits. And just to give an indication of the continued desirability of citrus, as late as 1705 orange trees were still being sold by a London nursery at a cost of £1 1s each. Sir Francis protected his treasures in a removable wooden shelter some 200ft (60.96m) long that was erected around the trees, and it was from such rudimentary shelters that the *orangerie* evolved. An early French example – an ornate stone structure with glass windows that faced onto its own small walled garden – was made for Diane de Poitiers at the château of Anet in 1555. Much more famous and far grander is Louis XIV's large *orangerie* at the Palace of Versailles. Built in 1685, it remains the winter home to a large collection of citrus that are grown in wooden tubs and grace the grass parterre in front of the *orangerie* in the summer months.

As the influence of Versailles spread across Europe, so the *orangerie* became a must-have garden feature. It developed into an ornate structure, often located near the house and designed in a classical style with a solid roof and a frontage of large windows. Many also became locations in which to entertain and take meals throughout the year, and within such structures in the early years the citrus made friends with other incumbents such as myrtles (*Myrtus* spp.), pomegranates (*Punica granatum*), oleander (*Nerium oleander*), Canary Island palm (*Phoenix dactylifera*), sugar cane (*Saccharum officinarum*), the Marvel of Peru and canna.

Another branch of the evolution of the glasshouse was the design and construction of protective structures solely for the purpose of cultivating tender and exotic plants. By the end of the seventeenth century, any establishment hoping to be of repute had some form of structure or 'houses' that was glazed with 'glass' and heated by 'stoves'. Within this 'hot' environment the 'greens' were 'conserved' – all words that contributed to the plethora of somewhat confusing names used to identify the glasshouse. The first detailed instructions for building a greenhouse were given in 1600 by Olivier de Serres (*serre* became the French word for 'greenhouse') in *Le Théâtre d'Agriculture*. His lean-to structure had rafters supporting and a gently sloping thatched roof that contained skylights. In the front, between the columns of stone or wood were walls of expensive glass or less expensive waxed canvas. Extra insulation could be gained by covering these with mats of straw and the interior was heated by open braziers of burning charcoal or wood.[9]

From this somewhat primitive structure, greenhouse design steadily improved. To take maximum advantage of natural warming by the sun it became accepted that greenhouses be placed against south-facing walls. As glass became cheaper so the ratio of glass to frame increased, thus enabling more light to penetrate; and brick, which absorbs the sun's heat during the day and radiates it out at night, replaced stone as the infrastructure. Heating technology, too, improved. Braziers were not only an uncontrollable source of heat, but produced a dry heat which was unsuitable for plants from the moist tropics, and fumes of combustion which were a source of damage to the plants. By the mid-seventeenth century open fires were replaced with a sort of hypocaust – flues running under the floor and the heat rising through. This concept was improved by John Evelyn (1620–1706), who made a great breakthrough when he invented the hot-air convection system, publishing the details in 1691. Evelyn placed the furnace outside the house and piped in not combustion gases, but heated air. As it cooled and fell, the air was conducted back to the furnace by pipes situated below ground level. Evelyn's innovation worked perfectly, but was quickly followed by a major obstacle placed in the way of the evolution of the glasshouse, for in 1695 William III levied a punitive glass tax. The huge unemployment it caused in the glass industry forced its repeal in 1698, but no greenhouses were made during the lifetime of the tax.[10]

Advances in greenhouse architecture and design gathered pace throughout the eighteenth century, and at the Chelsea Physic Garden, Miller, as was commonly the case, was in the vanguard of developments. Once again, the various editions of his dictionary are a mine of information. In the first edition (1731) Miller describes his range of glasshouses at the Chelsea Physic Garden. Minimally heated, the central greenhouse was built of stone, with an imposing central ornamental pediment, large windows and his accommodation on the first floor. Either side were stove houses, also with large glass windows, solid roofs, and kept at a higher temperature than the greenhouse. One housed those plants requiring humid heat, the other, those such as aloes and cacti (and later sedums and euphorbias) which required dry heat. Miller's plant collection was exceptional, and amongst his treasures were avocado pear (*Persea amencon* 'Puerte'), cabbage tree (*Cussonia pomiculata*), cashew (*Anacaidium occidentale*), Indian date tree (*Tamarindus indica*), and mahogany (*Swietenia mahoganii*).[11]

A year later Miller was granted a hefty £1,550 to erect a new range consisting of a greenhouse and two stoves. This is likely to be the range depicted on Hayne's engraving of 1751, which shows the stoves were lean-to structures with glass roofs, flanking either side of an imposing greenhouse. In the sixth edition (1752), Miller recommends two furnaces per stove – one heating an underfloor flue, the other a 'fire wall' or hollow wall. This new heating concept used the gases of combustion produced by an external furnace which were channelled into a series of flues built within the back wall of the greenhouse itself. As the gases passed up through the zig-zag of flues, their heat was transferred through the bricks and into the house. Miller's dictionary was widely read and the Physic Garden widely visited, and his set-up seems to have been adopted as a 'national standard' for much of the rest of the century. The range at Gopsall Park (Leicestershire) completed in 1749, for example, bore a remarkable resemblance with its classically elegant greenhouse and plain stoves. Both stoves had deep bark-pits (see pages 42–4), but the stove for tropical fruit – guavas, mangoes and pineapples – has two furnaces, the other, only one. Similarly at Burton Constable (Yorkshire), a greenhouse-and-two-stoves structure was erected from 1758 with a total length of 206ft (62.79m). Heated with fire walls, both stoves were used to raise pineapples.

In the second half of the eighteenth century a range of lean-to and freestanding heated glasshouses, hothouses or stoves became an essential feature of any self-respecting walled kitchen garden. One visitor to Wallington (Northumberland) in the 1760s, enviously noted that the walled garden had 'an abundance of stoves and hot walls so they have cucumbers daily throughout the year'. Other houses were home to tropical fruit, for example passion fruits were harvested at Gawthorpe Hall (Yorkshire) in 1766, together with exotic flowers. But much emphasis was also placed on extending the harvest season – both bringing it forward in spring and extending it into winter. Some hothouses (also known as forcing houses) were used for forcing vegetables, as well as ornamentals such as spring bulbs and early summer flowers. Others housed fruits such as apricots, cherries, dwarf currants, , figs, gooseberries, nectarines, peaches, raspberries and strawberries. And then, of course, there was the new favourite – almost as popular as the pineapple – the vine. From the 1770s dessert grapes were raised in separate structures called vineries or 'graperies', which could be up to 40 to 50ft (12.19 to 15.24m), 12 to 14ft (3.66 to 4.27m) wide, and 10 to 12ft (3.05 to 3.66m) high at the rear, sloping to 6ft (1.83m) at the front in order to maximise light penetration. Planted outside, the vines were trained into the structure, and during the winter months, when vines were bare, the floor space in the houses was taken up with pots of crops being forced.[12]

LANCELOT 'CAPABILITY' BROWN

Just as the head gardener's workload increased in the kitchen garden, so it did in the ornamental department. The creation of an expansive designed landscape was a major undertaking, both in terms of cost and manpower, and the head gardener was often tasked with overseeing the work, adding the role of Supervisor of Works to his portfolio. Indeed, Lancelot Brown (1716–83), the eighteenth century's most famous landscape designer, began his professional career as head gardener to Lord Cobham (1669–1749) at Stowe in Buckinghamshire.

A look at Brown's life prior to his appointment in April 1741 provides an indication of the level of schooling and range of skills learned during an apprenticeship required in order to become a head gardener. Brown was baptised in St Wilfrid's Church, Kirkharle (Northumberland) on 30 August 1716, and given that he was born to 'yeoman farming stock'[13] he enjoyed a good education both in the village school, and later in near-by

Cambo, where the school 'was an establishment of some repute'.[14] Leaving school at the age of sixteen, Lancelot decided not to follow the family trade, but instead was engaged on the Kirkharle estate of Sir William Loraine. Sir William had begun a major remodelling of his demesne from house to heath in the 1720s, and working on these improvements, Brown now spent seven years learning his practical crafts of horticulture, land reclamation, forestry and building. Within a few years Loraine entrusted Brown with a boggy tract of land to the north of the house, and here Brown created his first landscape. But with Loraine's catalogue of improvements completed, Brown left Kirkharle in 1739 and headed south. Following a commission from Lady Mostyn of Kiddington Hall (Oxfordshire) to create a lake, Brown took up his appointment at Stowe at the tender age of twenty-four. He was in charge of a staff of forty and received a salary of £35 per annum plus £9 for lodgings; this was a position he was to fill for a decade.

Numerate, literate and in possession of a wide range of horticultural, land, fiscal and people management skills, Brown nonetheless continued to 'improve himself', becoming a proficient self-taught architect. As paymaster for the grounds staff, Brown demonstrated another character trait essential in a head gardener – that of honesty. Cobham, who had had a celebrated career as a soldier serving under Marlborough against the French, and later became renowned as an MP, was in the process of creating arguably the eighteenth century's grandest landscape garden, also entrusted Brown with the implementation of many of William Kent's proposals for his new and classically inspired landscape. On one occasion, when theory did not transpose to on-the-ground reality, it was Brown who saved the designer's blushes. The Grecian Valley, now regarded as one of Brown's earliest pieces of design work, was in fact a fix. Intended by Kent to be a lake, Brown discovered during the course of construction that it would not hold water and so adapted the contours to create the sublime meadow we now see. Cobham evidently recognised and appreciated Brown's skills and strengths. Having a head gardener who was able to take your garden to another level in design and style was a popular form of one-upmanship in the nineteenth century, and it is evident from the fact that Cobham 'lent' Brown to design grounds for family and friends, that he also enjoyed showing off his head gardener. Amongst Brown's designs carried out whilst 'on loan' were Wotton (Buckinghamshire, 1740s) for Cobham's nephew, Richard Grenville (later Earl Temple) and Newnham Paddox (Warwickshire, 1745) for Lord and Lady Denbigh.

Following Cobham's death Brown left Stowe in 1751, establishing his own design office in Hammersmith near London. He spent the next thirty-two years criss-crossing the country, laying out magnificent landscapes on a vast scale. Gently massaging contours, planting trees, sowing grass and digging lakes may not sound like much, but Horace Walpole's words upon hearing of Brown's death cannot be bettered when it comes to giving a description of his style: 'Such was the effect of his genius that when he was the happiest man he will be least remembered, so closely did he copy nature that his works will be mistaken.' Brown became famous and rich as a landscape designer rather than a head gardener – but it was this fame which somewhat paradoxically secured him his royal appointment on 16 July 1764 as 'Chief Gardiner' (*sic*) at Hampton Court Palace, a post recently vacated by John Greening. Brown's contract provides a detailed summary of the gardens, what was expected of him, and what he was to receive in return.

*An extract from the six-page contract signed on 16 July 1764 appointing Lancelot 'Capability' Brown as the Chief Gardiner (*sic*) at Hampton Court Palace. Brown was also paid £40 p.a. to maintain the garden adjoining the Treasury at Whitehall.*

The gardens under Brown's control were distributed thus:

	Acres	Rods	Poles
The Melon Ground	2	3	0
Kitchen Garden	8	1	24
Wilderness & Grove	9	0	10
Great Fountain Garden	24	0	19
Privy Garden	4	2	8
Glass Case Gardens & Pheasant Court	2	2	6
Quadrangle Princes Court & Tennis Court	0	3	18
Great Terras & Bowling Green	5	0	33
Lower Wilderness	16	1	13

And his responsibilities were described in detail:

> The Melon Ground, Kitchen Garden and Fruit Garden in six divisions. To be dunged digged and cropped with the several varieties of eatables most proper for his Majesty's use, & the trees pruned and nailed.
>
> The Wilderness Grove, Great Fountain Garden, Privy Garden & Pheasant Court, Quadrangle Princes Court and Tennis Court, Great Terras and Bowling Green. The grass to be mowed, swept and rolled, the ground rolled and weeded, the Borders dunged, dug, hoed, raked and weeded, the several hardy Evergreens and other Plants to be staked, tied up and clipt, and to keep in good Order the several Collections of housed greens and flower Roots.
>
> Lower Wilderness. The Quarters and Sand Allies to be kept clean from Weeds, the Grass mowed and the Hedge Lines clipt.

As well as paying the gardeners' and labourers' wages, Brown was expected to supply tools, materials and fuel for the hothouses and fruit trees, replace any dead plants, and 'provide carriage of the Kings Summer Fruit...daily by relay of Men on foot to the Court'.[15] One legacy of Brown's work is, of course, the famous Great Vine – a 'Black Homburg' which he planted in 1768, and which continues to produce an annual crop.

In return 'for the whole charge of maintaining, keeping and upholding the said gardens' Brown was given use of Wilderness House and various 'sheds and places', and received £1,107 6s per annum (a rate of £15 per acre per year) with two 'extraordinary charges' or additional payments of £100 for raising pineapples and forced fruits. Exactly how much Brown personally made depended on how efficiently he ran the gardens, but based on the fact that on several occasions he returned money to clients because the actual cost of making a landscape was less than his original quote, he probably did pretty well for himself. Yet for a man whose design business had an average turnover of nearly £11,000 per annum in the three decades to 1780, the position was probably more about the kudos than the cash. Just to put Brown's business successes and royal payment in context, the accounts for Dunster Castle (Somerset) for the years 1749 to 1764 reveal the weekly wage of the under-gardeners who were, unusually, girls, was 6d a day, while John Morris, the head gardener, received 1s a day or £18 5s per annum.

FRAMES

The special payments to Brown reflect the extra effort and skill required in producing fruits, and especially pineapples. To achieve successes Brown would have used two forms of protected environment which evolved from the straightforward hotbed (see pages 6–7) – the frame and the pit.

In *The Gardeners Labyrinth* Thomas Hill noted that the Romans used glass to protect cucumbers from 'boisterous windes, yea, frosts'. Indeed, it was from classical sources that Hill drew heavily for his first book. *A most briefe and plesaunt treatyse teaching how to dresse, sowe and set a garden* which appeared between 1557 and 1559 and was essentially a collection of writing by authors including Palladius, Varo and Cato.[16] However, the Romans never devised a technique for mass-producing panes of glass and so it is likely that Roman gardeners glazed their wooden structures not with glass but mica, a type of rock that splits easily into transparent sheets. Thus the combination of a hotbed on top of which sat a structure that provided additional protection to the plants grown within was in use as early as the first century AD. Using such an apparatus, gardeners were able to provide the Emperor Tiberius (42 BC to AD 37) with the cucumber a day his doctors prescribed. No doubt such a charge made the gardeners very nervous for Tiberius was wont to deal with those who displeased him by throwing them off a high cliff! Forcing plants using artificial heat and a protective environment, rather than just protecting them from the ravages of winter frosts, was one of so many classical developments that became lost for over a millennium until rediscovered during the Renaissance. Yet it was not until the early seventeenth century that the glass bell jar was introduced into the English garden. The famous botanist and writer John Parkinson (1567–1650) author of *Paradisi in Sole Paradisus Terrestris* (1629) – the title of which was a pun on his name, Park-in-Sun's terrestrial Paradise – refers to 'Greate hollow glasses like unto bell heads' being used to protect melons in 1629. Half a century later, square glass cases or 'hand glasses' – an early form of cloche – were being specially manufactured for use in gardens.

The same century also saw the development of the 'frame' with its glass 'lights'. The glazed light was a horizontal window that sat on top of a frame. The frame was a hollow wooden box that was placed on top of a hotbed, its height dependent on what was grown within. The size of individual frames was determined by the light. Lights had to be moved and their size was limited to what could be lifted by two men, to about 4ft (1.22m) wide and 6ft (1.83m) deep. The length of the frame, however, was variable, as any number of 4ft (1.22m) sections could be built one after the other until the required area was covered. The combination of hotbed and frame was a powerful tool that aided the head gardener's ability to produce a wide range of crops for as long a season as possible. The advantages were quickly realised, and in addition to many of the crops Miller recommended for hotbed cultivation, aubergine, capsicum, cauliflower, potato, sea-kale and mushrooms were also raised in frames. However, two crops were perennial favourites for frame growing – the cucumber and the melon. Indeed, because each melon hotbed took up a considerable space, the frame yard also became known as the melon ground or melonry.

PITS

Another way of providing a protected growing environment was mooted in the seventeenth century by John Evelyn, but did not come into its own until the eighteenth. Instead of erecting raised hotbeds and frames, sunken pits were dug, lined with bricks and covered with lights. In a pit the heat source was kept separate from the growing medium: heat from the decomposing dung or tanners' bark (see below) was isolated within its own chamber and warmed the air within the growing chamber without coming into direct contact with the plants. Such an arrangement not only enabled the provision of heat without disturbing the crop, but also helped to reduce two of the gardener's major problems caused by hotbeds. First, how to re-warm a hotbed once it had cooled – now fresh fermenting or decomposing material could simply be added to the heating chamber. And second, how to manage the temperature within a frame in order to prevent leaves being scalded by steam or the roots roasted – such damage was far less likely in a pit because the growing chamber was warmed by dry heat and the plants were placed at a greater and safer distance from the heat source.

The man who perfected the pit was head gardener James MacPhail (1754–1805). A native of Aberdeenshire and from a very humble back-ground – in his own words 'educated and trained up amongst the lowest classes of society' – MacPhail rose from a farm labourer 'earning 23s 4d for the half year' in 1771 to become head gardener to Charles Jenkinson, Lord Hawkesbury (later Earl of Liverpool) at Addiscombe Place near Croydon (Surrey) in 1785. MacPhail was a renowned grower of melons, pineapples and cucumbers, and gained justified fame for his innovation in pit design when he published the design in his *A treatise on the culture of the cucumber* (1794). Running along the front and back of a central growing pit (covered with lights) were the two pits which held the heat source. These were 3ft (0.91m) deep and separated from the growing pit by a pigeon-holed brick-work wall – that is to say a wall with gaps where bricks have deliberately been omitted. It was for this innovation that MacPhail was duly lauded, for this arrangement not only enabled a more efficient heat transmission, but also provided side heating rather than bottom heating as was the case with a hotbed (and some later nineteenth-century designs for pits). In his *Vegetable Cultivator* of 1839 John Rogers noted 'That excellent invention has certainly rendered the forcing of this vegetable more simple, and reduced it to a more regular and certain system; so that at this time few gentlemen's gardens and few of the principal market-gardens in the vicin-ity of London and various other large towns are without them.'[17]

Another reason why MacPhail's new system worked so well was because pit cultivation had eagerly adopted an alternative heat source to manure. Until the 1680s hotbeds had been warmed by dung (various mixes of dung from different animals, including pigeons, being tried to extend the warm-ing period). Then in the late seventeenth century John Evelyn recommended something that had been tried and tested by Dutch growers for some time – tanners' bark (or tan bark). Evelyn died in 1706, and it was not until 1717 that tanners' bark was first experimented with in Britain. A by-product of the tanning process, this sludge of coarsely chopped oak bark ferments to produce a fierce heat. It was usually left to cool and drain for a period of about ten days before being put into pits on top of a layer of rubble. A further five weeks passed before the pits were planted, but this preparation time was worth the effort because tanners' bark kept a pit warm for up to six months – considerably longer than a filling of dung. Moreover, bark fermentation could be simply reactivated by stirring the mix, or adding fresh, thus keeping a pit going for up to a year with a constant bottom heat of 24–30°C (75–82°F). Bark had one other advantage – it produced less steam, which could cause potential harm to plants. It was an advance that rapidly caught on.

NURSERYMEN

As we have seen with the case of London and Wise, and 'Capability' Brown, head gardeners made their fortunes by becoming nurserymen and/ or designers. At the turn of the eighteenth century there had been just the one great establishment – the Brompton Park Nursery, but, as the century progressed, so commercial nurseries flourished – particularly in the vicinity of the capital. Located within easy reach of London's docks – the entrepôt for the vast majority of new plants – many nurseries specialised in supplying rare and exotic plants to the wealthy all over the country. The most successful were run by ex-head gardeners, and the most notable of these were James Lee and Lewis Kennedy, James Gordon, and Joachim Loddige.

Kennedy and Lee

James Lee (1715–95) was a native of southern Scotland, and about the age of seventeen he moved to London. The differing accounts of his employment have him working as a gardener for Archibald Campbell, Earl of Islay (later the third Duke of Argyll) at Whitton Place near Twickenham, at Syon House in Isleworth for the Dukes of Somerset and under Philip Miller at the Chelsea Physic Garden. Whatever his exact movements, by about 1745 Lee, in partnership with Lewis Kennedy (1721–82), who had been head gardener to Spencer Compton, Earl of Wilmington, and possibly for Lord Burlington at Chiswick House, established a nursery in Hammersmith on a plot of land called The Vineyard, from which the nursery took its name, and which is now under the Olympia Exhibition Centre.

Kennedy and Lee soon became noted for their successful culture of exotic plants, and the nursery for its ability to supply newly introduced plants. Vineyard Nursery is credited with the first introduction or commercial propagation of 135 new taxa, including *Buddleia globosa* (1789) and fuchsia. Lee also authored *Introduction to Botany* (1760), the first general introduction to the Linnæan system of nomenclature in the English language. Not only did this bring Lee some notoriety and help establish the Linnæan system in Britain, but it also increased interest in the nursery, and hence business. One amusing side story is that Lee was guardian to an attractive young lady called Miss Blosset to whom a young Joseph Banks pledged his troth and left a ring before scuttling off with Captain Cook in 1768. Upon his return three years later, Banks did not solemnise his vows and was forced to pay a sum rather than wed.

James Gordon

A contemporary of Lee and Kennedy, and another Scot, was James Gordon (*c*.1708–80). Gordon had been head gardener to Lord Petre at Thorndon Hall (Essex) until his employer's untimely death in 1743, aged only thirty. Lord Petre had been the foremost collector of American plants and had partly financed John Bartram's collecting work which had been organised by the London-based merchant Peter Collinson (1694–1768). On Petre's death the auction of his collection numbered a staggering 220,000 specimens. By 1748 Gordon had established a highly respected and very successful nursery in Mile End in east London, with a seed shop in Fenchurch Street. According to Collinson, himself the owner of one of the most famous gardens of the time, at Ridgeway House, Mill Hill, north London, and responsible for (re) introducing nearly 200 new taxa.

> The skill and ingenuity of some men is surprising; on Aug. 30, I was at James Gordon's, gardener at the last house on the left hand at Mile-end; there he shewed me a pot of seedlings of the cactus, or great melon thistle, perhaps the first ever raised from seed, but what shews his great knowledge and experience in vegetation is his way of raising the finest dusty seeds; before him, I never knew or heard of any man that could raise the dusty seeds of the kalmia's, rhododendrons, or azalea's [*sic*]. These charming

hardy shrubs, that excel all others in his care, he furnishes to every curious garden; all the nurserymen and gardeners come to him for them; and this year, after more than 20 years' trial, he shewed me the loblolly bay of Carolina coming up from seed in a way not to be expected; this elegant evergreen shrub is next in beauty to the magnolia's, and his sagacity in raising all sorts of plants from cuttings, roots, and layers surpasses all others by which our gardens are enriched, with an infinite variety, and for many years I have not been a little assistant to him in procuring seeds and plants from all countries.

This honourable mention of Mr Gordon, who is now in his 56th year, is an act of gratitude due to his memory from his old friend.

So well respected was Gordon that the naturalist John Ellis had no hesitation in recommending him to Linnæus as a correspondent, observing 'This man was bred under Lord Petre and Doctor Sherard, and knows systematically all the plants he cultivates. He has more knowledge in vegetation than all the gardeners and writers on gardening in England put together, but is too modest to publish any thing.'[18] Today, Gordon is widely forgotten as the man who introduced the ginkgo or maidenhair tree (*Ginkgo biloba*) into Britain around 1754. The specimen he gave to Kew still grows there today.

Loddiges

In the second half of the eighteenth century, the then-village of Hackney in Middlesex (now a suburb of London) had a reputation for horticultural excellence and boasted two famous gardens: the physic garden of Edward Lord Zouche, under the control of Matthias de l'Obel (after whom the genus *Lobelia* is named); and the garden developed by the family of nurserymen, the Loddiges.

Loddiges of Hackney was founded in 1771 by Joachim Conrad Loddiges (*bap.* 1738–1826.) Joachim grew up in Vrisbergholtzen in Hildesheim, Hanover, where his father was a gardener to a nobleman. Completing his apprenticeship in 1758, Joachim travelled to Holland, and eventually came to Britain in 1761, whence he was appointed head gardener to Hackney resident Dr (later Sir) John Baptist Silvester, to whom he had been introduced while working in Velzen, Haarlem. Silvester had Loddiges re-design his grounds in Mare Street from 1762, and when he sold the property in 1771, the gardens were notable:

> delicately laid out, and abound with the best of fruit & c, are two
> Greenhouses, a Fruiting-house, and Succession-house. A curious Grotto,
> with a constant Stream murmuring through, replenishing a Canal well-
> stored with Fish; and at the entrance thereof a Willow of magnitude, with
> extending branches, affording a refreshing Shade. A Farmyard with Barn,
> Stable, Cow- house &c and 15 acres [6.07ha] of land in high manurage;
> running through the centre thereof a Brook making five falls, the last in
> clamorous murmur; a Gothic Hermitage faces this cascade; which with
> ease may be converted into a Cold Bath. A Shrubby and Serpentine Walk
> (with flowering shrubs) nearly encompass the whole.[19]

Loddiges now took over the nursery that had been established by Johann Busch (anglicised to John Busch or John Bush), another Hanoverian. In 1771, Busch was head-hunted by Catherine the Great of Russia – he spent the next eighteen years as her Imperial Head Gardener and landscape designer. Nonetheless, Busch retained close contacts, acting as an agent, supplying rare seeds and plants, and in 1830 Loddiges' son, George, named *Lilium bushianum* in his honour. Loddiges bought land and expanded until the nursery covered about 15 acres (6.07ha) by 1842. The nursery became famous for its rare plants, and in 1826 John Claudius Loudon observed in his *Encyclopædia of Gardening* that Loddiges had 'the best general collection of green-house and hot-house exotics of any commercial garden'. Loddiges of Hackney rose to the peak of its fame between 1820 and 1840, during which time it boasted an arboretum of over 2,000 taxa and a collection of greenhouses including the Grand Palm House which at the time was the largest in the world. A nursery catalogue lists 151 plants introduced into cultivation by the nursery between 1782 and 1806, including *Gentiana decumbens* and several heathers from the Cape. Loddiges also holds the dubious honour of being the first to sell commercially *Rhododendron ponticum*, which he may have introduced when he came to England. Certainly he was growing it in Silvester's garden in the 1760s.

PUBLISHING

The eighteenth-century publishing boom in gardening books reflected the continued desire of garden-owners to deepen their knowledge of gardening and to keep abreast of the latest advances in horticulture. It also marked the beginnings of a popular trade supplying the gardeners themselves with information. The first gardening instruction manual to be targeted directly at the gardener rather than his boss was written by Henry Stevenson who was not a professional gardener, but a schoolmaster and keen amateur. Costing a mere 1s 6d *The young gard'ner's director* first appeared in 1716, and Stevenson intended it 'to be carried in the pocket as a vade mecum to a young gardener without overloading him or emptying his pockets'. It was a publishing success running to eight editions by 1769, and demonstrates there was a demand for literary instruction by those who actually gardened.

Abercrombie

However, it was a gardener-turned-nurseryman-turned-writer who also became the eighteenth century's most successful author. John Abercrombie (1726–1806) was the son of a Scottish market gardener and served an apprenticeship under his father before travelling south to work at several establishments including Kew and Leicester House. From about 1763 Abercrombie lived in Hackney, working as gardener to Mr Alveres, before establishing a small market garden and nursery in 1770. Thus he was a contemporary and competitor of Loddiges. However, Abercrombie again changed profession after a couple of years, this time becoming a publican, but this life was not to his wife's liking and he soon returned to the nursery business, and turned his talents to writing.

Abercrombie's first book, *Every man his own gardener* (1767) became a runaway success, going through twenty-one editions during his lifetime, and was still in print a century after its first edition. However, it was initially published under the name of Thomas Mawe, who, as head gardener to the fourth Duke of Leeds, was a far grander and more respected figure than an unknown nurseryman. Mawe, who subsequently met and became a great friend and advisor to Abercrombie, had been asked by London bookseller William Griffin to read the manuscript. He was impressed both with Abercrombie's practical knowledge and literary skill, and bore testa-

The frontispiece of the sixteenth edition of John Abercrombie's Every man his own gardener *(1800), showing the great man himself aged 72 with wooden spade standing in front of a frame and lights, and in the distance a lean-to glasshouse.*

ment to 'the merit of the production, and prefixed his name to the publication in order to give it that celebrity to which it was so justly entitled, for which he received a gratuity of twenty guineas'.[20] As hoped, using Mawe's name gave the unknown author a degree of cachet and boosted sales; and it was not until the seventh edition (1776) that Abercrombie was acknowledged as the true author.

Abercrombie was the Dr Hessayan of his day – as prolific as he was best-selling, offering easy-to-digest practical advice on a wide range of subjects, and his list of publications offers an insight into the contents and diversity of a garden likely to be under the control of a head gardener, and the subjects of which he was expected to be a master. Between 1767 and 1789 he was the author of at least fifteen works, including *The*

British Fruit-gardener, The Garden Mushroom, its Nature and Cultivation, &c. and *The British Fruit Garden, and Art of Pruning, &c.* (all three 1779), *The Complete Forcing Gardener* (1781), *The Complete Wall-tree Pruner* (1783), *The Propagation and Botanical Arrangement of Plants and Trees, useful and ornamental* (1784, 2 vols), *The Gardener's Pocket Dictionary, &c.* (3 vols) and *The Gardener's Daily Assistant* (both 1786), and *The Hot-House Gardener, The Complete Kitchen Gardener, and Hot-bed Forcer, &c.* and *The Gardener's Pocket Journal* (all 1789). The last of these, as inexpensive as it was useful, regularly sold an edition of 2,000 copies a year.[21]

However, these very successful head gardeners-turned-nurserymen were the exception to the rule, and more typical, and less successful, were the experiences of Archibald M'Naughton also of Hackney, who in a letter dated 29 November 1825 entitled 'On the Life of a Jobbing Gardener' gives a glimpse into one man's 'upwards of fifty years in the line':

I left Edinburgh in the year 1777, and, after working some time in Mr Christopher Gray's nursery at Fulham, I got a very good place with a Mr Rolls, a great stock-broker, whose affairs went wrong after I had been six years with him, and I was obliged to quit. After going down to Scotland to see my friends, I came up again and got a place from Mr Hare, then a seedsman in St. James's Street, to go to Mrs. Wilson at Putney, where I remained till her daughter married, when her husband having an aversion to Scotch servants, I was obliged to leave. Soon after this, a fellow-work-man and myself attempted to set up a small nursery at Epsom, part of which is now occupied by Mr Young of that place; but, after struggling hard for little more than two years, we were obliged to give up, after losing all we had saved, and about £50 which my partner had borrowed from his aunt at Kinross, and which preyed so upon his mind, that I verily believe it was the cause of his death, which happened about a year afterwards at Windsor; where he got into a small place to look after a garden, and some fields in which vegetables were grown for sale.

Not liking to go into servitude again, I began jobbing on my own account, and a poor business I have found it ever since. When I first began, the highest wages I could get were 3s. a day, and obliged to find my own tools. I had a good deal of employment at first, partly from the circumstance of being a Scotchman, being called by the people who employ jobbers, a professed gardener.[22]

M'Naughton's experiences show that gardening in the eighteenth century was a hard profession and one generally poorly paid. The next chapters examine in detail the education of the head gardener and the conditions under which he trained and worked in the nineteenth century.

CHAPTER 3

Education and Apprenticeship

To understand how and why the head gardener's star rose to its zenith in the nineteenth century it is necessary to look at the wider picture and to put his realm into the broader context of the British Empire. The latter part of the eighteenth century saw the great technological breakthroughs that heralded the machine age. As processes of manufacturing, especially those of cotton textiles, were revolutionised, so international trade boomed. Simultaneously, associated industries such as coal mining, iron smelting and transportation (canals and later the railways) also grew dramatically. Between 1740 and 1848 the national output of iron increased from a level smaller than that of France to one greater than the rest of the world combined. In 1848 British coal output was two-thirds of the global total, and cotton more than half. Even as late as 1913 and on the eve of the First World War, Britain still accounted for 25 per cent of world trade in manufactured goods (albeit a marked reduction from the figure of 37 per cent in the 1880s) and a year later, total foreign investment by 'the City' in the 'formal and informal empire' still stood at £4 billion. By the mid-nineteenth century Britain was both the workshop of the world and the world's first super-power. Industrial innovations helped secure this position, while trade paid for much of it. 'Old money' continued to flourish and the wealth base widened. While land values had almost doubled between 1700 and 1790, so the average per capita income rose from £8 to £9 in 1700 to £22 by 1820.[1]

Certain industrialists, financiers, merchants and other entrepreneurs made very wealthy through various endeavours, together with others such as retired military staff, politicians and the literati, became the *nouveaux riches*. Many of these 'new arrivals' wished to display their wealth, and perhaps more importantly, desperately craved respectability and acceptance into the upper echelons of established society. The eighteenth-century cachet of land ownership still held fast – 'a gentleman did not work' – and so the purchase of a country estate (in tandem with a town house for the

Season) became an essential accoutrement for the socially aspirant. An intrinsic part of this status symbol was the garden, which itself offered further scope to demonstrate one's learning and to celebrate one's financial success, while simultaneously conforming to expected social norms.

The swelling ranks of the wealthy estate owners thus created a demand for more gardeners. *The Horticultural Directory* (a 'who's-who-and-where' of owners, head gardeners and country gardens published annually by *The Cottage Gardener*, continued as *The Journal of Horticulture*) listed *c.*1,056 head gardeners in 1867, rising to *c.*1,831 two decades later, *c.*3,720 by 1907 and a peak of *c.*4,199 in 1914. And even this was not a complete catalogue, for absent in 1914 are Miss Jekyll's own Munstead Wood (Surrey), together with the gardens she co-designed for Marsh Court (Surrey), The Deanery (Berkshire) and Lindisfarne Castle (Northumberland).

This widening of garden-ownership (and the acceptance that women could also be interested in gardening) was commented upon as early as 1828 by the head gardener and author, Charles McIntosh (1794–1864, also variously spelt M'Intosh and MacIntosh) in the Preface of his first major work *The Practical Gardener and Modern Horticulturist*.

> The gardens of the great were formerly under the sole control of a well-educated scientific man, but now we see the peeress directing the management of her own gardens and greenhouses, by the force of her own knowledge and experience; we see her ransacking the most distant quarters of the world for those beautiful exotics, which are now the pride and beauty of our gardens; we see the opulent merchant, after a meritorious life spent in the harassing and uncertain walks of commerce, retiring to his suburban retreat, and there passing the evening of his life in the cultivation of his garden, or the management of his hot-houses. [2]

Indeed, what could make a *nouveau riche* garden-owner feel more smug than to invite his aristocratic neighbour to view his most recent, most expensive and thoroughly fashionable horticultural purchases and successes. And who was given the responsibility of creating and nurturing such displays of one-upmanship? Why, the head gardener of course! It was the head gardener's job to ensure that the formal gardens juxtaposed to the house and wider pleasure grounds looked at their peak whatever the season or weather. It was the head gardener's job to ensure the grounds reflected, or better yet, set the latest style. It was the head gardener's job to ensure the ornamental gardens were filled with the latest, rarest and most expensive plants. It was the head gardener's job to fill the glasshouses and conservatories with rare plants in their prime. It was the head gardener's job to ensure the kitchen gardens produced the blooms and foliage that he carefully transformed into elaborate decorations which graced the house. It was the head gardener's job to cultivate the greatest diversity of vegetables and fruits to the highest level of perfection, in and out of natural season so that the dining table both when in the country and in town was laden with the unusual and the tasty.

CHANGING TIMES

But a head gardener's duties did not end there, for just as the wider world was changing rapidly and dramatically, so was the realm of the head gardener. This was a great age of scientific enquiry and experimentation, of a growing understanding of how the natural order of things was arranged and how it all worked. It was also a time of quandary – how did art and nature relate to one another, should the genius of man be clearly stamped on the natural, or was a synthesis or symbiosis possible? Down the century the rapidly advancing art and science of gardening transformed both how the garden looked and how plants were grown, and consequently put ever-increasing demands on the already heavily burdened shoulders of the head gardener. Perhaps McIntosh was only somewhat exaggerating when he suggested that were a gardener from the mid-eighteenth century suddenly to be placed in a garden 'cultivated on the principles of the present day' he would be as surprised as 'the untutored savage seeing a gigantic fabric moving on the waters, impelled by a little steam issuing from a cauldron of boiling water'.[3]

John Claudius Loudon (1783–1843) provided a more rounded summary in 1826 when he said that gardening was quite different to what had been twenty years ago. To back up his assertion he cited that more than double the number of exotic plants were in culture, and nearly the same proportion of new fruits, that 'Forcing by flues, steam, fermenting substances, &c. is now carried to an extent never before contemplated', and that garden buildings, structures and implements had all improved and increased in their variety. Add to this discoveries in chemistry, 'the doctrine of heat', meteorology, geology and plant physiology, and Loudon could claim with justification that 'there is not a single operation, whether on the soil or on plants, that has not undergone improvement'. Loudon finished by asserting that in addition to a mastery of these new subjects, the head gardener was now also 'employed as an artist, or man of taste, in designing and laying out walks, roads, and plantations of various kinds'.[4]

JOHN CLAUDIUS LOUDON

Described by his contemporary, the highly influential American landscape designer, Andrew Jackson Downing (1815–52), as 'the most distinguished gardening author of the age', Loudon was not a head-gardener-turned-writer in the mould of Abercrombie or McIntosh. Rather, he was a garden designer turned author, yet played a pivotal figure in the story of the head gardener, where his two spheres of influence revolved inseparably around one another. As a hugely prolific writer – he published approximately 60 million words on subjects including gardening and horticulture, architecture, farming and rural improvement in the four decades before his death – his publications were the definitive source of reference for a generation of head gardeners, their subordinates and their employers – in particular those new to gardening who knew nothing, but wanted to. And while Loudon was often opinionated, authoritarian and censorious in his proclamations, his zeal was tempered with a great and genuine humanity and life-long dedication to improving. As his wife, Jane (1808–57), observed without the need of a proud spouse's bias, 'there never lived a more liberal and thoroughly public spirited man'. This aspect of Loudon's character played a large role in his second realm of influence. For through his writings Loudon emphatically encouraged and berated those amongst his readers who were landowners that they had a duty and responsibility to improve the lot of, amongst other groups, gardeners. Other entries on the long list of liberal causes advocated by Loudon were the provision of public parks in the rapidly enlarging cities and the improvement of rural workers' living conditions, including the provision of a garden.

The son of a farmer, Loudon arrived in London in 1803 determined to be a landscape designer in the Picturesque style, and that year the *Literary Journal* published his first treatise 'Observations on laying out the Public Squares of London'. A monograph appeared in each of the successive three years – *Observations on the formation and management of useful and orna-*

mental Plantations, &c. (1804), *A short Treatise on some improvements lately made in Hot-house* (1805), and the two volumes of *A Treatise on forming, improving, and managing Country Residences, &c* (1806). As a consequence of a bout of rheumatic fever Loudon left London for Oxfordshire in 1806 where he exchanged his drawing board and pen for horse and plough and began to farm at Pinner, and later at Tew Lodge. Assisted by his father, Loudon proved to be a successful farmer, for five years later, when he did not renew the farm lease, he was able to use his savings of £15,000 to fund extended tours of the south of England in 1813 and through Europe as far as Moscow the following year.[5]

The decade also yielded four more books – *Hints on the formation of Gardens and Pleasure Grounds, &c.* (1812), *Remarks on the Construction of Hot-houses, &c.* (1817), and *Sketches of Curvilinear Hot-houses, &c.* and *A comparative view of the Curvilinear, and common mode of Roofing Hot-houses* (both 1818). Indeed, Loudon was a pioneer in glasshouse design, inventing not only the ridge-and-furrow style of roofing, which he claimed maximised light penetration, but also patenting in 1816 his flexible wrought-iron glazing bar. Loudon was convinced that metal was the material of the future as far as glasshouse frameworks were concerned, and his glazing bar, which could be bent into any direction without loss of strength, enabled the design of metal-framed structures of curvilinear and conical form.[6]

Encyclopædia of Gardening and The Gardener's Magazine

However, it was the 1820s that saw Loudon achieve two of his greatest publishing triumphs. His massive *Encyclopædia of Gardening*, described as 'the first book to treat the subject comprehensively from the historical, technical, aesthetic, and horticultural points of view' first appeared in 1822; and, four years later he launched *The Gardener's Magazine* of which he remained Conductor until his death (and the demise of the magazine). *The Gardener's Magazine* was not strictly the first gardening periodical – William Curtis had commenced his *The Botanical Magazine* in 1787 (it continues to be published to this day). Nor was it the first weekly published gardening newspaper – that honour belongs to George Glenny (1793–1874), a watch-case maker and later a wine merchant with a passion for tulips, who started the *Gardener's Gazette* in 1837. A year later Glenny courted notoriety when he received censure from the council of the Horticultural Society for daring to criticise the judging at the Chiswick show![7]

Where *The Gardener's Magazine* proved innovative was in its market position and contents. Filled with information on a vast range of gardening topics – accounts of new plants, garden visits, plans of bedding schemes, designs for head gardeners' houses, discussion about artistic garden design, detailed advice on the culture and cultivation of all types of plants, glasshouse architecture and heating, book reviews, etc., etc., etc. – it was the first periodical intended to be read by both professional gardeners and garden-owners alike. Through its pages, Loudon gave a mouthpiece to gardeners who broadcast their opinions and experiences, and to employers, who made suggestions – some judicious, many others patronising and pompous. But above all, *The Gardener's Magazine* gave Loudon a regular mouthpiece through which he could propound and disseminate his ideas and opinions.

THE EDUCATION OF GARDENERS

One of the topics about which Loudon and his correspondents regularly and fiercely beat the drum was the education of gardeners. So important did he consider it that he included it in his Introduction to the first issue of *The Gardener's Magazine*, which appeared in April 1826: 'Finally, there is one subject which, more than every thing else, will tend to improve gardening and agriculture, – the better education of gardeners… As gardening has advanced, as its productions and its province have extended, the situation of head gardener has become more and more important; he has become a more confidential servant; he is entrusted with more power, and is more frequently consulted by the master and mistress of the family, with whom his communications are more frequent than they used to be.'[8] Loudon was vehement in his belief that the good head gardener had to be possessed of a good and broad education in addition to fine horticultural skills. McIntosh was equally convinced that 'The knowledge of the management of a garden is not to be obtained by pertinaciously [*sic*] adhering to one particular system, however recommended by high and celebrated names.' Rather, it was 'only to be acquired by the most constant perseverance and the most unremitting industry, and by reducing the principles of theory to the certain and infallible test of practice'.[9]

The long, hard road to the top

Loudon also asserted that to achieve a headship required 'extraordinary exertion, and the denial, in great part, of even the necessaries of life for a series of years'. If such proclamations sound formidable, then they were nothing compared to the traineeship that the prospective head gardener had to endure. To ascend the tall ladder to the elevated position of a head gardener was a long and hard climb. It began aged twelve or fourteen when a young lad, already in possession of a good primary education, embarked on a traineeship that could last as long as they were currently old. Put simply and generally, the new apprentice began by spending a year as a pot boy, carrying out the most menial and unpleasant tasks – washing pots, stoking the boilers, etc. Next, he spent periods of a year or so gaining a basic grounding in the different divisions of the garden – the ornamental grounds, the kitchen garden, the glasshouses, etc. After about four years of mental and physical slog, the apprentice rose to the position of journeyman gardener. As the name would suggest, the following years were peripatetic, as the journeyman moved from one establishment to another, changing jobs in order to further develop his skills in the various disciplines of horticulture. Not all trainees could or would achieve a headship and many did not progress beyond the level of journeyman, as Loudon pointed out 'Many journeymen are unwilling or unable to undergo these privations; under their pressure the exertions of others are weakened; and in no case are they what they might be, or, what the art requires.'[10] For those who could stay the course, a talented journeyman of two or three years' experience could then take a head gardener's post in a small garden, perhaps alone or with a staff of one or two, or could move to another large establishment as a foreman of one of the garden departments. The penultimate rung on the ladder was that of general foreman or deputy head gardener. Following experience at this level he was ready to apply for his first major headship.

So who were the men who decided to pursue this tough path? Gardeners were male and usually from a rural, working-class background; many also had a father and/or brothers in the trade. To make it to head gardener, however, the prospective candidate had to be possessed of certain qualities of character. McIntosh gave an indication of these – a natural horticultural talent, determination, open-mindedness and adaptability, an ability to learn quickly, forbearance of working very hard, high levels of self-discipline and both personal and professional pride in the constant striving for self-improvement through reading and study.

Just such a man was William Miller, whose father had been gardener to three generations of the Lamont family at Knockdow, near Dunoon on the south-east coast of Scotland. While a journeyman at Erskine House, the seat of Lord Blantyre in Renfrewshire, he spent a year managing the forcing houses in which cherries, figs and vines 'were grown successfully on hot walls'. Miller, 'in consequence of having the care of the fires, which were all smoke flues' never went to bed very early, but rather than complain about this, he looked at it as a positive, for it afforded him more time for study. Later in his apprenticeship Miller moved to Dysart House (Fife) as the outdoor foreman, and was there when the head gardener, Mr Laing, succeeded in flowering *Rhododendron dalhousiæ* for the first time in Britain. According to Miller's dates of employ this must have been between 1853 and 1856, but taken in conjunction with the fact that seed of this epiphytic *Rhododendron* sent from India by Sir Joseph Hooker did not arrive in Britain until about 1849, it is more likely to be the later date.[11]

A glance through the pages of the gardening press reveals that the education of trainee gardeners was a particularly contentious topic, exactly because the debate over education was inextricably entwined with the issue of the hardships endured because of it – issues that are examined in the next chapter. But what exactly was the range of subject matter that an aspiring head gardener was expected to master? It was taken for granted that before entering a garden an apprentice was possessed of a tolerable school education including writing, arithmetic, geometry, drawing and some rudiments of Latin. Once in a position, education became a parallel track. During the day the trainee (apprentice and journeyman alike) had to work and master the diverse practical skills of gardening taught by means of instruction and experience. These long days (ten hours a day, six days a week) were combined with long evenings dedicated to self-improvement through the study of both horticultural theory and the wider set of subjects of which the head gardener was expected to be a master. A look at just some of the most influential gardening books of the time offers a small insight into how much horticultural knowledge a trainee was expected to add to his practical learning. The second edition of Loudon's *Encyclopædia of Gardening* (1824) runs to 1,233 pages of tiny, closely spaced print; the two volumes of McIntosh's *The Practical Gardener* (1828) run to 1,120, while those of his massive two-volume *The Book of the Garden* (1853 and 1855) contain 776 and 867 pages respectively.

The importance of books and the responsibility of the employer

Horticultural knowledge was just the start. Ideally, opined Loudon, 'wherever there is a tool-house, there ought to be a library', and in 1827 he considerately provided a preliminary reading list. In seventeen sections it ran to 167 titles covering subject matter from grammar through foreign languages, arithmetic and book keeping, mathematics, drawing, geography and history, oral and political science, taste and criticism, natural philosophy and chemistry, natural history, general knowledge, and professional books as well as general and professional periodicals.

Loudon placed the responsibility of its provision four-square on the employer, for the reason that: 'a gardener can no more acquire his profession without books than he can without tools, and because the wages of gardeners, and especially of journeymen, are inadequate to every individual's purchasing such books as are requisite for him'. Loudon further asserted that such a resource would have additional psychological benefits, for trainees 'would immediately proceed more faithful and industrious servants, because the library would be felt at once as increase of wages and an act of kindness; and gentlemen, however high in rank, cannot be ignorant, that in all kinds of labour, from the lowest and most mechanical to the highest and most intellectual, men work as they are paid, and are attached to their employers in proportion as they are treated by them with kindness'. Moreover, the moral welfare of trainees would also be improved, for their evenings would be spent in diligence in the library and not indulging in licentious behaviour in the pub. And last but not least, in Loudon's opinion, the provision of a library would mean that the trainees would no longer have to purchase books themselves, a practice that in many cases required trainees 'to deny themselves the requisite quality and quantity of food'. Thus would they be able to put the saved money towards food and 'be able to live better and work harder'. But, while many trainees did live up to the educational achievements expected of them by Loudon, few employers were convinced to part with their money and establish libraries.[12]

Loudon's last contribution to a trainee's education, was, sadly, a posthumous one. Two years after his death the 240-page *Self-instruction for Young Gardeners* (1845) was published, and its contents page provides a specific catalogue of the non-horticultural subjects that the apprentice was expected to master. In addition to the assumed knowledge of the 'geography of natural history, geology, chemistry, meteorology and physiology', the twelve chapters provide instruction on, in order, arithmetic, book keeping, practical geometry, mensuration, practical trigonometry, mechanics, hydrostatics and hydraulics, land-surveying, levelling, planning and mapping, architectural drawing, and isometrical [*sic*] and perspective, with examples, showing their application to horticultural and agricultural purposes.

Loudon was a hard task-master, and in 1861 William Keane, head gardener at Orwell Park in Ipswich, contributor to *The Journal of Horticulture*, and author of both *Out-Door Gardening During Every Week In The Year* (1859) and *In-Door Gardening During Every Week In The Year* (1860), issued *The Young Gardener's Educator*. Published in twelve monthly parts costing a shilling each, and thus clearly targeted at the none-too-well-off apprentice, Keane's syllabus was slightly less taxing. *The Young Gardener's Educator* he proudly claimed contained all the 'subjects generally considered necessary for the young gardener to understand', to whit, 'English grammar, geology, botany, vegetable physiology, horticultural chemistry, physical geography, entomology, land measuring, architectural drawing, letter writing, penmanship, and the measurement of artificers connected with gardening'. Written in a similar way to London and Wise's *The Retir'd Gard'ner* it took the form of questions and answers between an eager-to-learn journeyman gardener and the all-knowing head gardener, 'MrB'; and some of the language is wonderful. In this instance the journeyman, having received Mr B's introduction to the subject of plant physiology, replies 'I have listened most attentively, and endeavoured to understand all you have said, but I must confess that there were some crackjaw words that I could not comprehend.'

Gardeners' Improvement Societies

An alternative to solo-study was to learn with others in the same boat, and to join an Improvement Society. The concept for such societies for gardeners was another of Loudon's grand improvement schemes. He considered that they could be modelled on 'institutions like those recently established for mechanics, or travelling libraries', but added the caveat that, with the exception of large metropolises it would be unworkable to expect gardeners from various gardens to travel in order to meet because gardens and gardeners were so isolated by the very nature of their employ. However, Loudon's scheme proved more popular than library provision (probably because it cost employers little if anything) for thus was conceived the garden-based society. Many were formed across the country and enjoyed success. In 1865 'W.R.P.' of the garden at Shrubland Park (Suffolk), wrote to *The Gardeners' Chronicle* to say 'A society for the improvement of young gardeners has been established here, and is working well. Two are appointed to act as treasurer and secretary; subscriptions are required to purchase weekly papers, eight in number, including *The Gardeners' Chronicle*, *The Florist and Pomologist* and *The Journal of Horticulture*.' The article goes on to say an additional paper and books are presented by their employer, Sir G. B. Middleton. The society met twice a week to study grammar and once a week one member presented an essay – when attendance was compulsory.[13] And six years later, the gardeners at Drumlanrig (Dumfries and Galloway), formed their own Mutual Improvement Association. A decade later, the list of topics under discussion was extensive, and included 'Eradication of Garden Insects; Protection of Wall Fruits; Formation of Character; Certain Trades and Professions as Causes of Disease; Cultivation of the Cyclamen; Cultivation of the Azalea; Progress in Australia; The Pansy; Cultivation of the Strawberry; The Conservatory; Temperance; Forcing of the Fig; Government by Party; Does Civilisation necessitate Demoralisation?; Food; Potato Disease; Cultivation of the Balsam; Cultivation of the Bouvardia; Movements of Plants; Garden-Walks; Hardy Plants for Walls; Cultivation of the Raspberry; Pruning of outdoor Fruit-trees; The Camellia; Man's Inhumanity to Man; Hotbeds and their uses'; 'Cultivation of the Orange' and 'Window plants, and their Injuriousness to Health'. [14]

STANDARDISING EDUCATION

While it was roundly agreed that gardeners required a high level of education and that they had to endure undue suffering to achieve it, there was no set standard of apprenticeship, no national curriculum by which the lad would ascend the ladder of his chosen profession. Consequently, there was no standard terminology for describing the exact rung to which he had risen, nor what level of experience and skill was required or expected for its attainment. An early attempt to bring some order or standard to the profession of gardener was made in 1836 by The Horticultural Society of London (now the Royal Horticultural Society). Loudon was effusive when the Garden Committee decided 'to admit no young men into their garden, as journeymen, who have not received a certain degree of school education;

and to recommend no Journeymen from the gardens, to fill situations as head gardeners, – who have not been regularly examined as to their physiological and other scientific knowledge, and received a certificate stating the degree of proficiency they have attained'.[15] However, creating a national standard was something that took a further thirty years to bear any fruit, and even then, sad to say, the fruits were scarce.

In 1860 the debate over the education of gardeners, which had been smouldering away for over a quarter of a century, burst into flames again and raged hot and fast. The starting point was the well-rehearsed and often-opined view that gardeners should have a sound and broad education in horticultural and related matters. But since horticulture was now advancing so fast, more needed to be done. In fact, the first step towards a national standard had already been made in the 1850s when the Royal Society of Arts expanded its national system of artisan exams to include botany; and within the pages of *The Gardeners' Chronicle* there was mooted reproach that too few gardeners sat the exams, combined with concern that a trainee gardener's 'on the job' training was biased towards the empiric rather than the scientific.[16] In the issue for 9 June 1860 'Linager' – a well-meaning but somewhat misguided gent – put the cat amongst the pigeons by suggesting a three-tier set of national exams. The Preliminary Examination, to be taken between the ages of eighteen and twenty-one, would require 'little more than what every decently educated lad must learn if he is to rise to the level of a labourer' with additions of book keeping, land-surveying and timber measuring. The Pass Examination, not to be taken over the age of twenty-three, would be based on a candidate's 'Practical skill as a cultivator' and would include botany; and the final exam, the Examination for Honours, was not to be accessible to men under twenty-five and would comprise papers on vegetable physiology, plant geography, climate, and two optional subjects, pomology and mathematics 'not to go beyond the first book of Euclid'.

Knowing his readership was primarily professional gardeners and their likely response, the Editor, John Lindley, attempted pre-emptive mollification by acknowledging that Linager's system was not intended for:

the mature gardeners of England . . .whose knowledge goes far beyond what is required to grow a plant; excellent business habits, skill in construction, good taste in arrangement, sound knowledge of practical physiology, and acquaintance with various collateral matters . . .our own columns have for 20 years borne the strongest possible testimony to the justice of this representation. The best writers on practical subjects have been gardeners, or have been educated as such, who can lay down the pruning knife, or put aside the potting board and take up their pens with equal skill.[17]

Feathers were, nonetheless, very ruffled. The notion of a national curriculum was a good one, and had the objective been to devise a syllabus for full-time study at degree level, Linager's suggestions would have been an excellent starting point. But his syllabus was suggested in all seriousness to be applicable to employees (not students) who were already working more than sixty hours a week. No surprise, then, that Linager's well-intentioned but impractical suggestions received the scorn and ire of gardeners. Typical of the scathing rebukes was one from William Prestidge, who wrote to ask Linager 'what class of men' he thought were going to be trained as gardeners, 'for only the sons of middle-class men could ever afford the time and money to be educated as he proposes, and they will hardly go through all the high degrees mentioned in order to enter even a nobleman's garden at wages varying from £50 to £100 per annum, when they can clear above £1000 per annum in trade with less education than he insists on their possessing'.[18]

Another correspondent, 'A Gardener and Constant Reader', echoed Prestidge's criticisms that not only was Linager's suggested level of education unrealistically high and could only be acquired at an unaffordable cost, but even if such a goal were achieved, the subsequent financial reward would not be worth the hardships endured to have achieved it. Contrasting the practicalities of reality with the hypothetical desires of Linager, he sarcastically observed that if a trainee who had followed Linager's syllabus to the letter and passed with honours 'at last arrives at an age and possesses an amount of experience when he may justly expect a situation and remuneration commensurate with the trouble and expense he has been at to prepare himself for it. Does he get it ? Oh, no! . . . if he is clever and can produce testimonials to that effect, together, with being married and having no incumbrance, he may be fortunate enough to realise a salary of 18s per week, or perhaps £1.'[19]

Progress did continue towards developing a more realistic national system of exams, and on 9 December 1865 *The Gardeners' Chronicle* announced that the Royal Horticultural Society in conjunction with the Royal Society of Arts was to arrange the 'Examination of Gardeners' to be held for the first time in April 1866. Their aim was to: 'provide a more efficient and widespread means of bringing out the theoretical talent in the rising generation of gardeners'.

The system was a two-tier one. The first level was conducted by the Royal Society of Arts and candidates were invited to sit the three-hour exams for Diplomas in Mensuration, Book-keeping, Practical Geometry, Botany, Floriculture, and Fruit and Vegetable Culture. The Society, aware of the costs and difficulties of travel experienced by potential candidates, offered the exams in a range of locations all over the country. Not so the Royal Horticultural Society which oversaw the second level. This was a practical examination held in London open to those who had gained Diplomas in Botany and Floriculture or in Botany and Fruit and Vegetable Culture. Those who passed with a first- or second-class Certificate in 'the operations of the Fruit and Vegetable Garden' or 'in the operations of the Flower-garden' (including 'a fair amount of skill in Surveying and Plan-drawing, and taste in Laying-out Gardens') had their travelling expenses reimbursed and were admitted as Associates of the Royal Horticultural Society. The highest-scoring candidate was also awarded a medal.[20] An additional incentive to sit the exams was offered by *The Gardeners' Chronicle*, which, in the years until 1871, put up prizes of £3, £2 and £1 to 'bona fide' professional gardeners taking First Class certificates.

However, records in the Royal Society of Art's archives show that the exams were not well subscribed. Between 1866 and 1874 only seventy-seven candidates took the exam in Fruit and Vegetable Culture and seventy-eight in Floriculture. The numbers for 1867 were nine in each division, which given the fact that the *Horticultural Directory* for the year listed *c*.1,056 head gardeners, which would put the number of apprentices eligible to sit the exams at several thousand, shows a pitifully low take up. Thus, despite all laudable efforts, and so many print inches over the years, national exams were not a success. The conclusion must be that apprentices and journeymen continued to learn their craft 'on the job', and that the exams were not popular because trainees received no benefit sitting them, a problem exacerbated by a lack of a national pay structure linked to exam achievement – employers simply did not care about a bit of paper. As 'A Gardener and Constant Reader' pragmatically

BOTANY.

THREE HOURS ALLOWED.

The candidate is expected to answer correctly three questions in Section I, and six questions in Sections II. and III., including descriptions of at least two of the fresh specimens, Nos. 8, 9, and 10 each stand for an answer.

SECTION I.—STRUCTURE AND PHYSIOLOGY.

1. Define the following terms, and give examples in illustration as required.

Diadelphous. Give examples from two Natural Orders. *Orthotropous.* Give two Natural Orders in illustration. *Gynandrous.* Name fruits of genera belonging to two Natural Orders in illustration.

Anomous. Give an example.

2. What are *Stipules?* In which British Natural Orders are they generally present? In which absent?

3. Explain the structure and function of *Leaves.*

4. What is the function of *Albumen?* Name six British Natural Orders which generally have albuminous, and six which have exalbuminous seeds.

5. Name the essential elementary constituents of plants.

6. What functions are liable to be interfered with in *transplanting?* And how is fatal disturbance to be guarded against?

SECTION II.—SYSTEMATIC AND ECONOMIC BOTANY.

1. State the principles upon which plants are classed.

2. Which natural orders furnish the following products? State also the part of the plant affording each:— *Cotton, saffron, manna, colocynth, croton, sago.*

3. Distinguish *Ranunculus* from *Leguminosae.*

4. Distinguish the genera Oak (*Quercus*), Chestnut (*Castanea*), and Beech (*Fagus*).

5. Describe the usual structure of the flower in *Grasses.*

6. Describe the principal modifications of the *vegetation* and of the *fruit and its appendages* in British *Compositae.*

7. Name the *Natural Order* to which the plants marked A, B, and C respectively belong, with *reasons for your opinion.*

SECTION III.—DESCRIPTIVE BOTANY.

8, 9, and 10. Describe the three plants marked A, B, and C in the proper sequence of their organs, and in accordance with the examples given in Lindley's "Descriptive Botany" and Oliver's "Lessons" (Appendix).

FLORICULTURE.

THREE HOURS ALLOWED.

1. What are the conditions most favourable to the germination of seeds?

2. Describe the process of budding, and point out in what respect it differs from grafting.

3. How and by what means, if at all, may hardier races of any particular kind of plant be obtained?

4. For what special cultural purposes are "span-roofed" and "lean-to" houses most suitable?

5. Suppose a conservatory has to be decorated at Christmas with flowers, some in their natural season, others forwarded or retarded by artificial treatment. Name a few of the leading plants which will naturally be in a condition to be used for that purpose, and name also some of the most important of those which would have to be prepared artificially, indicating in general terms the mode of preparation.

6. The showy Pansy of the garden is understood to have been produced from one of our wild pansies. Describe how this change can have been effected.

7. What are the conditions and process, at the flowering stage of a plant, necessary to the production of fertile seed?

8. What system of treatment would be specially conducive to the production of abundance of blossoms, and what would be most conducive to a paucity of blossoms? Take greenhouse Azaleas and Pelargoniums as examples.

9. Name the principal decorative plants available for the garden, greenhouse, and stove, in the different months of the year, in establishments where both stove and greenhouse accommodation are provided.

10. How should forcing houses be ventilated, and for what reasons mainly is ventilation necessary in such structures—to which artificial heat, it is to be remembered, is being at the same time applied?

11. Describe the process of hybridising plants, and the conditions necessary to a successful result—that is, the actual production of hybrids.

12. In what way is bottom-heat important in plant-culture, and how is it best applied?

FRUIT AND VEGETABLE CULTURE.

THREE HOURS ALLOWED.

I.—FRUIT-TREE CULTURE.

1. Give a list of 12 varieties of dessert apples to ripen in succession from August till May, and in the order in which they are ready for use.

2. The same of pears.

3. Give a list of eight varieties of kitchen apples to come into use in succession from August of one year till August of the year following.

4. Give a list of six varieties of dessert plums to ripen in succession from July till November, arranged in their order of ripening.

5. The same of cherries from May till September.

6. Name six varieties of the best peaches and state the order in which they ripen.

7. The same of nectarines.

8. The same of apricots.

9. What are the various stocks used for the propagation of the apple, and what is the effect each has on the scion?

10. What is the best form in which to train fruit trees for open fruit garden culture; and when ought the pruning of these trees to be performed so as most effectually to economise the vigour of the tree and develope the greatest amount of fruit-bearing wood?

The question paper for examinations in botany, floriculture, and fruit and vegetable culture set in 1866 by the Royal Society of Arts as part of its programme of examinations for artisans.

11. What is the object for which root-pruning is practised, and at what season and in what manner is this operation to be performed?

12. Describe the process by which trees absorb moisture by their roots, and by which the sap circulates throughout their system.

13. Why are the upper shoots on a branch developed with greater vigour than the lower?

14. How is a branch increased in thickness?

15. How is a branch increased in length?

16. What are the functions of the leaves, and what is the influence that stimulates their operation?

17. Do trees absorb moisture by their roots and leaves only; and, if not, through what medium?

18. What are the substances that constitute the food of trees, and how are they conveyed and assimilated into their system?

19. What are the causes that induce canker and gum in fruit trees, and how are these causes to be removed or prevented?

20. Describe in detail, as concisely as possible, the forcing of vines for a crop to be ripe early in February, stating the period when the vines are started, the various degrees of temperature employed, and every operation practised in the course of the process.

II.—VEGETABLE CULTURE.

21. Give a list of six varieties of peas to furnish a supply in succession from May till October, and state the periods when the seed of each should be sown.

22. Describe the cultivation of broccoli, stating the soil best adapted for it, and the mode of its preparation; also the varieties to be employed in securing a succession of supply throughout the year, beginning in August.

23. Describe in detail the process of making a hotbed.

24. Prepare a list of the kinds and quantities of vegetable seeds and roots necessary for cropping a garden of half an acre throughout the year.

ANIMAL PHYSIOLOGY.
(IN RELATION TO HEALTH.)
THREE HOURS ALLOWED.

1. Describe the structure of the human lung, commencing at its root, and including the air tubes, air cells, blood-vessels, lymphatics and nerves.

2. When, where, and how, is the gastric juice formed? Give an account of its composition and its action in the economy.

3. Enumerate the parts which serve as protective organs to the eyeball. Describe briefly their position and structure, and give the use of each.

4. Suppose a person to be suddenly immersed in carbonic acid gas, how and by what form of nervous and muscular action is suffocation produced? Name the parts which are concerned in the stoppage of the breath, and say how each acts.

5. What poison or poisons destroy human life in the case of exposure to the fumes of burning charcoal, or to the smoke of accidental fires in close rooms? What preliminary and other precautions can be taken to enable one to enter such apartments to save human life?

Exam question paper set by the Royal Society of Arts

pointed out 'if there is a prospect of corresponding remuneration young gardeners will not be found backward in applying themselves with diligence and ardour in order that they may be competent to fill first-class situations'.[21]

CHAPTER 4

———◆•◆•◆———

The Practical Working Life of a Trainee

To become conversant with all aspects of a garden's operations, the trainee spent time working in the different departments of a garden – each of which, depending on the size of the establishment, was under the supervision of a foreman or senior journeyman. An indication of the different departments that made up a garden is given by *The Gardeners' Chronicle*, which published a weekly calendar of operations, dividing the theatre of operations into six divisions: the planting department, the forcing department, the flower garden and shrubberies, florist's flowers, the hardy fruit garden and the kitchen garden. Reading such periodicals kept the trainee informed and up to date, while the keeping of a daily journal or log book of all the garden tasks carried out when, how and why was often encouraged as both an educational tool and as a source of reference for later in life when the apprentice had become a foreman or head gardener.

It was also an apprentice's lot to do the least pleasant and most mundane tasks, which in the ornamental gardens included weeding the flower beds, weeding and raking the paths and keeping lawns free of fallen leaves. In the kitchen garden there were pots to wash, the boilers to stoke or vents to open at night, and plenty of lifting – the coal and, of course, manure and tan bark for the hotbeds and frames. One of the less fond memories of David Thomson (1823–1909), who became head gardener at Dyrham Park in Barnet, London at the tender age of twenty-four having spent eight years as a journeyman (at Bothwell Castle, Kew and Wrotham Park), was helping to carry in 'all the bark for the pine pits . . . tons of it . . . up steep stairs . . . in December with stinging frosts, and the sweat dripping off my nose like peas'.[1]

While certain aspects of an apprentice's existence came under the microscope within the pages of the horticultural press, it is not common to find a description of an apprentice's life during the first half of the century. An

An extract from the garden journal for January 1881 kept by William Henry Winter, an undergardener in the vegetable garden at Frogmore. The entries list where and when the diverse tasks were carried out.

The most unpleasant, in this case most hazardous, tasks befell the junior apprentices. Here a young lad is applying a dusting of powdered pesticide to the crop from a very rudimentary applicator.

exception, albeit a somewhat florid and indulgent one, was provided by Peter Mackenzie who in 1842 introduced the 'four young lads' who inhabited the bothy (or apprentices' accommodation, see page 83), at Dinbur Castle.

Sandy MacAlpine, the foreman of the gardens, was at one time intended to be something else than a gardener, and was kept longer at school than boys are generally kept; but, like many a novice, he forgot to strengthen his muscles when he was endeavouring to inform his mind. Close application in the study of Latin and Greek, and one season at college, gave him every appearance of a blanched student. He found his health under-mining rapidly; he was advised to try something else; he chose the occupation of a gardener, and his health recovered; but, in-stead of leaving it when he got better, he continued to love his employment.

Colin Forbes was another inmate of the bothy at the time we refer to. He was a stout active young man; the spade appeared as light in his hands as if it had been a child's toy, and he could use it to good purpose: he did not, however, forget the education he received in his early days; he was fond of mathematical studies, and liked well to talk about square roots and cube roots, equations, involutions of quantities, circles, angles, pyramids, cylinders, cones, polygons, &c.

Walter Glenesk, another of the four, when alone, occupied his time differently from any of the rest: he was in love with the study of natural history. He made himself pretty well acquainted with the botanical systems of Linnæus and Jussieu: but he did not stop there; he acquired a knowledge of Cuvier's system of geology, Jameson's system of mineralogy, and an outline of zoology. Leach's *Arrangement of Insects* came in his way, and from it he gained some knowledge of entomology: the *Elements of Conchology*, by Brown, made him acquainted with the Linnæan arrangement of shells, also the description of the genera, and the explanation of terms used in the science of conchology. Often would he wander along the sea-beach collecting razor-shells, cockles, muscles [*sic*], oysters, &c.

The last of the four was Bauldy Black: he differed from all the rest; he did not pretend to be a book-learned man, but, for strength of body, he would match with any of his comrades; he was a good-natured lad, and took things very easy. He lost his father when he was young, and he had nothing but hard work before, and few opportunities for improving his mind. However, he had formed a love for the fiddle, and with it he used to chase away dull care, but his music was not at all times acceptable to those who lived with him.[2]

Far more convincing are the recollections of the group of noted gardeners, who having risen to positions of eminence in their profession, were asked by *The Gardeners' Chronicle* in 1874–75 to contribute autobiographical notes to a series entitled 'British Gardeners'. These recollections are first-hand accounts of the realities of trainees' experiences, albeit those of a group whose later successes demonstrably prove that they were all far-above-average trainees. All had in common a sound basic education based firmly on the 3Rs, and several were also the sons of head gardeners or nurserymen who spent their summer school holidays working in their father's gardens or business before undertaking their apprenticeship 'at home'.

William Tillery (*b*.1808), was one such who served his apprenticeship under his father, who was manager to Mr Gemmell, a nurseryman of Kilmarnock, and described his subsequent training as:

two years at Eglinton Castle under Mr Rose, who was then gardener at that place [then] employment in Malcolm's Nursery, Kensington . . . After leaving . . . I got into Caenwood [*sic*], the then refuge for destitute young gardeners, and had Mr Philip Frost, of Dropmore, for my foreman, and a friendship arose between us that has never yet been severed. Mr Frost came from Dropmore, where the bedding system had just commenced under Mr Baillie...After leaving Caenwood I was in Miss Longman's garden at Highgate for a short time, and often used to meet Coleridge the poet walking like a half-dead man on the arm of Mr Gillman, a doctor, in whose house he was an inmate. From Highgate I went to Oakhill, to be under Mr Dowding, who was then growing some of the finest Grapes in the kingdom. He was a very worthy and strict old gentleman, giving us young gardeners every information as regards the formation of his Vine borders for growing his famous Grapes.

In 1837 and at the age of twenty-nine Tillery achieved his ambition, and became head gardener to the Duke of Portland at Welbeck Abbey (Nottinghamshire). It was a position he was still holding some thirty-six years later when he wrote his account, in which he also noted that when he first arrived, as well as enjoying 'every opportunity of growing fruits, vegetables, and plants to supply the wants of a very large establishment' he also had 'frequent opportunities of visiting him [Joseph Paxton], and his then foreman, Mr Gibson, of subtropical celebrity' at Chatsworth.[3]

Also a Scot, John Webster (*b*.1814), later head gardener to the Duke of Richmond at Gordon Castle (Morayshire), began his apprenticeship under his father at Manderton, the home of General Maitland. From the age of thirteen to sixteen he worked in the gardens in the summer then 'schooled in the winter' before gaining regular employment at Manderton. At the age of eighteen he left home for Dalquharran Castle (Ayrshire) as journeyman, under David Dick, and remained there until November 1833 when he went to Whittinghame (East Lothian), under William Rintoul. 'The place was then in high keeping, and had a good range of vineries, Peach-houses, Pine-stoves, Pine-pits, &c. I derived considerable advantage during my services here from my having to assist in the laying-out of a new flower garden, of which I had the principal superintendence.' After three years, the last as foreman, Webster moved south to Claremont (Surrey) where 'all the Grapes and Pine-apples had to be sent during the summer and autumn months for the supply of the Royal table

at Lacken' where he acted as foreman 'in the houses of the fruit department' under McIntosh.[4]

A somewhat different path was trod by Archibald Fowler (1816–87) of
Castle Kennedy (Dumfries and Galloway), who began his horticultural
training at the relatively late age of sixteen. Upon the payment of ten guineas 'for apprentice fee' (see page 78) and receiving 5 shillings a week in
wages 'the first year, 6s per week the second, and 7s, per week the third'
Fowler joined the Royal Botanic Garden in Glasgow as an apprentice in
November 1832. His training was 'under the late able and accomplished
curator, Mr Stewart Murray', who presented all the apprentices with a
large ruled book, which they were expected to fill with names of plants
learned. On the first page was a set of rules, including one that said the
names learned were to be tested on 'pay nights, and if the examination did
not prove satisfactory he was to receive no pay'.

Scotland was regarded throughout the century as fertile ground for the
training of young gardeners, and Glasgow offered Fowler two further
advantages. He had 'the great privilege of attending every alternate day
Dr., afterwards Sir William Hooker's annual course of extremely popular
botanical lectures, which he delivered to crowded classes in the hall of the
Botanic Garden' and 'in the winter evenings a night school was generally
organised for three nights in the week. Practical geometry, plant and plan
drawing, mathematics, land surveying, &c., were taught.' Fowler's apprenticeship lasted four years, at the end of which he was engaged at Cadden
House near Glasgow as a journeyman gardener for nearly a year, during
the course of which he was promoted 'to the charge of the forcing houses'.
From here, in the spring of 1837 he moved to gardens of Lord Cloncurry
at Lyons, County Kildare in Ireland as foreman to Duncan M'Naughten.[5]

Yet another Scot, but one who had a famous gardening brother (Robert,
1808–73) on whom he could call for favours, was David Taylor Fish (1822–
1901). Born at Old Scone, Fish began his training at Scone Palace, the seat
of the Earl of Mansfield and famous for producing prodigious horticultural talents. Famous alumni included Fish's brother and plant hunter
David Douglas (1799–1834).

Fish's description of his formative years is particularly detailed, both in
its content and how he was treated. He trained under the 'able management of Mr James Dodds' who insisted that no 'scamping' was ever allowed
and ensured work was plentiful and done well, whether 'mowing from 5 to
9 in the morning, hoeing, digging, raking, nailing'. Fish seemed particu-

larly fond of Dodds, who was both 'able and energetic' and seldom gave direct instructions but taught by example, and occasionally by 'a pregnant saying' such as addressed to Fish one Saturday when he was cleaning the long range of glasshouses '"That's right, Davy; cleanliness is the parent of health" a sentiment that was soon made the common property of all the lads and men on the place.' During the three years of his apprenticeship, Fish also learned much from Dodds's three 'most efficient foremen': W. Purday, who later 'succeeded to the curatorship of the Botanic Gardens in Calcutta', Alex Blackie later of Revesby Abbey and John Lamont of Dickson & Company in Edinburgh. This trio 'of worthy men did much by their own enthusiasm in botany, floriculture, and kitchen gardening, to evoke similar qualities in the young men under their charge'. The curriculum for apprentices was also a useful and an unvarying one. The first year 'fires and houses', the second 'serve the kitchen' and the third 'work in the flower garden'. Custom generally gave a fourth as a journeyman, to establish more perfectly 'prentice hands' by practice in all departments before changing to another place, or going into an Edinburgh nursery.[6]

JOURNEYMAN YEARS

Moving on from an apprentice position, a journeyman gardener would travel to work in different gardens. He would apply for a specific position in order to get as broad a range of experiences as possible; it was useful to work in different parts of the country to learn about the different climates and soils, and thus what could be grown and how; while to work in a garden of renown was useful as much as a source of learning as to have as a future reference. A stint in a good nursery was also considered invaluable, for as David T. Fish observed:

> The nursery is a most useful school for young men, and all ought to pass
> through it. A fuller knowledge of men, business, and plants can be gleaned in
> nurseries than in private gardens. The mental culture and intellectual
> advancement of the men in the nursery were also stimulated and cared for at
> that time, and in the prizes of books for drawings of hothouses ... the
> establishment of the study, &c., we had the germs of those more perfect
> arrangements that have been made by the Messrs. Veitch and others for the
> intellectual culture and physical comfort of the men in their employment.[7]

As well as learning the technical aspects of garden culture and cultivation, there was always plenty of mundane work for the apprentice to carry out in the kitchen garden, be it shovelling, barrowing, stoking boilers or washing pots.

Following his apprenticeship, Andrew Turnbull spent time working at 'Selkirk Nursery until I went to Dalkeith Park in March, 1821, under the late Mr McDonald, who was undoubtedly a very good kitchen and fruit gardener, and an active pushing man'. Here Turnbull began to develop his plantsman skills, taking fullest advantage of the 'excellent collection of herbaceous plants in the old garden' and 'the privilege of staying in the gardens after working hours to learn the plants, which opportunity I fully embraced, and often remained alone'. Turnbull generally learned fifty plants an evening, repeating the names the following evening before learning the next batch, and clearly had a talent in this department, for 'not quite eighteen years of age'. McDonald placed him as foreman in the flower garden. Here he further developed his propagation skills, recalling later that 'the three years that I held that situation I have often looked back as to a very pleasant period of my life'. The next step for Turnbull was promotion to the position of general foreman, which gave him responsibility over 'the whole of the men and women employed in the garden and grounds, and conducted the work as arranged by, keeping all accounts of time, &c., which he was kind enough to say I managed to his entire satisfaction'.[8]

The experience of Thomas Speed, who became head gardener at Chatsworth in 1868, gives an insight into the hierarchy of the different departments, suggesting that only when a journeyman was considered capable and competent did he progress to a position of responsibility in those departments deemed to require higher levels of skill and proficiency. Engaged as a journeyman in the kitchen garden by William Thomson of Wrotham Park (Hertfordshire), it was 'after being in that position for twelve months' that Speed was promoted to foreman of the department. Afterwards, he advanced to foreman of the flower garden and subsequently the conservatory department, and from there the forcing department. Speed acknowledged that his nearly four years spent under Thomson and the excellent practice he experienced and learned 'owed no little of my after success – so much so, that I have always felt a deep debt of gratitude to that gentleman'. From Wrotham Park, Speed moved to Belvoir Castle (Leicestershire) in 1856, to be foreman of the glasshouses under William Ingram (see page 131) a position he held for nearly four years. One of the many lessons he learned from Ingram, who was a 'good practical geologist' was 'the different geological formations, and their bearings upon horticulture'. From Belvoir, Speed gained his first headship, to Sir Edward Walker at Berry Hill (Nottinghamshire), where he remained until 1868. During his stay he 'laid out the flower garden anew, replanted all the vineries, built a range of Pine-stoves, replanted all the Peaches, and, in a word, remodelled the whole place'.[9]

David T. Fish was more fortunate still, for following his apprenticeship at Scone Palace he moved to Putteridgebury (Bedfordshire), then under the control of his elder brother, Robert. Arriving in the middle of November 1842, he remained until the spring of 1845, rising through the ranks from second to first foreman, and according to Fish, 'These years were among the busiest and happiest of my life.' From Putteridgebury Fish moved to the famous Royal Exotic Nursery run by Knight and Perry, which was situated on King's Road in Chelsea (and subsequently taken over by Veitch in 1853). This new position was, Fish recalled, very different to what he was used to in a garden. The spring of 1845 was so severe that the foremen had to take turns staying up all night to ensure the fires did not go out. To 'fortify (so it was thought) us youngsters, the man on night duty went in at 11 P.M. to Mr Perry to report temperature, and drink up or carry forth with him an enormous glassful of brandy and water – a sure recipe for stupidity or the sleep of insensibility to duty to those who drank it off.'

Fish also recalled that Knight was a canny instructor – never letting pass an opportunity to impart 'a word of reproof, instruction, or correction'. 'Old Joe' as he was called was also a bit of a card. On the occasion of introducing Fish to the 'application of closet sewage to pot plants at an old pump behind the orangery' he could see that Fish found the whole procedure distasteful, so he gave him the job of liquoring the young camellias twice a week. From then on Old Joe gave him 'many a sly smile as he passed the pits ... stopping to point out one day how much darker green the foliage was since the rich food had been given them in their liquor'. It was this introduction that inspired Fish to later make a study of fertiliser applications.[10]

THE APPRENTICE FEE & OTHER CHALLENGES

However, even before an apprentice passed through the kitchen garden gate, it was likely that he would have been extorted. As the correspondent 'R.S.E.' noted in 1830, 'Some gardens which are celebrated for their extent, superiority of management, or for the ability or character of the superintendent, are those into which young men are anxious to gain admittance; but before they can obtain this advantage, they must submit to bribe the master by a douceur of a sum beyond their ability to pay, or to be able to furnish must suffer the most rigid self-denial and inconvenience.'[11] This sum was the 'apprentice fee' (which was also levied on many journeymen) charged by head gardeners. An example has already been cited – the ten guineas Archibald Fowler paid to Mr Murray at the Royal Botanic Garden, Glasgow (see page 74). In this case the sum was paid 'up front' on the principle of 'no fee, no position'. Other times the fee was taken as a weekly deduction from the apprentice's already-meagre wages.

The argument put forward for the practice was that the fee was ostensibly charged by the head gardener as recompense for training given, since no apprentice could gain a knowledge of his art or trade without instruction from their master. In Fowler's case it was money well spent for he received an excellent training. However, numerous correspondents to various periodicals complained that the system was so widely abused it was often viewed as nothing more than a simple and exploitative means by which unscrupulous head gardeners supplemented their income.

In 1832 it was stated that a fee as large as £20 was not uncommon, and that often the trainee received little education in return as in the case of a:

> much praised establishment not a hundred miles from London, where the young men must pay a large premium before they are admitted into the grounds, and yet the individual who exacts this sum considers it beneath him to hold any intercourse with his men, and (as I have been informed) deigns not to hear a request or grant a favour, unless submitted to his consideration by being sent upon paper, in the form of a petition. I am at a loss to know how any young man can receive the worth of his money in such a place as this.[12]

Others were far harsher with their criticism of the practice, 'R.S.E.', considered that 'exacting this oppressive tax, as the absolute passport to their favour…it is as degrading to themselves as it is oppressive to their journeymen'.[13]

Without excusing the iniquity of the fee, some readers also pointed out that if head gardeners were properly recompensed by their employer in the first instance, they would not need to supplement their income this way. Others were saddened, seeing the charging of fees as a major failing amongst head gardeners who were generally lauded as men of great moral fibre and upstanding. Verbal broadsides, gentle persuasion and moral pressure achieved little, and the apprentice fee remained an ingrained but generally reviled part of the training process.

An editorial in 1850 suggested a fee should be charged only if it were done with the permission of the employer (which a head gardener was unlikely to secure), and in such a circumstance, a portion of the fee should be shared amongst the various foremen. The closing comments, however, reveal what more commonly continued to happen 'to take money of men for their places clandestinely is not only a direct fraud, but a dirty trick, disgraceful to all concerned in it'.[14] A decade later, when a typical journey-man's fee was put at a shilling-a-week or between £5 and £10 upfront, a correspondent who called himself 'Crostonians' took a pragmatic approach. Thinking it acceptable to charge a reasonable fee, so long as the trainee actually got training in return, he suggested 10 per cent of a trainee's salary over three years, but added the rider that to 'demand 1s 6d or 2s per week for an indefinite length of time is certainly unjust'. Crostonians goes on to give a personal example of such unjustness.

> I served an apprenticeship of five years, for my parents, being poor I was compelled to begin to 'scratch' when only 13 years of age. After that I went to a place in Yorkshire as an 'improver', served three years as pleasure-ground man, received 11s. per week, and paid 1s. 6d.; and then three years as stove-man, when I had 12s. per week and paid 2s. per week to the gardener, besides a premium of £3. The evils arising out of this system of weekly payment are numerous. Young men cannot afford to buy books for instruction, and the first place, which offers itself is accepted. Thus the country is overstocked with gardeners (?) who are inefficient and inexperienced. They got low salaries, but quite as much as they are worth. In short the supply is increased while the quality is deteriorated, an evil which is to be attributed chiefly to the 'stop weeks'.[15]

Yet there were benevolent head gardeners – many of those featured in the 'British Gardeners' series had fond memories of their mentors. George Johnston, for example, recalled that while a journeyman at Balbirnie (Fife) where he was first in charge of flower gardens for a year and subsequently the forcing-houses, Mr Edwards the head gardener was 'a highly educated man, and offered his aid frankly and freely to any of his men who wished to improve themselves'.[16]

More specific about how he executed the duties of pastoral and educa-tional care towards his trainees was the self-titled 'nobleman's gardener', who wrote a rebuttal in 1826 to accusations laid by the journeyman 'G.R.G.' that head gardeners did not act generously towards their trainees, neither stimulating or encouraging, nor disseminating knowledge to them. Proudly stating that he acted from 'unselfish motives', having never charged an apprentice fee in his ten years as a head gardener, this humanitarian went on to say he worked hard to improve those under his charge, noting that 'When they first come to me, I tell them that the more they learn, and the faster they improve themselves, the more I shall approve of them.' He goes on to give the example of the 'young lads', currently in his care – three at 8s. per week, two at 12s., 'and to the oldest hand, who I make my foreman' 13s. All six worked until 'nine o'clock at night – studying their books', and since our philanthropist was 'anxious they should improve every minute of their own time, I allow an old woman to prepare their meals, &c.' As a rule the lads were expected to keep 'a journal of the work, &c.; and seeing them almost every night, I now and then examine their journals, and put questions to them as to the meaning of botanical terms, or upon any subject they have been reading. I sometimes also hear them read aloud, and examine and instruct them in every thing I think useful.'[17]

POOR PAY

It was accepted practice for apprentices and journeymen in many other crafts to pay their masters a training or apprentice fee. But such trainees also earned considerably more than their gardening counterparts, on average nearly three times as much. Writing in 1826 and in praise of gardeners and in particular their phlegm in the face of low wages, an architect by the name of I.P. Burnard of Formosa Cottage, Eden Grove in Holloway offered hard facts.

> If we take a carpenter, bricklayer, mason, or smith, and compare the wages usually paid them through their apprenticeship, and while they are journeymen, with the wages of a gardener during these states of progression; and compare also their intellectual state, the difference between the two classes is almost incredible. A bricklayer who cannot write, and who has not the least knowledge of figures, or geometry, receives from five to seven shillings a-day, as the common price given by master builders. A journeyman gardener in one of the first nurseries, who has gone through a course of practical geometry and land surveying; has a scientific knowledge of Botany, and has spent his days and his nights in reading books connected with his profession, gets no more than two shillings or two and sixpence a day.[18]

One of the reasons that apprentices from other crafts received higher wages was to enable them to purchase a set of tools of their trade. Garden tools were provided (usually only the head gardener had his own set), but even discounting this cost, the low wage endured by trainee gardeners left very small provision for purchasing the equally necessary tools for learning – books and periodicals. Yet, the trainee gardener was expected to have a far greater knowledge than those in other crafts or that expected of domestic staff – and this knowledge had to be gleaned through determined 'self-improvement' at no extra wage. Indeed, the trainee gardener incurred extra costs in the pursuit of this knowledge – books, periodicals and candles by which to study at night, all cost money.

William Miller, an apprentice in the 1840s at Erskine House, the seat of Lord Blantyre, recalled that 'in the evenings we read greedily, each paying for a pound [weight] of candles in turn. Our wages were not much, so they were easily taken care of.'[19] Sometimes the low level of income was almost beyond belief. When Andrew Turnbull began his apprenticeship at Haining near Selkirk in 1813 he was 'bound for two years, and paid £4 as an apprentice fee. I got my bed and board, but the only cash that came to my share was 2 shillings a year given in two payments, being 1 shilling at each of the two leading fairs.' And this is not a mis-quote.[20] Or take the example from 1824 cited by Burnard of 'an Irish lad working in Jenkin's nursery, was summoned before the Mary-la-bone [*sic*] police magistrates, to provide for an illegitimate child, and being required to allow the mother two or three shillings per week, assigned as a reason why he could not afford it, that his wages were only 10s. per week! The magistrate would not believe him; he had but a small plot of a garden, he said, but he paid the gardener who did it up 4s. a day: this unfortunate lad, therefore, had the alternative of paying the money, going to prison, or marrying the girl; in the simplicity and goodness of his heart he chose the latter.'[21]

In reply to the complaints of insufficient recompense made in 1827 by the journeyman 'G.R.G.' whom we have already met (see page 80), Loudon puts forth a counter-argument, or more accurately, a sop. While admitting that he knew that 'a journeyman gardener can barely exist on his wages' and believed wages for gardeners at all levels should be raised, Loudon argued that a good journeyman of two or three years' experience and at the age of twenty-five could expect to become a head gardener and thus, if he attained a first-rate situation he was 'as well off at twenty-five as an industrious journeyman carpenter of forty-five, because it would probably require that time before the latter could save sufficient money to enable him to become a master ... Knowledge, therefore, to the gardener is money as well as knowledge.'[22] But put under scrutiny, Loudon's argument simply does not hold water, for the comparison is not a fair one. If, instead, the comparison is made between the head gardener and his equal in the ranks of domestic staff, the butler, a different picture emerges. This was highlighted in 1828 by another correspondent 'A.S.', who, while observing that a trained butler earned between £5 and £10 more per annum, goes on to make an interesting contrast between the costs of training two such employees. Assuming a starting point of two boys aged fourteen and a seven-year apprenticeship, the result is that 'the house servant will be found to have cost the gentleman more by £115 12s. to qualify him for being his butler, than the other has to qualify him for being his gardener'. Sadly, no explanation was offered for why a more costly apprentice was subsequently paid more, just a resigned sigh that gardeners were under-paid.[23]

In time wages did improve, but not substantially in comparison to other trades. William Taylor, who undertook his apprenticeship at Shrubland Park in the 1850s (a garden made famous in the previous decade by Donald Beaton), received 2 shillings a week – a quarter of the wage paid to the garden labourers. A decade later, in October 1860 *The Gardeners' Chronicle* put wages of an apprentice boy at between 3 and 4 shillings a week, those for a journeyman at 10 to 14 shillings.[24] And two decades after this, a journeyman gardener's wage had risen minimally to 12 to 18 shillings a week, while those for other crafts such as carpenter, smith, printer, weaver, painter or bricklayer ranged from 25 to 30 shillings a week.[25]

LONG HOURS AND BOTHY ACCOMMODATION

In addition to low pay, another disadvantage often faced by trainees was long working hours. It was generally accepted that a fair working week was sixty hours – Monday until Saturday, 6am to 6pm, with an hour for breakfast and dinner. However, one of the other regular complaints voiced by trainees was that they were often kept working overtime with no recompense. Andrew Turnbull, for example, recalled that 'during the season of cutting the short grass, which lasted most of the summer, we commenced work at 4 A.M'.[26] Such regimes were called 'slavish and unjust' and deprived 'them of those hours of relaxation which ought to be devoted to mental improvement'.

However, given the accommodation that some trainees had to endure, returning home after work would not have been a pleasant experience. A 'bothy' was a sort of hut in which the trainee garden staff or 'bothy boys' lived, ate and studied together. The quality of bothies varied enormously; at the luxurious end of the scale were structures such as the Hansel and Gretel picturesque bothy erected in the early 1880s at Ascott (Buckinghamshire) by Leopold de Rothschild, who also provided educational classes and a cricket pitch for recreation. Bothy boys usually had to do their own victualling and cooking, but the lucky few had a woman 'who did'. At Drumlanrig (Dumfries and Galloway) the fourteen under-gardeners had a housemaid employed full time to care for them; while at Wimpole Hall in Norfolk, part of the job description of the woman who looked after the boys was that she be employed for her advanced age and acute ugliness in order that no temptation befell the testosterone-fuelled inmates! Sometimes, too, bothy life offered a new life experience – it was in the bothy at Polesden Lacey (Surrey) that a particular garden boy took his first-ever bath with running water. However, such civilised conditions were the exception, and the antithesis far more common.

In 1834 there was criticism of the 'very uncomfortable hovels in which, in many instances, the young men are lodged [were] often so cold, damp, and gloomy as to be totally unfit for human habitations'.[27] And three years later, when appointed foreman to Duncan M'Naughten in the gardens of Lord Cloncurry at Lyons, Fowler had but one complaint – the bothy – which by all accounts was similar to many in the area. But that did not make it any the easier to bear.

> It was a lean-to, against the north side of the north wall of the kitchen garden, 10 or 12 feet in length by about 8 feet in breadth, with an earthen floor below and only the slates above, the inside walls unplastered; with a small window without a frame, set in lime, let in some light; the door was low and narrow, minus about 1 foot at the bottom, which in the course of several generations had gradually decayed. The table was formed of a few pieces of deal board, nailed together by two cross bars of the same material, hinged to the back wall on one side, and when in use supported by one foot, also moving on a hinge; the seats were stumps of trees, a fire-place near one corner but no grate in it, the remainder of the scant furniture made to correspond.[28]

Yet, little seems to have changed in half-a-century. This in *The Gardening World* in 1884 was clearly penned from experience:

> We have one in our mind as we write . . . a true type of a bad bothy. It faces north and is near the stoke-hole, and so shaded by a high wall that a gleam of sun-shine seldom reaches it. Its roof is leaky and its walls damp, and it is altogether a disgrace to the garden. Within such hovels living conditions could also be diresome. A lad, and a big boy, and a single woman live in one room, which is badly furnished. There are two benches or forms, which supply the place of stools or chairs, but there is no table. The inmates make use of a chest lid as a substitute. There are two beds of coarse unplaned deals. All the sheets and blankets must be provided by the lads themselves, and all the bowls, plates and spoons. Their food consists of milk, when it can be got, and oatmeal. Beef, mutton, pork or fish or flesh of any kind they rarely taste. The bothy may not be cleaned out or whitewashed for years, and their bedding is washed but seldom.[29]

Not only were such conditions unpleasant to bear, but they provided little incentive to stay in of an evening and study. No wonder then that 'young men, being incited to seek that pleasure abroad which they cannot enjoy at home, are often thus driven to form those habits of unsteadiness and dissipation which are both ruinous to themselves and prejudicial to the interests of their employers'.[30]

Perhaps, though, we should finish with Norman Thomas, who was a bothy boy at Penrhyn Castle (Gwynedd) in the 1920s and who provides not only a personal and detailed insight into the living conditions of a bothy boy but also what was expected of him on a day-to-day basis:

> The bothy was a fair sized house, with the facilities to accommodate eight gardeners. The foreman, Teddy Jones, the garden boy and six journeymen gardeners. The house comprised of a large kitchen, also a large dining room, another room on the ground floor was called the study, which was seldom used for the purpose of studying, with one exception, Kenneth a Welshman from Rhyl was studying for his RHS certificate, would sometimes use this room, for quiescence. There was one large bedroom, Teddy's, another large bedroom with two beds, one for the garden boy and the last journeyman to arrive, I slept here for a period of around two

months. Another large space to accommodate five journeymen, each bedroom was separated by a partition; there was also a bathroom.

My first morning at work, commenced with a hurricane lamp in hand leaving the bothy just before seven o'clock, anyone leaving the bothy after the official time of seven would soon be in trouble…The seven o'clock start was a very sore point with us bothy boys, as the other workmen did not start work until seven thirty.

I well remember my first job, with the garden boy (Tommy Thomas) I was instructed to remove bulbs in pots from an ash bed where they had been covered for some weeks, for them to form roots before foliage, now they were to be allowed to see the light and the growth of foliage would commence. These pots were put onto a hand barrow (a barrow without wheels) and removed to a green house for gentle forcing. The bothy boys work was chiefly in the greenhouses, occasionally other duties outside the greenhouses were undertaken especially the one hour before tea, compulsory, during the summer months, for which we did not receive any extra pay, another sore point.

The senior journeyman's first duty in the morning at six o'clock was to unlock the three doors that lead into and out of these gardens. He would then attend to four green house fires, clean out their ash and clinker, open the dampers to get the fires burning brightly before the man in charge of a certain section commenced his work at seven o'clock.

All journeymen had to see to their charges every Saturday and Sunday mornings until midday, then henceforth all work had to be done by the duty man. Consequently a whole day from work was not possible, albeit it was surprising what one could achieve in the way of entertainment in the hours available.

No wonder after being on duty all the week, one endeavoured to get away from the bothy as soon after midday on a Saturday and Sunday as possible. This early getaway was frequently stymied by Teddy who invariably would find something wrong with your morning's work to get you out of the bothy if you were preparing yourself for an afternoon's entertainment. Sometimes one would be lucky if one could get away by two o'clock.

My wage was twenty two shillings per week with an extra five shillings for the week's duty. On this amount of money we were able to live reasonably well, our weekly bill from Teddy's catering was well under twelve shillings I would say the average would be ten shillings. The remainder of the remuneration's sufficed for our clothing and entertainment.

The growing of fruit was a speciality, outside and under glass. Under glass we grew pineapple, grapes, peach, nectarine, fig and less important fruit, such as the humble tomato...To illustrate, how the tomato was so important to this family. His Lordship at the time of my stay there was the chief official of the Jockey Club, he travelled the country from one race meeting to another. Fresh fruit, vegetables and flowers had to be at the place he was visiting one day prior to his arrival. The packing of these items was an interesting and educational experience. Everything had to be done in a professional manner. Teddy was the expert here, he undertook the packing of the most important fruit and flowers. Grapes had to arrive at their place of destination with their bloom intact. Peaches, figs and similar fruit required special attention in their packing. All fruit was placed in special paper with wool and wood wool surrounding them, they were then placed in special boxes....Packing took place three times a week. On a Sunday this operation could take five hours to complete. Owen Morris would come in specially to take these boxes to Bangor station....(In) 1926 there was a national strike, and sending goods by rail was not possible, and only a few ounces were allowed through the post. To get over this difficulty each tomato was sent separately. One tomato was wrapped in cotton wool and put into a small cardboard box, each box with an addressed label. Scores and scores of these boxes were sent by this method. They arrived at their place of destination in perfect condition.

Now for the composition of the greenhouses and the type of plants grown therein. The chief emphasis being on the cultivation of fruit. At the south side of the garden were a range of lean to green houses, each of a good size. The individual houses were, three vineries, one peach, one nectarine, one fig. At the rear of the tall back walls of the greenhouses were two mushroom houses, a fruit store, packing shed, two stokeholes, and the Head Gardeners office. In the individual houses of this range was a pineapple house, one vinery, one each of peach, nectarine and fig, and two boiler houses. Adjacent was the melon ground, this contained a number of green houses dotted about. A number of melon houses, other houses for the growing of tomato, cucumber, etc. A large house for the growing of flowering plants suitable for cutting for floral work, these were sent three times a week with the vegetables and fruit. Incidentally only one variety of melon was grown, Hero of Locking. There were numerous pits and cold frames, a lot of violets were grown in the cold frames. In the melon ground was a large potting shed, men's mess room, W C, store and tool shed.

Cultivation (of the fruit) was superb, everything so methodical and timed down to the tiniest detail. Water given to individual plants was recorded. In the vineries, peach houses and others. On the wall in each greenhouse was a slate and pencil. When watering, say the vinery, every gallon of water put on the border had to be recorded and written on the slate, this was frequently scrutinised by Teddy. The setting of temperature in greenhouses were set to a stipulated and uniform temperature, I should know, I was in charge of the early vinery in the spring of 1926. To maintain the correct temperature stipulated could be most frustrating. One had to open ventilators when the sun came out and close them again when the sun went in. Later in the season when shading of the greenhouse was required to protect the plants from the excessive hot sun it was a case of, shading on when the sun was visible, shading off when the sun went in. One can visualise the situation when the sun made up its mind to be awkward. One minute the sun could be shinning brightly the next minute it could disappear behind a cloud, resulting in a rise or drop in temperature as the case may be. Many a dinner time [lunch] I have had to leave my meal a number of times to carry out these unwelcome operations, which could be very annoying to say the least. Night temperatures could also be a headache, trying to maintain a set temperature. When on duty, the final stoking of the greenhouse fires could not be contemplated until the proper temperature had been obtained. I well remember one night when there was a sudden drop in the outside temperature due to an unexpected frost. I had great difficulty in trying to reach the required temperature in the early vinery. A temperature of fifty degrees Fahrenheit was required at this time of year. I had had difficulty in trying to reach the stipulated temperature that was required this night. It was now ten thirty and I was tired out after a hard day's and the extra evening duties. The temperature was at forty seven degrees, three degrees under the stipulated temperature. I knew from experience that at this temperature no harm could be done, so I banked the fire for the night, banking and filling the boiler with coal to last throughout the night, until seven o'clock the next morning.

The gardens also included a number of vegetable plots with their highly productive crops. There was a large area for the growing of soft fruit. On each side of the garden footpaths were concrete posts supporting wires to these were trained, apple, pear, plums, red and white currants, black currants, gooseberries etc: all trained in a characteristic manner, most suited for obtaining of high quality fruit as cordons, fan type and espaliers.

The walls round the gardens were also furnished with fruit trees. On the south side peach, nectarine and fig. On the east and west-side apples and pears and the north side the large variety, many of them in fruit aviaries. The individual attention paid dividends in the producing of superior fruit. All the maintenance of fruit trees and bushes and the cultivation of the vegetables was done by the outside staff, and a wonderful job they did. With the large amount of gardeners, farm workers and foresters. His Lordship truly had a fairly high wage bill to pay each week, just for labour alone.[31]

CHAPTER 5

The Head Gardener

GETTING A POSITION

Having survived a decade or so of training as apprentice, journeyman, foreman and perhaps deputy head gardener, the ambitious gardener could now apply for a headship. The 'Positions Vacant' section of *The Gardeners' Chronicle*, which carried advertisements for Second Gardener, Third Gardener, Under Gardener, Foreman and Journeymen, as well as Head Gardenerships, was a good place to start. A sound reference, for preference from a head gardener or nurseryman of note or renown, would help enormously with the application. Another route was to tap into the 'word of mouth' network. The most straightforward route to advancement in this case was promotion – Mr Beesley moved up the ladder from foreman upon the retirement of James Drewett, the noted exhibitor of Muscat Grapes and for nearly twenty-four years head gardener at Denbies near Dorking (Surrey). This was the residence of master builder Thomas Cubitt (1788–1855), whose work included designing the east front of Buckingham Palace and, with Prince Albert, Osborne House on the Isle of Wight.[1]

Another channel of advancement was recommendation by the aspirant's current boss – and such a system made even more sense if the landowner possessed more than one property. In 1828 as a twenty-four-year-old foreman, Andrew Turnbull was sent to his headship at Bothwell Castle by his boss at Dalkeith Place; a post he continued to hold in 1874 when interviewed by *The Gardeners' Chronicle*. Another who obtained their position by this route was George Johnston, who had been foreman to Archibald Fowler at Castle Kennedy (Wigtonshire), and to whom he owed his headships first to Henry Fernie of Mill Bank House in Liverpool, and subsequently to the Earl of Strathmore at Glamis Castle (Angus).[2]

However, it was not always a smooth transition. William Miller had worked as a foreman under John Fleming (*d*.1883) of the celebrated gardens at Trentham (Staffordshire), before Fleming recommended him as

Ground Foreman.

WANTED, IMMEDIATELY, a married MAN, thoroughly practical in Forest Tree and general Nursery-work. Well up in Roses, Fruit Trees, and Hardy Stock.—JOHN CARTER, Nursery, Keighley, Yorkshire.

WANTED, a Young MAN for the Garden, to live in the bothy with another. Must thoroughly understand the Vinery, Peach-houses, and Plants. Wages £1 per week, and milk. Must have a good character from last employer.—A. B. C., Mr. Bedbrough, Butcher, High Street, Windsor.

WANTED, a good steady Working MAN—who can Bud, Graft, and Layer, and act as Salesman occasionally—to look after a small Nursery. Must have a good character.—G. SMALL AND SON, Nurseries, Harston.

WANTED, a steady MAN, accustomed to Garden Work, who also understands the Care of a Cow and Poultry.—State age, with wages required, to B. A., Post Office, Kingston-on-Thames.

WANTED, as IMPROVER, a young Man from 18 to 23, with some knowledge of the Nursery Trade.—Apply, with testimonials, &c., to GODWIN AND SON, The Nurseries, Ashbourne.

WANTED, a good handy GARDEN LABOURER. Constant employment. — Apply to L. J. WALKER, The Nurseries, Wood Green, Waltham Abbey, Essex.

WANTED, as KNIFEMAN, a steady and industrious Man. Must be a successful Budder and Grafter. Wages, 20s. per week.—State age, and where last employed, JOHN JEFFERIES AND SONS, Royal Nurseries, Cirencester.

Bouquet Maker.

WANTED, IMMEDIATELY, a young Woman as BOUQUET MAKER. Must be a good hand at the Business, and a sharp Saleswoman, with good address. Age not under 25 years. Liberal wages will be given to a suitable person.—Address, stating experience, &c., to TURNER BROS., Florists, &c., 21, Bassett Street, Liverpool.

Looking something like a poster from the Wild West, such job advertisements were a weekly feature in The Gardeners' Chronicle. The range of positions on offer reveals much about the diversity of the horticultural industry at the time.

head gardener to the Viscount Clifden at Gowran Castle (County Kilkenny, Ireland), a position he held for four years. In 1858, when Fleming was promoted to the position of 'resident agency' on the Trentham estate, he recalled Miller 'with a view to my filling his shoes'. Miller was 'brought before the Duchess of Sutherland', but sadly for Miller Her Grace took against him – perhaps because of his 'Irish brogue, which I had caught strongly, or perhaps from my awkwardness'. But whatever the reason, Miller returned to Ireland a disappointed man.[3]

On other occasions it was not the head gardener who recalled and advanced a previous member of staff, but the landowner himself. Philip Frost (1804–87) began his training in the garden of Lord Grenville at Boconnoc (Cornwall) in 1817, before moving to his lordship's garden at Dropmore (Buckinghamshire) in 1822. After six years, Frost 'wished to go, for improvement, into a kitchen-garden' and moved to Caen Wood, making 'a sacrifice of 6s. per week' in wages. He spent a year there. In the autumn of 1832, and after a stint at the Chelsea Physic Garden, Frost received a letter from Lord Grenville informing him that for reasons undisclosed he had dismissed Mr Baillie, his head gardener at Dropmore, and he would take Frost 'in preference to any one he knew'. Frost jumped at the chance not only of promotion to such a respected garden but also to work for someone whom he so clearly had a liking and enjoyed an excellent working relationship.[4]

Once ensconced in his new position, a head gardener had to find his feet, establish a rapport with employer and staff, instigate his own form of garden and personnel management, and prove himself. John Cameron, a gardener from Grove Lane, Camberwell in London, stated that:

> it is a well known fact that the proprietor cannot find out the merits of his gardener in less than four or five years; and experience has proved that it is better to keep a bad gardener than be often changing. By changing, as some do every three or four months, they totally destroy their gardens; for how can so many gardeners, having different methods and intentions, and entering at every stage of the cultivation, avoid entirely to do so? Every new gardener must make a change . . . and hence these repeated innovations, carried on by a succession of gardeners, shortly present to the owner the total destruction of his garden, and which destruction, on taking a retrospect, he can only attribute to his own imprudence in so often changing his gardener.[5]

As we have seen, many head gardeners remained at the same establishment for many decades, but inevitably situations arose where clashes of personality occurred or a better offer came along – it was not unknown for visiting guests to 'head hunt' their host's head gardener! At Heligan (Cornwall), the Tremayne family employed ten head gardeners in the forty-seven years between 1867 and 1914, with their length of employ varying from a year or so up to six: Francis Enston (1867–73), George Newman (1874),

W. Hovel (1875–77), Henry Hill (1878–84), the position was vacant in 1885, W. Osborne (1886–97), R. Andrews (1898–1902), T. Preece (1903–07), S. Gordon (1908), R.W. Norman (1909), the position was vacant in 1910 although Norman was listed for 1911–13, and in 1914 the post was held by H. Griffin. Cross-referencing the names reveals that both Hovel and Hill left Heligan for Glyn Park near Bodmin, Osborne went to Fota Island (Co. Cork, Ireland), Gordon went to Monreith House (Wigtonshire), while Norman went to nearby Trelissick.

The corollary of appointment was termination of employment upon the death of one's employer. A famous example was Sir Joseph Paxton's 'jump before being pushed' at Chatsworth upon the demise of the sixth Duke of Devonshire in 1858. Paxton had been there for thirty-two years. However, Anthony Parsons, the head gardener at Ponders End in the London Borough of Enfield, was dismissed upon the death of his employer A.R. George, after forty-two years. Parsons was pragmatic and found a new post, but as a well-renowned and experimental plant breeder he was aggrieved at being forced to dispose of his 'un-bloomed seedlings . . . into the hands of [the nurserymen] Messrs. Paul, who, I believe, found them to be a very fine lot'.[6] However, a death of an employer or change of ownership did not always result in dismissal, for according to *The Horticultural Directory*, Thomas Evans, head gardener at Gwydir Castle near Llanrwst, served three owners between 1890 and 1916: Lord Willoughby d'Eresby, Lord Carrington and the Marquis of Lincolnshire.

TYPES OF ESTABLISHMENT

It was not just the large country house that required the services of a gardener. Urbanisation had brought about the construction of thousands of suburban villas, with gardens ranging in size from a quarter to 10 acres (0.10 to 4.05ha) all of which required a gardener as much for the cachet of having a gardener as for having someone to do the gardening! The 'Positions Vacant' advertisements in *The Gardeners' Chronicle* shed some light on the various classes of headship, listing 'Head Gardener', 'Head Working', 'Head or Singlehanded' and 'Singlehanded'. The categorisation is clarified further by 'Paul' writing in 1860, who wistfully noted 'we cannot all be head gardeners, with 20 or more men under us, however we may sigh for so blissful a position. The majority of places at the present day are – a gardener and a boy, or perhaps one, two or three men, and where the most particular work has to be done with the gardener's own hands.'[7]

In the same year, Roaldus of Preston who 'had a good deal to do with and among gardeners during the last quarter of a century' offered additional clarity, perhaps tinged with jealousy, stating that 'the whole body [of head gardeners] may be divided into three classes: - 1. Gardeners who have charge of first-rate establishments, and do not work. 2. Gardeners who have a man or several men under them, but are expected to take an active part in whatever is going on. 3. Men who take single-handed places and work hard.'[8] No doubt the fortunate members of the first class would not have agreed with Roaldus's opinion of their workload, and in fact such a statement was ludicrous. To effectively and successfully manage a sizeable 'first-rate establishment' required the continual application of both superb horticultural and excellent management skills, as well as the self-discipline to continue to improve and develop one's own skills.

THE HEAD GARDENER'S DOMAIN

Such a head gardener was in reality the managing director of a small- to medium-sized complex business. As well as the grand formal gardens, the wider pleasure grounds and the conservatories or winter gardens, a large country house boasted extensive productive gardens. This realm was composed of three sub-businesses. There was the market garden – the open space and glasshouses growing all the vegetables and fruits for the dining table; the floristry – cut flowers and pot plants raised for house decorations and to fill the conservatory; and the nursery – each year (tens of) thousands of seasonal bedding plants had to be raised in order to fill the formal gardens. And everywhere the head gardener had to meet his employer's expectations, which were as easy to state as they were hard to achieve. Exceptional quality and unmatched uniqueness was demanded at all times. To meet such exacting standards, the head gardener commanded a large staff over which he had complete authority. John Jaques, at the turn of the twentieth century, commanded a small army of a hundred at Waddesdon Manor (Buckinghamshire), while at Cragside (Northumberland) Henry Hudson's minions numbered seventy. At Clumber Park (Nottinghamshire), twenty-eight men were employed in the walled garden alone, with foremen in charge of the three divisions – fruit, vegetables and glasshouses; and at Frogmore (part of the Windsor Castle estate) Owen Thomas had eight foremen under him and a total staff of fifty.

THE HEAD GARDENER AS MANAGER

The head gardener would undertake practical work, applying his skills and experience to the most complex and delicate jobs, which were often conducted within the greenhouses, and included, for example, nurturing new arrivals, performing hybridisation procedures, or establishing and maintaining heating regimes for the various incumbents. Another of the head gardener's prerogatives, albeit in close co-operation with his master or the lady of the house, was to design the seasonal planting schemes for the formal beds on the terrace. Or if very lucky, to design a new garden – when head gardener to the Duke of Richmond at Gordon Castle (Morayshire), in the 1850s, John Webster was asked to 'layout for the Duchess a new flower garden in the Italian style'. In this Webster had 'the guidance of the good taste of the Duchess, in deciding upon plans for the balustrades, fences, fountain, and ornamental work'.[9] Given the diversity of his domain and the seasonal nature of gardening, in order that all the gardening activities were carried out at the appropriate time and to impeccable standards, it was imperative that the head gardener was also an adept and adaptable manager. Perhaps this is what Roaldus was referring to – the fact that a successful head gardener would spend much time walking the gardens, notebook in hand, monitoring and planning.

Then, of course, there was the matter of managing his employer and wife, whose demands he was there to meet. No doubt there were many frustrating days when a head gardener had to reschedule, as minds in the house were changed on a whim; when harvesting plans had to be changed because 'someone' had come into the glasshouses and helped themselves to the ripe crop without asking; or when beds had to be repaired as a result of damage – it was commented upon how destructive a sweeping crinoline dress could be to a display of bedding plants. At trying times like these it was wise to follow the sage advice of William Taylor, head gardener at Longleat (Wiltshire): 'There is often great and frequent provocation from unsympathetic employers, employers' friends and their children [but] self control in the presence of employers is particularly to be insisted upon.'[10]

However, gardeners did not always keep their cool. In one incident at Chatsworth in July 1839 George Norkett an under gardener of thirteen years' standing was taking a party of visitors around the garden – something he had done numerous times before. But on this occasion, when he turned on the joke fountain in the Cascade House, one of the men was inadvertently soaked. Not seeing the funny side of it, the man thought Norkett had drenched him deliberately and ran at him brandishing his stick. To defend himself, the hapless gardener pulled out a knife and an altercation followed. Eventually, after complaints and questions, and an apology from Norkett, the matter was considered by his boss, Joseph Paxton, to be closed and no further action was taken.[11]

An alternative employer-management technique was to develop such a tyrannical manner that neither master nor mistress dared gainsay their head gardener. P.G. Wodehouse's truculent and tyrannical Scot, McAllister who appeared in *Lord Emsworth and Others* (1937) and ruled his employer with a rod of iron, was not entirely apocryphal. Thomas King of Devizes Castle (Wiltshire) not only flouted his employers' wishes by growing only the flowers he liked, but also denied them their desire to encourage birds into the garden by felling roosting trees and breeding cats![12] Then there was the rogue, Samuel Braker of Clumber Park (Nottinghamshire). In addition to falsifying his tax returns and writing vitriolic letters to his employer, when without his permission she harvested and ate 'his' prize bunch of grapes, he was also caught cheating at the Royal Horticultural Society's Westminster Show![13]

The head gardener also had to establish relations with the domestic staff in the house. It was a deeply held conviction within the gardening fraternity that because of his level of education, expertise and independence, the head gardener was a class of servant above the rest. In many ways he was, but the reality of the situation within the social hierarchy of the country estate staff, was that the head gardener ranked equally alongside the butler and the cook. However, this did not always prevent problems and conflicts, such as a careless member of the household staff harvesting and damaging delicate crops, or deciding who was in charge of making the floral arrangements, the head gardener or the butler. In the latter case at Cragside, it was most certainly the head gardener, Hudson. His walled gardens included a Cane Room and Basket Room where he stored his flower-arranging paraphernalia, and the Flower Room in which he gave his creations form. From here they were very carefully transported in a specially designed sedan chair-like contraption the half-mile (0.80km) to the house, where Hudson made finishing touches in the Butler's pantry before they were installed.

In these relations, William Taylor's advice was once again wise, acknowledging that servants 'ranging from the scullery maid to the agent' could also cause great annoyance, but he recommended that the gardener must 'keep on good terms' with all of them 'if he would live in peace and have the most made of his produce'.

Nevertheless, the canny head gardener took precautions to 'cover his own back'. James Barnes (1806–77) of Bicton Park took it upon himself to produce a 'weekly Vegetable and Fruit List'. This he acknowledged was partly so 'that my employer's housekeeper, butler, and cook should know what is in season, and fit for table every day in the week or year'. But it was mainly so that 'they should know what they have had, and what they ought to have' and Barnes' way of producing a paper-trail for self-preservation. For as he noted, the household staff were not always as attentive as he:

> I have taken or sent in a dessert to the housekeeper's room, and, having occasion to go in afterwards . . . have seen one third or half; of this dessert gone, by first one person, then another, taking article after article. But that is not the worst; for what fruit is left, in such a case, I have seen pinched or squeezed and bruised to that degree that it was not fit to send to a nobleman's or gentleman's table, or, indeed, any other . . . I have seen the very best of vegetables, of all kinds, and at all seasons, come from the scullery in the hog-tub; never having been touched after leaving the garden basket, except being bundled into the hog-tub; at the same time I have been complained of because there was such a short supply of fruit, salads, and vegetables.

On other occasions Barnes had arisen before dawn to collect mushrooms only to find later in the morning 'stablemen, footmen, and women-servants having a feast of the very mushrooms I took the trouble to get while they were in bed', and as a result mushrooms had to be purchased 'because it had been said that I could not get them. Now is not that enough to cause one to establish rules of some kind?'[14]

It was with his staff of foremen, journeymen and apprentices that the head gardener had to exercise his man-management skills most frequently and adeptly. Once again, Taylor's words were apposite:

'Management of oneself and the management of those under our command are mixed together so intimately ... that if we succeed in doing the first the other becomes very much simplified.' If it is taken as read that the head gardener was well-organised, how did he apply his rule to his staff? For the self-assured and resourceful James Barnes, arrival at Bicton was a time to show he was as forceful as he was determined. To his horror he found not only the gardens in a poor state, but the gardeners had an even worse work ethic – tools dropped where a job was finished, dirty pots just thrown together and the men themselves dishevelled, 'never ... satisfied except they were tossing, and guzzling, and smoking'. Telling his foreman of each department that 'I must have a little better order in every place' he received the reply that it was impossible 'for there were not half hands enough to do the work'. So Barnes sacked the 'most factious' men and replaced them with 'good young men' who were motivated and enjoyed their work, and instigated sets of Rules (for Barnes it was rules with a capital 'R') for both the kitchen and ornamental gardens and enforced them with a system of fines. Initially, he recalled that 'to establish [them] was something like my going into the garden on a hot day, and after kicking against the bee-hives to stand in front of them, and let the bees exercise themselves freely on myself'. Certainly his no-nonsense approach 'caused a great stagnation and blight with both foremen and men. I was the whole talk of the neighbourhood round: it was said that my long ugly legs would not be walking Bicton gardens long.' However, Barnes did survive and not only transformed the garden, but also converted his men. 'The difference in the industry, cleanliness, happiness, and contentment amongst my men is truly astonishing. They are always in time of a morning, as clean as I can expect labourers, merry, whistling, singing, going to work as if they were taking an interest in doing good, and always knowing where to put their hand on any tool that is wanted, which you observed when here. It is one of the greatest pleasures to me that can possibly be imagined, to see such a change.'[15]

Barnes' approach to man-management was so efficacious that he was emulated. In 1858 Robert Fish visited Bicton and observed that 'a number of years ago, I tried some of these rules, and found they saved a great deal of annoyance. They did then work with me, and then got into disuse, but I think of reviving them.'[16]

Another very important aspect of managing a large garden were the finances, especially so if the grounds were undergoing improvements or developments. In such circumstances, just as in 'Capability' Brown's days at Stowe, the head gardener would often act as estate paymaster with 'two or three hundred men under his direction for executing improvements. The work of all these men, or their time, he has to measure, or to calculate; and perhaps £60 or £80 a week passes through his hands for their payment.'[17]

The sum spent on the moderate-sized garden at Linton Park (Kent) in 1873 by the head gardener John Robson (*d*.1886) was £680 13s 1½d , of which by far the greatest proportion went to pay wages which, for a dozen or so full-time staff, came to an average of £10 per week. This left Robson with about £160 a year to spend – a very moderate sum for what was expected, and when compared with what was spent elsewhere on the estate. Just one bill for 'replastering kitchen, doing roof, carting coals and other stuff to house, brewing, [and] cleaning windows' came to £344 10s 4½d. On another occasion Robson's employer, Lady Holmesdale, spent £106 15s at the Veitch nursery just on new ferns for her conservatory. This last example reveals a head gardener's budget generally did not include 'special' purchases such as expensive new plants or large-scale construction projects such as new conservatories or greenhouses, but did have to cover all other expenses. Therefore thrift and extra revenue generation were both essential weapons in the head gardener's armoury. At Linton, for example, Robson sold excess produce to the tune of £23 7s 6d in 1865.[18]

Given the fact that such large sums passed through their hands, it was admirable that head gardeners did not succumb to temptation and indulge in widespread embezzlement. As a correspondent to *The Gardeners' Chronicle*, a Mr Burnard, rhetorically asked in 1826: 'Would any mercantile man or manufacturer consider it safe to entrust so much power in the hands of a man so ill paid, and consequently so exposed to the temptation of dishonesty? Yet how seldom do we hear of gardeners falling short in their accounts. So rarely does that happen, that I do not recollect of a single instance; this must be attributed to the high moral character of gardeners, which may be traced in part to the recluse way in which they are brought up, and in part to the nature of their profession.'[19]

ACCOMMODATION

The word recluse is an apt one, for while the head gardener may have left the estate occasionally to visit other gardens, exhibit at shows, or participate in a plant auction, he essentially 'lived above the shop' in a tied cottage or house. The accommodation was usually close to the walled garden, if not actually built into it, and so the head gardener was on hand to monitor everything and take any decisions that required immediate attention. The moral fibre of the head gardener was of great importance, and certain writers suggested that keeping a head gardener isolated from the house had the added advantage that he was less likely to be 'led astray' by the morally depraved domestic staff. As 'Common Sense reforming Gardener' put it in 1826 'gardeners are often led away by servants and lose their places, more through this than any other circumstance'.[20] As revealed by 'Positions Vacant' advertisements, certain employers were insistent that their head gardener came with 'No Incumbents'. However, when Mr Addison applied for the post at Lyme Park (Cheshire) in the early 1900s, his employer was far more concerned at his prospective employee's ability to play cricket than his five children!

Many magazines and books (in particular those published by Loudon) offered designs for head gardeners' houses. An example from 1833 recommends it be built into the kitchen garden wall and contain an office, kitchen, parlour, master and two additional bedrooms, and entrance porch from the garden. Beneath it was a fruit cellar and at the back of the house a lean-to containing coal-bin, wood-bin, dust hole and privy.[21] More luxurious and grand was the house John Fleming designed for himself at Trentham in the early 1840s. In contrast to the Italianate mansion, he chose a Tudorbethan or Gothic look, the same style as the substantial two-storey brick house that was built into the wall as part of the development of the kitchen garden at Frogmore and in which Thomas Ingram entertained Queen Victoria and Prince Albert. With a more Italianate look was Barbrook, the large head gardener's house that Paxton designed for himself at Chatsworth at about the same time, and which was sadly demolished in 1963.

Another long-standing tradition had it that the head gardener also received produce for his table. An agreement from 1768, between John Carew and his gardener Philip Langdon, captures something of the flavour of life at Antony House (Cornwall). In Carew's absence Langdon was 'to provide the servants with all manner of kitchen and garden stuff (the wall

The apprentice and journeyman may have suffered dreadful living conditions, but a lucky few head gardeners lived pretty well. This splendid head gardener's cottage was designed and occupied by John Fleming while incumbent at Trentham.

fruit and table fruit saved for Mr Carew with all things from the garden when the family was in residence). He was to have use of garden produce for himself, to leave all in good order, not to diminish any of the trees, etc., and to have meat and drink in the house.'

STATUS AND CONDUCT, RESPECT AND POOR TREATMENT

All the evidence examined would suggest that (with the exception of the issue of apprentice fees, about which most employers never heard) head gardeners should have commanded the respect and loyalty of their employers. The reality was that head gardeners generally gave far more than they received. Or more pertinently, received far less than was their due, given their achievements and successes, and their high levels of expertise, experience and management abilities.

101

The horticultural press regularly published articles and correspondence to the effect that a head gardener required 'incomparably greater application of mind than that of a butler' and that 'a gardener is also expected to have attained a greater stock of general knowledge than the other, and not to be behind him or any servant in attention to his duty, fidelity to his master's interest, and general trustworthiness'. Such praise for the moral fibre and intellectual standing of head gardeners was frequently accompanied by complaints that head gardeners were not accorded their true position in society, nor were they paid sufficiently well. Mr Burnard rhetorically asked in 1826: 'With respect to master gardeners, to what class of gentlemen's servants, is there so much confided, and so little paid? . . . Is there not something very extraordinary in this?' Seventeen years later his sentiments were echoed by Mr W. Sherwood, gardener to Mr Millis of Stamford-hill, who claimed (without bias, naturally!) that 'there is no class of rural operatives, or masters, whose moral character stands so high, and whose remuneration is so low' adding 'As a body, Gardeners are more respectable and better informed than any class of servants'. And in 1870 A.D. Maybush moaned that 'The social status of gardeners is not a high one, at least not such as will induce them in youth to look forward to it with any large amount of enthusiastic inspirations'.[22]

WAGES

As for the trainees, so for the head gardener – their main source of complaint was low pay. The head gardener received a salary rather than a weekly wage, which provided a modicum of security – four months' notice rather than possible instant dismissal. Yet the going salary for the period seems to have been about the £100 per annum mark (compared with, in the 1870s, about £36 for a skilled journeyman and £20 for apprentices). Given that this was the same sum awarded to John Tradescant the Elder when appointed Keeper of the Royal gardens for Queen Henrietta Maria at Oatlands in 1630, wages clearly had not kept pace with the times. In the 1820s Loudon acknowledged that there were valid complaints against the low sums paid to head gardeners, noting that there were 'some noble-men who do not allow their head gardener more than the wages of a servant in livery'. Sadly, though, Loudon's solution to the problem was as hopelessly optimistic as it was unrealistic 'but this evil we trust to see reformed; for if good gardeners be not sufficiently paid, they will soon cease to be produced. If a class of superiorly educated gardeners were to come forward, they would create a demand for themselves, on the principle that demand is influenced both by the supply and the quality of the article.'[23]

As we have seen, the numbers of head gardeners rose dramatically as the century progressed, but not so their remuneration. This matter became more galling to head gardeners as the century wore on. For not only were head gardeners now better and more comprehensively educated than their predecessors, they also had a constantly increasing workload, without a commensurate rise in wages. Moreover, there seemed little relationship between size of establishment and wage – a head gardener in charge of a 'small' suburban garden of a few acres would receive only slightly less than a head gardener of a 'first rate establishment'. One head gardener complained to *The Gardeners' Chronicle* in 1841 that he and one assistant had to work 4,848 square yards (4,053.55sq m) of kitchen garden, 548 yards (501.09m) of wall trees, a 38-yard (34.75m) long range of pines, vines etc., an area of frames, 1,200 pots of plants, 2 acres (0.81ha) of lawn, shrubbery and coach drive.[24] Yet in 1873 there was some astonishment at the high level of salary paid to the head gardener at Hampton Court Palace – £130.

Some head gardeners did make a good living – from 1849 until 1858 Joseph Paxton received the substantial sum of £500 a year from the Duke of Devonshire. But this amount was not just for his responsibilities as head gardener at Chatsworth, but as agent for the whole estate. At the other end of the scale, the salary offered was sometimes nothing less than insultingly low. When, whilst a foreman at the Royal Exotic Nursery in the mid-1840s, David T. Fish was offered a situation paying '£30 per year, with board, and the half of a footman's room for lodging', he refused point blank and his 'indignation blazed forth'.[25] Even so, ingenious incumbents made up for their meagre salaries in other ways. An example was Mr Kneller of Penrhyn Castle, who in the mid-1920s was in charge of a staff of fifty and recipient of the Royal Horticultural Society's highest honour, the Victoria Medal of Horticulture. He had 'a man from the gardens to assist in the house and do any other odd jobs, a workman to look after his two cows and poultry. A lot of surplus garden produce helped to feed these. A weekly hamper to butcher and baker, with something in return.' And just to put the head gardener's salary in context, an 1828 'Priced List of Florist's Flowers' gave the most expensive cultivar, *Auricula* 'Lee's Colonel Taylor', at 60s or £3 a plant. Thus you could have purchased 33 auriculas for the same amount as you paid your head gardener each year.[26] And at the turn of the twentieth century new orchid cultivars were changing hands at 1,000 guineas (£1,050) each.

While the criticisms levied against stingy employers were justifiable, the behaviour of another sector of the horticultural industry was reprehensible. '"Save me from my friends" is an old proverb never more true than when applied by gardeners to those gentlemen in the trade who compete with each other in keeping down a just remuneration to qualified gardeners,' said Zadok Stevens (*c*.1833–86), head gardener at Trentham in 1885.[27] This was one of the frequent accusations of collusion between employers and nurserymen. Two familiar scenarios went something like this: were a journeyman gardener to leave his post, he had often to resort to taking employment with a nursery, where he would be paid considerably less than were he employed in a garden. Other times the advice of a nurseryman was courted by a prospective employer who wanted a head gardener 'on the cheap'. Many nurserymen would betray a head gardener to an insufficient salary and suggest a man, rather than, 'in a reasonable and candid manner, remind their applicants of the nature of the services which they require; and that these services, if paid below their fair value, will never be performed so well as if the performer were conscious of being properly treated'.[28]

The head gardener's impecunious position had another impact – it prevented their rise through the social ranks. As 'W.S.' bluntly put it 'what we want is an increase of money; without this, vulgar and unsentimental though it may appear, gardeners may be educated *ad lib.*, but they will ever remain the socially lean creatures they are till the end of time'.[29] Some gardeners did achieve middle-class respectability – but they were the exception. John Spencer, head gardener to the Marquis of Lansdowne at Bowood House (Wiltshire) became the director of a bank; John Robson was treasurer of Linton Parochial Church Council and Chairman of Maidstone Gardeners' Society; and James Leighton who left Kew in 1880, migrated to South Africa and established a nursery, was elected mayor of King Williams Town in 1910. And, of course, Joseph Paxton retired a knight and millionaire.[30] Others were on occasion treated most foully by their employer. Again it is Mr Sherwood who provides a particularly contemptible example:

One of the richest if not the very richest nobleman in England, has just parted with his gardener upon the subject of wages. This gardener, it was stated where I dined, is among the most intelligent of those of your country; he went to the situation about seven years ago; and besides doing the common routine of a nobleman's gardens, he laid out an immense park and pleasure ground, from his own designs; and that in such a way as to give universal satisfaction. The place, in short, is talked of, and we all know how proud Mr P. is of the share he had in the architecture of the house. The gardener went there on wages which he felt to be low; but which he trusted would be raised as he displayed his talents. With the most honourable feelings he declined asking for an advance while the great works he had in hand were going on, least it might be considered as a sort of threat to leave in the midst of them; but when the whole was completed, he then respectfully represented to his employer that he found great difficulty in supporting himself, his wife, and three children on forty pounds a year, and eleven shillings a week board wages, for he had no perquisites, not even milk or a pig. The magnificent and generous nobleman, not more rich than pious, after several weeks' consideration offered an addition of £121 a year. Such is the liberality of a man who is said to have upwards of £100,000 a-year…Had this gardener not been an honest man, he might, out of the thousands a year that passed through his hands, in the multifarious payments of from 250 to 300 men weekly, easily have helped himself: Is not such treatment enough to tempt men to dishonesty? And is it not astonishing that gentlemen, when they hire servants, do not take these things into account in adjusting their remuneration? In a word, there is no class of servants so ill paid as gardeners, and none, who from their general good conduct, and the long study and attention required to excel in their profession, deserve to be so well paid.[31]

BENEVOLENT INSTITUTION

And, so, after a life of hard toil, poor pay and under-appreciation, what did a retiring head gardener have to look forward to? The occasional employer did take care of their old retainers – Lady Lothian of Blickling Hall (Norfolk) was so kind-hearted that at one point she had fifteen old gardeners about the place doing light work. Much more common was, if anything, a send-off. Perhaps a celebratory dinner hosted by his employer, a whip-round, and a small token. In December 1872, for example, Philip Frost of Dropmore House retired, and to celebrate this event, friends and admirers presented him with a 'handsome silver cup, of the value of £25, on which were engraved the portraits of two of his more remarkable nursings *–Araucaria imbricata* and *Abies douglasii*, together with an annuity purchased with the sum of about £200. Long may he live to enjoy it, and to care for the wants of the magnificent trees at Dropmore.' John Robson, when he retired four years later from Linton, was presented by friends and neighbours with 'a handsome silver inkstand, and a purse containing £126, with a list of 160 subscribers'. In 1910 when Edward Butler retired from Surrenden Manor at Pluckley (Kent) after fifty years' service, a dinner was held in his celebration at which Mr and Mrs Butler were presented with their portraits, Mr Butler with a gold watch and an illustrated album containing the names of subscribers and an illuminated address.[32]

Usually the retiree had no pension and was often obliged to move out of his tied accommodation. What of the under-gardeners, or those unfortunate to fall ill or suffer injury or disability? The workhouse or starvation on the streets was a reality. It was in order to provide a modicum of succour to unfortunate gardeners of all levels of employment that in 1838 a group of philanthropists banded together under the Chairmanship of the landscape designer and author George Glenny to form The Gardeners' Benevolent Institution (the name was changed to the Gardeners' Royal Benevolent Society in 1960 and Perennial in 2003). It took until late 1840 to raise sufficient funds to enable the first three pensioners to share £75 as an initial instalment of a pension. By 1852 over £500 per annum was being spent on caring for the Society's pensioners, average age of seventy-seven. Nine years later income had reached about £1,000, dependent on voluntary contributions and the major fundraising event, the Annual Dinner; and by 1899 the number of pensioners had risen to 154.[33] Today, Perennial continues to be the United Kingdom's only charity dedicated to helping horticulturists in need, and continues to do great works, so please visit www.perennial.org.uk

CHAPTER 6

The Head Gardeners' Contributions

Before examining the major contributions made by head gardeners to the evolution of the garden, it is germane to offer an overview of the nineteenth century garden. The development of these gardens, in particular the Victorian garden (Queen Victoria reigned from 1838 to 1901), is as complex as the gardens were varied, and the variations on a theme can confuse the observer from another millennium as much they did the gardenmakers of the time. Generally speaking, by the mid-1800s the standard arrangement of the country house and garden was a formal terrace with geometrically laid-out flower garden providing a setting for the architecture of the house. This arrangement could be augmented by a conservatory, although it could also be detached and located within the pleasure grounds. Seminatural by design, the pleasure grounds were set beyond the terraces to create a buffer between, and link with, the wider countryside, which in many instances was a designed landscape left over from the eighteenth century. Within this transition zone would also be found the kitchen gardens.

GARDEN STYLE

When it came to the design of the ornamental garden, one theme or question loomed large throughout the whole century: what was the correct relationship between art and nature? Or put another way, how were the two contradictory modes to be reconciled within a garden setting? With the death in 1818 of Humphry Repton, the last great landscapist, there was deliberate rejection of the more-natural-than-nature landscape and the embrace of a deliberate display of artistry within the garden. Thus, until the 1860s when the wheel of fashion began to turn full circle and the cry for a return to a more natural approach grew louder, art, rather than nature, was the order of the day. To ensure that a garden was a work of art and not just an imitation of nature, the hand of man needed to be manifestly visible; and the artistic garden was given its first major fillip by Loudon, who devised the Gardenesque. This was a term he coined in his *The Gardener's Magazine* in December 1832 and further defined it in *The Suburban Gardener and Villa Companion* (1838) 'As a garden is a work of art and a scene of cultivation every plant or tree placed in it should be so placed as never to be mistaken for a plant placed there by nature or accident or as to prevent the practices of cultivation being applied to it.' The Gardenesque was, therefore, in essence a new planting style in which plants were positioned in such a way that was clearly not natural, and such that the individual artistic beauties of the (often foreign and therefore exotic) plants could be admired to their fullest. Indeed, simply by planting those taxa which were not native (or naturalised) helped enforce the statement of artistry, for non-native equated to not natural, and if not natural, by default, the subject had to be artistic.

Loudon also stimulated changes in fashion indirectly through his *Encyclopædia* (1822), which contained one of the earliest, and at the time, most thorough chronological appraisals of international garden history. The subject was picked up by George W. Johnson (1802–86) who published *History of English Gardening* in 1826, and in so doing became the torch bearer and foremost authority on the subject for the next thirty years. The principal areas of garden history that most caught the public's imagination, and the stylistic differences between them, were spelled out by Charles McIntosh in his *Flower Garden* (1837–8):

ITALIAN: characterized by one or more terraces, sometimes supported by parapet walls, on the coping of which vases of different forms are occasionally placed, either as ornaments, or for the purpose of containing plants. Where the ground slopes much, and commands a supply of water from above, *jets-d'eau* and fountains are introduced with good effect.

FRENCH: The French partially adopt the Italian style close to their chateaux and houses; and, beyond the terraces, layout parterres, sometimes in very complicated figures.

DUTCH: The leading character of the Dutch style is rectangular formality, and what may sometimes be termed clumsy artifice, such as yew trees cut out in the form of statues, though they require a label to inform the observer what they mean to represent.

ENGLISH: It is generally understood, that the style termed English in gardening consists in an artful imitation of nature, and is consequently much dependent on aspect and accessaries [*sic*]. In the true English style, accordingly, we have neither the Italian terrace, the French parterre, nor the Dutch clipt evergreens. ... The pretended adherence to nature... is wholly a style of conventional artifice, not so stiff and formal, indeed, as the Italian terraces, the French parterres, or the Dutch clipt evergreens, but still strictly artificial.[1]

FORMAL TERRACE GARDENS

The realisation that there was a back catalogue of historical styles to plunder excited garden designers and architects alike, and by the 1840s the natural genius of the place had given way to the artistic and inventive genius of man. Two styles came to dominate: Gothic for public institutions and the Italianate for private commissions.

In the case of the latter, the terrace made a triumphant return as the most suitable setting for the house, and the leading proponent of the Italianate garden was the architect Sir Charles Barry (1795–1860). Barry's first great Italianate creation was Trentham, where from 1833 he remodelled the house, adding the garden from 1840.

His masterstroke was to carefully manipulate the gently sloping site in order to create two broad and shallow terraces which he augmented by gravel, balustrading, statuary and, of course, formal flower beds. He intended to extend the scheme right down to the shore of the Brownian lake, but was overruled by the writer-of-cheques, the second Duke of Sutherland (1786–1861). When in 1849 the air had grown so foul as a result of the pollution from the potteries that the Duke was forced to relocate to Cliveden (Buckinghamshire), Barry's services were called upon once again. Initially Sutherland intended to simply revamp the house, but when it burned to the ground during the works, a new Italian villa was commissioned, together with an appropriately terraced setting.

But after Trentham, Barry's most celebrated garden was Shrubland Park (Suffolk), and here he took fullest advantage of a steeply sloping site and

Taken from E Adveno Brooke's The Gardens of England *(1857), this is Trentham in all its Italianate glory as seen through the shrubberies of the pleasure grounds, and as depicted on the Duke's letterhead from the estate.*

installed a vast staircase off which ran a series of terraced walks that led to other areas of the garden. With its different components drawn from different cultures and different ages as categorised by McIntosh, the Italianate received the royal seal of approval when Prince Albert used the design for the house and garden at Osborne House (from 1845). As Bisgrove eruditely explains, the style 'found favour all round: the patron could ostentatiously display his wealth and good taste; the architect could display his classical learning and geometric inventiveness; and the gardener found the large level terraces ideal for exuberant displays of plants'.[2]

However, plants did not always enter into the picture, especially if the terrace garden was designed by one of Barry's associates, William Andrews Nesfield (1793–1881). His elaborate scroll-work parterres drew heavily from the French Renaissance designs of Le Nôtre and Mollet, and Nesfield was not above excluding Flora entirely, favouring instead of plants with their wild-growing ways, inanimate and controllable materials such as painted gravel, coal, chalk and powdered brick. His most ironic design was for the Royal Horticultural Society's new gardens in South Kensington, which not only had no plants but also nearly bankrupted the Society.

PLEASURE GROUNDS

Juxtaposing a formal garden and country house, be it old or new, was not much of a design challenge, for the architecture of the house could be subtly melded with that of the terrace. However, to artfully and harmoniously unify this combination with the wider countryside posed more of a challenge, especially in the cases where the setting was nature designed left over from the eighteenth century. We shall see how Paxton solved the issue at Chatsworth. Barry almost got away with it at Trentham by making the two shallow terraces especially broad. At Osborne House, however, the large sloping lawn provides a somewhat unconvincing link between terrace garden and distant seashore, and at Bowood House, George Kennedy 'sort of' solved the problem by restricting the size of his terrace and positioning it so that it deliberately did not look out over the Brownian lake. However, whatever solution was attempted, there was always at least a slight jarring where garden ended and countryside (designed or not) began.

The most widely used solution was to develop a pleasure ground in which the style was semi-natural or nature-controlled. As well as providing a transition zone between formal terraces and informal nature, the pleasure grounds offered a further opportunity for a display of horticultural novelty – this time of hardy plants. To provide an appropriately artistic show, designed to be visually harmonious, mentally stimulating, and above all expensively novel, nature was embellished. Natural (native) woodland could be pierced by walks and rides of gravel or grass laid out to open and close specially devised vistas, while the grounds were ornamented with rustic wood constructions, rockwork, water features and, of course, plants. The plants could be botanical collections such as an arboretum, pinetum or an American garden; or the natural setting could be tempered by the creation of curvaceous shrubberies and sinuous beds of flowering shrubs and hardy exotics, of which from the 1850s onwards, rhododendrons and those taxa with coloured foliage proved particularly popular.

KITCHEN GARDENS

According to Robert Fish, writing in *The Cottage Gardener and Country Gentlemen* in 1857 'the first duty of a gardener is to provide his employer's table with plenty of good-flavoured vegetables; the second importance is plenty of good fruit; and the third is an abundance of beautiful flowers to crown the whole'.[3] Placed at a distance from the house, but often closer than its eighteenth century counterpart, the kitchen garden remained a feature on the garden tour itinerary. The meticulously maintained open ground with its neatly raked paths, and weed-free straight rows of crops and cutting flowers looking like some exotic regimental parade, was always a stirring and impressive sight, and one that demonstrated man was very much in control of nature. And the results of such mastery were impressive. At Frogmore in 1895, the royal gardener Thomas Owen produced, in addition to vast quantities of apples, pears, and a wide variety of soft fruits, 4,000 lbs (1814.4kg) grapes, 520 dozen peaches, 220 dozen nectarines, 180 dozen apricots, 239 pineapples and 400 melons. And two years later the 'List of Fruit and Vegetables served from the Royal Gardens' and sent to Balmoral for the period 30 August to 9 November listed £396 4s worth of fruits, £375 16s 6d worth of vegetables and £80 worth of flowers, making a grand total of £852 0s 6d at average market prices.[4]

Within the kitchen gardens the extent of the ranges of glass increased. At Trentham, where the kitchen garden covered some 5 acres (2.02ha), Robert Fish estimated a third to be under glass. Here were plentiful vineries to supply a 'regular succession of Grapes...throughout the year'. On 18 February 1854 the grapes in the early vinery were colouring, while large bunches of Barbarossa remained 'still fresh and plump'. Peaches in the first house had set their fruit and would be harvested in May, while strawberries, melons and cucumbers were all 'in a forward state'. The latter two were grown in low pits 'with a path in the interior for facilitating their management' and provided with bottom heat from hot water pipes. Numerous similar pits were used for 'the propagation and wintering of the thousands of bedding plants, which are yearly wanted to furnish the beds of the extensive parterres', and of course, there were several ranges of pits devoted to pineapples.[5]

When, in 1869, Cliveden was sold to Hugh Lupus, the first Duke of Westminster (1825–99), he sensibly retained the services of John Fleming, and perhaps as an incentive for him to stay, allowed him to entirely redesign and rebuild the glass department. This was described some eight years later as 'very extensive, as needs must be to meet the large demands made upon it for fruits and flowers . . . and now forms one of the most compact and complete departments to be found in the three kingdoms.' The department comprised some thirty-two structures including one of the 'most

LIST of FRUIT and VEGETABLES served from the ROYAL GARDENS at
Windsor from *August 30* to *Nov 9* 1898

FRUIT.

DESCRIPTION	QUANTITY DELIVERED (average prices)		£	s.	d.
	FROM HOUSES OR FRAMES	FROM GARDEN			
APPLES		305 Dozen 82 Pecks	43	10	-
APRICOTS	Dozens	Dozens			
BANANAS — CURRANTS	13	Quarts	1	12	6
CHERRIES	lbs. oz.	lbs.			
CURRANTS—BLACK		12 lbs.	-	6	-
Ditto RED	lbs. oz.	12 lbs. oz.	-	6	-
Ditto WHITE		lbs. oz.			
Ditto GREEN		Quarts			
DAMSONS		Quarts			
FIGS	20 Dozens	Dozens 4	6	-	-
FILBERTS		lbs. oz.			
GRAPES	423 lbs. oz.	lbs.	105	15	-
GREENGAGES	Dozens	Dozens Quarts			
GOOSEBERRIES		lbs. Quarts			
MELONS	No. 113 weighing lbs.		34	11	-
MULBERRIES		lbs. oz.			
NECTARINES	Dozens	40 Dozens	24	-	-
PEACHES	Dozens	106 Dozens	63	12	-
PEARS		93 Dozens	18	18	6
PINE APPLES	No. 57 weighing 209 lbs.		50	-	-
Ditto for Preserving	No. weighing lbs.				
PLUMS	Dozens	245 Dozens 48	26	18	-
QUINCES		Dozens			
RASPBERRIES	lbs. oz.	lbs. oz.			
STRAWBERRIES	19 lbs. oz.	lbs.	9	10	-
WALNUTS		12 Hundreds	1	4	-
FLOWERS	236 Dozens		59	-	-
WREATHS	12				
		£	476	14	-

The fruit part of the Fruit and Vegetable List recording the produce, worth £852 0s 6d, which was dispatched from the walled garden at Frogmore to Balmoral. The vegetable section includes entries for 552 bunches of carrots, 150 hundredweight of old potatoes and 206 dozen lettuces.

comfortable bothies it has been our good fortune to see in any garden'. The productive glass comprised five vineries – a Muscat-house, long, early, second and late; three peach and nectarine houses – early, second and late; an apricot-house, a fig-house, a cucumber-house, a melon range, and a span-roofed pits used in spring to force early vegetables. The flower houses numbered an exotic fernery, plant stove where 'are to be seen the usual order of flowering and fine-foliaged subjects, all, with few exceptions, being grown specially on account of their usefulness either for table decoration…or for furnishing cut flowers', two houses dedicated 'mainly in the culture of Pelargoniums and Carnations', one devoted 'exclusively to Gardenias and Stephanotis', a 'handy structure…in which Tea Roses are planted', and between the packing-shed and potting-shed a north facing glass corridor 'filled with a collection of good-sized specimen Azaleas'. Finally there was a frame 'used for every conceivable purpose', an intermediate house 'turned to useful account in a variety of ways' and, of course, Fleming's office.[6]

Even far less grand establishments such as Underley Hall (Lancashire), the seat of the Earl of Bective, where 'the many improvements recently made here have been well carried out by Mr Sandford', boasted a new range of seventeen glasshouses erected by Weeks of Chelsea in 1870. Just the two vineries and four peach and nectarine houses grew seven types of grape (Black Alicante, Bowood Muscat, Gros Colman, Hamburghs, Lady Downe's, Madresfield Court, Muscat of Alexandria), ten types of peach (Alexandra, Dr. Hogg, Early Alfred, Early Beatrice, Grosse Mignonne, Lord Palmerston, Louise, Noblesse, Prince of Wales and Rivers' Early) and five types of Nectarine (Downton, Elruge, Lord Napier, Stanwick and Violette Hâtive).[7]

Such produce would be destined for the dining table, or meticulously packed, and sent up to the town house during the 'season' – or to wherever it was needed. In the 1920s when the third Baron Penrhyn of Penrhyn Castle was chief official of the Jockey Club, he travelled the country from one race meeting to another, and so fresh fruit, vegetables and flowers had to be at the place he was visiting one day prior to his arrival. As Norman Thomas recalled, 'grapes had to arrive at their place of destination with their bloom intact. Peaches, figs and similar fruit required special attention in their packing. All fruit was placed in special paper with wool and wood wool surrounding them, they were then placed in special boxes.' In 1926 the National Strike prevented the sending of large hampers of produce by rail, and the mail restricted packages to a few ounces, and so to overcome this obstacle, 'each tomato was sent separately. One tomato was wrapped in cotton wool and put into a small cardboard box, each box with an addressed label. Scores and scores of these boxes were sent by this method. They arrived at their place of destination in perfect condition.'[8]

CONSERVATORIES OR WINTER GARDENS

Ornate conservatories or winter gardens were an adjunct of any garden that desired to be of note. They were sometimes attached to the house or detached and set in the pleasure grounds. These great glass structures were home to many exotic and tender new arrivals brought from jungles and tropical regions across the world. Indeed, be they tender, half-hardy or hardy, the wealth of new plants brought to Britain by the plant hunters excited botanists and garden-owners, and provided head gardeners with a

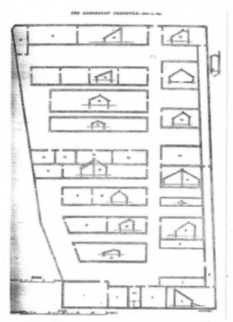

An illustration from The Gardeners' Chronicle *dated 21 July 1877, showing the disposition of the new range of glasshouses and buildings designed by and erected for John Fleming at Cliveden soon after the purchase of the estate by the Duke of Westminster.*

constant onslaught of challenges. These expensive treasures required careful and skilled nurturing to survive. Often in the vanguard of those attempting to cultivate such tricksy rarities, the head gardener had to rely on his experience, a modicum of experimentation and an ability to learn fast.

At Trentham the conservatory was large and square, formed a connecting link between the ornamental grounds around the house and the kitchen garden, and was 'chiefly devoted to the growth of arborescent kinds of conservatory plants, which are principally planted in open borders: Acacias, Camellias, Orange-trees, Polygalas &c.' The temperature was kept surprisingly low – just sufficient to exclude frost, but for a good reason. While the plants did not bloom early as they would have in a hotter environment, they came into their peak at the time when the family was in residence and able to enjoy it'.[8] The century's largest and grandest private conservatory, the Great Stove at Chatsworth, is examined in Chapter 7 (see page 158).

ORNAMENTAL GLASSHOUSES

As the description of the range at Cliveden reveals, it was not just edibles that were grown under glass. Table decorations and cut flower arrangements were becoming popular. From the mid-1860s onwards, the fashion of *service à la russe* at the dining table saw food served rather than the dishes being left on the table. The empty space now on the dining table had to be filled with something, and so floral table decorations of increasing complexity became popular. Thus the head gardener had to master yet another skill. The pioneer of such decorations was not a head gardener but a civil servant in the Lord Chamberlain's office, Thomas March. In 1861 March took first prize in the Flower Arranging Competition, held as part of the inauguration of the Royal Horticultural Society's new garden in Kensington. His entries were based around a flower stand of his own devising – two shallow glass dishes, a smaller one raised about 2ft (60.96cm) above a larger one by a glass rod. The gardening press raved about his exhibits.

Demand grew for the stands, and a year later March published *Flower and Fruit Decoration* which became a must-read for head gardeners who were now expected to produce table decorations of great artistry. Head gardeners also set about using their horticultural skills to create ingenious living ornaments, such as the 'novel feature in Grape culture', developed by Mr Sage of Belton Park (Grantham) – 'fruiting canes in 7- and 8-inch pots for table decoration', and for which he was awarded a Silver Medal from the Royal Horticultural Society. In addition, the flowers grown under glass were mainly chrysanthemums and pot roses, 'largely grown for cut flowers', together with 'an immense quantity of Marie Louise, Count Brazza, and Neapolitan Violets'.[10]

The conservatory had to be kept filled with plants in a perfect state. Thus provision had to be made within the glass range for raising flawless exotics which were temporarily transplanted to be admired in their fullest glory before being removed and replaced at the first sign of fatigue. At Trentham a large range of plant houses occupied a site at the rear of the kitchen garden 'from which they are separated by a belt of low evergreens and American plants'. The range consisted of a stove, geranium houses, heathery, camellia house and a 'long house' devoted to plants in bloom, and which contained 'many excellent specimens of popular greenhouse plants' including 'the newer kinds' of Chinese azaleas, daphnes, epiphyllums, forced roses, *Magnolia conspicua*, bulbs, primulas, which 'gave the house a very gay appearance, reminding us much more of May than February'.

Less magnificent but no less fit for purpose was the plant stove at Underley Hall. This was positioned at the centre of the principal range. It measured 30ft by 20ft (9.14m by 6.10m) and contained 'good plants of Ixora coccinea, I. javanica, Anthuriums, Crotons, Eucharis amazonica; Bougainvilleas, Stephanotis, some large healthy plants of Dendrobium nobile, Dracaenas, Dieffenbachias and Palms, conspicuous amongst which latter were fine plants of Kentia Canterburyana and Chamaedorea Ernesti Augustini'.[11]

Then there were the tender plants raised in the greenhouses to be transplanted *en masse* into the summer bedding schemes. In many gardens the quantities required were staggering. Ernest Field, head gardener to Alfred de Rothschild at Halton (Buckinghamshire), 'Once heard it said that rich people used to show their wealth by the size of their bedding plant list: 10,000 for a Squire, 20,000 for a Baronet, 30,000 for a Lord, and 40,000 for an Earl.' Alfred had 41,000, but Alice Rothschild at Waddesdon had a planting list that ran to 50,000. Just consider the greenhouse space such tasks demanded, the devastating consequences of a boiler going out on a cold night, the tricky hardening off process, and finally, the complex planting out.

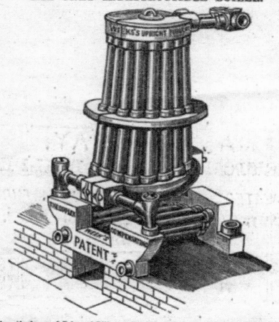

A glance through the pages of the horticultural press of the times is as interesting for the advertisements as for the factual content. One area of great choice was the range and type of boiler with which to heat the glasshouses.

Apricock	ADEW	6 Roman	ADEW	16 Noblefs	ADEW	Plumbs	LDEW	27 Blue Perdrigon	ADEW	Pears	SDEW
1 Bruſsels		7 Peas		17 Groſs Minion		20 Royal Dolphin		28 Peach Carbeon		1 Rochea	
Grapes		8 Scarlet come clean		18 Nivitte		21 Matchles		29 Marvileſs		2 Callow Roſe	
2 White Sweet Water		9 Small Scarlet		19 Royal George		22 Prune Royall		30 Larryall		3 Black Mulberry	
3 Black Sweet Water		10 Italians		20 Mongeard		23 Fotheringhall		31 Black Damaseen		A The Apple Roſe	
Nectarines		11 Arpells		21 Double Swalow		24 Elvert		32 Damaz: Nordlux		B The Medli Pfaeen	
4 Nimington		Peaches		22 Mountaignes		25 Damask Violecour		33 Mitre Claude		C The Virginaux	
5 Peterborough		12 Perrigue		23 S.t Laurence		26 Hatfield Blue		34 Rein Claude		C Mespheles	

AUGUST 1732.

A work of science and art, as innovative as it was attractive, the Great Stove at Chatsworth was, when completed in 1841, the world's largest greenhouse. The men standing on the frame halfway up the building provide scale!

Perhaps even more stunning inside than out, the Great Stove was home to a vast collection of tender plants. A coach and horses could be driven through it and the heating system burned a tonne of coal a day.

Imbued with a sense of grandiose nature, The Wellington Rock is in fact an artful construction, and perfectly demonstrates how Joseph Paxton so successfully and harmoniously assimilated these two design influences in the gardens at Chatsworth.

Designed in the early 1850s by John Fleming, the spring bedding display at Cliveden used over 20,000 plants and nearly 10,000 tulips to fill the 3 1/2-acre (1.42 ha) parterre (above). This arrangement (right) was one of several bedding innovations devised by Fleming.

RHS Linley Library

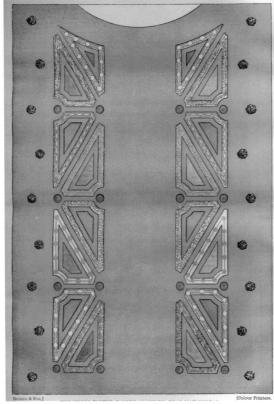

Benson & Son.]   [Colour Printers.

Designed by Sir Charles Barry and planted by John Fleming, the great terrace gardens at Trentham were arguably the apogee of the Italianate, a peculiar amalgam of various historical styles from around Europe. RHS Linley Library

Painted in the mid-nineteenth century, the formal terrace at Eaton Hall with its large size and complex pattern was typical of its time. Keeping it immaculate was just one of the head gardener's many responsibilities. RHS Linley Library

The planting craze of the nineteenth century was
bedding, and head gardeners were in the vanguard of its
development. In the 1830s early pioneer John Caie set
the fashion for 'massing' together bold clumps of bright
colours in formal beds.
RHS Linley Library

1. Echeveria glauco-metallica.   5. Pyrethrum Golden Feather.
2. Coleus Verschaffeltii.   6. Alternanthera amœna.
3. Cineraria maritima compacta.   7. Lobelia pumila grandiflora.
4. Alternanthera paronychioides major. 8. Antennaria tomentosa.

1. Coleus Verschaffeltii.   6. Mesembryanthemum cordifolium variegatum
2. Lobelia pumila grandiflora.   7. Alternanthera paronychioides.
3. Alternanthera amabilis.   8. Sempervivum montanum.
4. Cerastium arvense.   9. Sempervivum subtubuliæforme
5. Sedum glaucum.   10. Cerastium tomentosum

Another bedding method, invented by
John Fleming at Cliveden, was
named 'carpet bedding' in 1868.
Using low-growing foliage plants, the
aim was to devise patterns as
colourful as they were intricate.
RHS Linley Library

The great range of glasshouses at Waddesdon boasted some fifty different structures and was as much a feature of the tour of the garden as a place of cultivation. Sadly, the glasshouses were demolished in the 1970s. Waddesdon, The Rothschild Collection (The National Trust)

From the walled garden at Frogmore successive head gardeners supplied the Royal residences with vast quantities of fruits, vegetables and flowers. In the early twentieth century Edward VIII spent over £65,000 developing the garden and its glasshouses.
The Royal Collection © 2007 Her Majesty Queen Elizabeth II

Head gardeners were also inventors. William Barron of Elvaston Castle devised a system for lifting, transporting and transplanting large trees. His greatest triumph was the relocation of a 1,000 year-old oak in Buckfast Abbey churchyard. RHS Linley Library

A picture from another world that has sadly vanished forever. Taken in 1917, this photograph features four esteemed head gardeners, each of whom was an octogenarian. The group had a collective age of 336! RHS Linley Library

If there was no grand conservatory, as was the case at Waddesdon, glasshouses within the kitchen garden performed the role. Here there were more than fifty glasshouses, of which forty had been erected by 1885; the flower houses were an especial marvel and an essential part of any garden tour undertaken by guests. The tour started in the vestibule, with its tiered show of formally arranged potted flowers, and thence along a similarly adorned main corridor, glancing to left and right to admire the contents of a series of 80ft (24.38m) long glasshouses that adjoined the corridor. These were filled with a fiesta of potted ornamentals and of course the specialities of the mansion – Malmaison Carnations (Souvenir de la Malmaison) of which many new varieties were raised at Waddesdon, the exotic climbing Glory Lily (*Gloriosa rothschildiana*), a native of South Africa and now the national plant of Zimbabwe, and of course orchids.

The orchid houses were designed to provide the specific climatic conditions desired by each different orchid genera cultivated, in particular, cattleyas, miltonias and odontoglossums. The collection was gathered with the assistance of Frederick Sander (1847–1920), one of the greatest orchid experts of his day, and from 1891 Royal Orchid Grower. The main corridor terminated in the high-domed palm house, dominated by a fern-encrusted rockery-cum-grotto made of Pulhamite (an artificial but incredibly realistic stone) and a waterfall which *The Gardeners' Chronicle* found 'too realistic and too noisy'.[12]

AGGRANDISEMENT

The enthusiastic 'W.S.', a gardener from Kincardineshire cried in 1866 that gardening 'has progressed more during the last 10 or 15 years than ever it has done in the same period before'. And it had been the nation's head gardeners whose hands had lifted up gardening to this 'point of excellence never anticipated even by their more recently departed predecessors'.[13] Head gardeners were, without doubt, instrumental in driving forward advances in all aspects of the art and science of gardening. However, at a less altruistic level a head gardener, if he wished further advancement, needed to develop a professional reputation. Such a reputation not only helped secure better future employment prospects, but more immediately, placing one's current garden firmly on the horticultural map brought kudos to, and, it was hoped, gratitude from, one's employer. Once a position had been secured, a talented, energetic and ambitious gardener made certain that the garden under his command excelled, or as Thomas Speed decided upon his appointment at Chatsworth in 1868, 'to rear a mount of excellent gardening on which I could stand and be seen'.

To attain (and to a certain extent to maintain) perfection in all departments of the garden under one's command required a combination of skill and the study and application of the latest developments, be they horticultural, scientific or artistic. Or as Robert Fish encouraged, to keep 'pace with the onward march of discovery and improvement; ought to be the heartfelt desire of every gardener worthy of the name, or in whose breast one spark of true and elevated ambition resides'.[14]

Gardening periodicals, of which there were a growing number, were a convenient way in which to obtain the latest information. Some, such as Loudon's influential *The Gardener's Magazine* (1826–43) and *The Floricultural Cabinet and Florist's Magazine* (1833–59), came and went; others have exhibited extraordinary longevity. The best-known and oft-quoted

Bloxham's fumigator as endorsed in 1866 by Mr Coleman, head gardener at Eastnor Castle. The diversity of horticultural sundries available was remarkable and included glass tubes for growing straight cucumbers!

Technology moves ever forward. It was in October 1830 that Edwin Beard Budding received his patent for the first cylinder lawn mover, and 1833 when he sold a licence to manufacture to Messrs Ransomes of Ipswich. The rest is history!

The Gardeners' Chronicle continues today as *Horticulture Week*. Beginning life as the *Transactions of the Horticultural Society of London* in 1807 and passing through a number of titular incarnations including *Journal of the Royal Horticultural Society* (1865–1975), *The Garden* is still widely read. Packed and printed in squint-formingly tiny fonts, the periodicals were a mine of useful facts and figures, including for example: descriptions of newest plant arrivals and hybrids; suggestions for the design of anything from flower beds to housing for head gardeners; questions and answers; book reviews; reports from garden societies and shows; meteorological statistics; experimental results on the research into fertilisers or plant trials; market prices, the merits or not of boilers; discussion about gardeners' conditions, etc., etc., etc.

Periodicals were not just a source of information, they were also outlets through which a motivated and skilled head gardener could self-promote. Thus gardening correspondents (often head gardeners themselves) were invited to visit and to assess the establishment under the headship of Mr So-and-so. But in terms of reputation-building, more important were the communications from head gardeners themselves. To enter the most pressing debate of the day, to exchange ideas or pass comment got one's name in print, but still most noteworthy were the reports published of advances made. And exactly because gardening had so many branches of investigation, there was ample scope for anyone with sufficient dedication and drive to use their garden as a laboratory and undertake research, make developments, advances or discoveries, and to be published.

John Fleming and Trentham were a case in point. In 1854 the garden (and by inference the head gardener) was described as 'a great school of horticulture, where every thing relating to the art is put to the test of practical experience the results of which show how carefully every detail of management is carried out by Mr Fleming'.[15] Accordingly, as the century progressed, many of the plant sciences – botany, plant physiology and nutrition, pathology, entomology and pest control, became increasingly understood. Thus the words of Robert Fish uttered at a lecture given to the West London Gardeners' Association on 19 December 1836 proved to be prophetic. For not only had 'a knowledge of the sciences upon which the first principles of gardening are founded' led 'to greater unanimity upon points [of gardening] which are subjects of dispute', but also that the gardener who aimed 'at excelling must act upon the principle that his profession is one of enquiry, one in which practice ought to be based upon scientific induction'.[16]

PUBLICATIONS

Some head gardeners did more than pen the occasional missive, they founded, edited and wrote columns for periodicals. Robert Marnock of Sheffield Botanic Garden started the *Floricultural Magazine* (1836–42) and *United Gardeners' and Land Stewards' Journal* (1845–48), while Joseph Harrison of Wortley Hall (Yorkshire) established *Gardener's and Forester's Record* (1833–36), *Floricultural Cabinet* (1833–59) which continued as *Gardener's Weekly Magazine* (1860–65) and *Gardener's Magazine* (1865–1916), and Joseph Paxton founded three magazines (see page 180). *The Cottage Gardener* was founded in 1848 not by a head gardener but the barrister and keen garden historian George W. Johnson (see page 108), who is not to be confused with the head gardener George Johnston. Its original title was *The Cottage Gardener*, but following the waggish yet accurate comment by E.S. Dixon that its contents were 'more suitable for a double-coach-house' than a cottage, it was renamed in 1861. Amongst its editorial board were some head gardeners of note – Edward Luckhurst, Warrington Taylor, David Thompson and Robert Fish. Fish penned between two and three thousand words a week on top of running a garden. Thus were born gardening's first 'media stars' – so popular was the journal's regular contributor, Donald Beaton, that when he retired from Shrubland Park in the early 1850s, an admirer offered him an experimental garden in Surbiton, London, the records of which he communicated through his column. And so held in esteem was the team of experts who wrote 'The Week's Work' for *The Gardeners' Chronicle* that they were proudly paraded on the opening pages of the first issue for the year 1910: 'Plants Under Glass' by John Donoghue at Hardon Hill (Yorkshire); 'The Hardy Fruit Garden' by A R Searle at Castle Ashby, Northampton; 'The Flower Garden' by E Beckett at Aldenham House (Hertfordshire); 'The Kitchen Garden' by John Dunn (kitchen garden foreman) at Frogmore (Windsor); 'Fruits Under Glass' by B Goodacre at Moulton Paddocks (Newmarket); 'Public Parks and Gardens' by W W Pattigrew, Superintendent of City Parks in Cardiff; and 'The Orchid Houses' by W H White at Burford (Surrey).[17]

Head gardeners also became respected authors. We have met Charles McIntosh who was one of the century's earlier successful authors with a string of titles under his belt, including *The Practical Gardener* (1828), *The Flower Garden* and *The Greenhouse, Hot House and Stove* (both 1838), *The Orchard and Fruit Garden* (1839) and the mammoth two-volume *Book of the Garden* (1853 and 1855). Other head gardeners who successfully ventured into the world of print included John Fleming whose *Spring and Winter Gardening* (1864) cost a mere 2s 6d, William Taylor whose detailed description of grape culture appeared as *Vines of Longleat* (1882) and David Thomson who published *Handy Book of the Flower Garden* (1868) and *Fruit Culture under Glass* (1881) both of which were very popular tomes.

One ex-head gardener managed to combine two successful new careers – as an author and nurseryman. Whilst head gardener to Charles B. Warner at Hoddesdon (Hertfordshire), Benjamin S. Williams (1822–90) had honed his skills on Warner's famous orchid collection and in 1852 published *The Orchid-Growers Manual* based primarily on his series of articles 'Orchids for the Million' that had appeared in *The Gardeners' Chronicle*. By 1865 he had left his position, and had established Victoria and Paradise Nurseries in Upper Holloway (London), specialising in orchids, and continued to write. *The Orchid-Growers Manual* was updated twice, and Williams also published *Select Ferns and Lycopods* (1868 and 1873) and *Choice Stove and Greenhouse Plants* (1873, 1876 and 1883) which in its third edition cost 7s 6d and contained descriptions of upwards of 1,300 species and cultivars.

THE ART OF HORTICULTURE

The design of the ornamental gardens and grounds was generally the reserve of the architect or garden designer, but head gardeners were sometimes asked to lay out new grounds. The new ornamental gardens, kitchen gardens and orchard at the Denbies (Surrey), were designed by James Drewett, and Archibald Fowler did the same for the Earl of Strathmore at Glamis Castle.[18] However, the greatest contribution made by head gardeners to the style of the nineteenth-century formal garden was the development of the bedding system.

Bedding

The use of plants *en masse* to create a striking effect was not something new to the nineteenth century. Islamic garden designers had planted sunken beds filled with tulips and other plants whose flower heads were at ground level to create the impression of a living carpet of flowers. And at Versailles, for the flower garden at the Grand Trianon alone, 1.9 million plants were raised every year just so the king could have the colour scheme changed on a whim. But bedding as an art form rose to dominance in the nineteenth century, and head gardeners devised the new stylistic forms.

In 1830 Loudon was making excited noises about experiments being made in various gardens where plants were massed together in blocks of a single colour to create a bold show. One of the gardens which, in Loudon's opinion, most perfectly demonstrated 'the advantage of placing beauty in masses' was Dropmore. Here, the head gardener William Baillie had designed the new rococo bedding scheme in 1828, which was a part of the flower garden under the foremanship of Philip Frost, who eventually replaced Baillie in 1832.

Mixing vs. massing

Throughout the decade the concept of filling formal flower beds with a show of flower colour for the summer months garnered increasing enthusiasm and stimulated a debate which centred on whether the plants should be mixed or, as Frost advocated, massed. Mixing took for its inspiration naturally occurring riotous shows of colour such as the annual transformation of the veldt of South Africa or the vivid blends of *Coreopsis, Eschscholitzia* and *Nemophila* that erupt on the Mexican prairies. Such displays were most definitely not British, occurring as they did in foreign countries, but perhaps just because there was a hint of imitating nature, albeit an un-natural one, mixing lost out to massing. Massing could be described in no other way than purely artistic, and it was another head gardener, John Caie (1811–79) of Bedford Lodge in Kensington, who by the late 1830s had become the doyen of massed bedding. Caie spread his ideas to a wide audience through the pages of *The Gardener's Magazine*, and to a receptive professional audience through his establishment and membership of the West London Gardeners' Association. Of his influence on the development of bedding David T. Fish later wrote:

> Take, for example, the bedding-out system, of which in its best form he was undoubtedly the originator. He was literally possessed with, lost in it, for years. He would talk for hours of the proper proportion of green to grey, of light and shade, the contrasts and harmonies of colour, the relative breadths of flower-beds and shrubberies to open spaces, of gravel to grass, of life and repose in landscape, of cold colours and warm, of the proportion

of tall trees to dwarf bushes and flowers, &c., until the Dowager Duchess of Bedford's garden . .... became a lesson-book of decorative landscape art for all England.

Caie's golden rules were: solid masses of 'clean, simple, and intelligible' colours, arranged contrast and planted in beds of simple shapes whose size and position were relative to the visual impact they gave. That is to say both plant heights and colour intensity had to be in proportion to the bed size, and the overall colour scheme. Thus equal-sized beds had masses of equal brightness, while large beds of muted colours could be balanced by a small one of bright ones. The overall aim was a balanced and proportional show in which 'order' was 'the source of peace'.

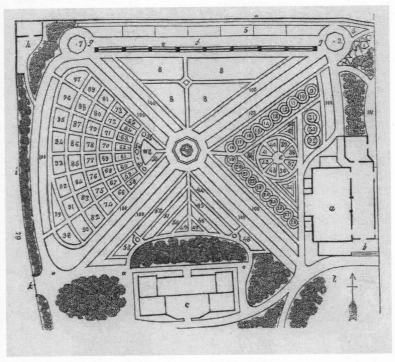

John Caie's plan for the extensive bedding scheme to be laid out in the flower garden to the west of Bedford Lodge, and which was published by Loudon in his The Gardener's Magazine *in 1838.*

In the same year as Caie's plan for Bedford Lodge, Joseph Paxton offered this layout of a large flower garden. Published in his periodical, Paxton's Magazine of Botany, *the scheme is generally more complex and ornate.*

TYPES OF PLANT

What was not in question was the type of plant which should be used. The word from the editor of *Paxton's Magazine of Botany* made it clear to his readers in 1838 that 'We propose banishing entirely from the flower-garden all such plants as are perfectly hardy, or, in other words, those which are termed hardy herbaceous plants, and supplying their place with the more showy and favourite kinds which require protection during the winter.' But it was Caie, again, who was responsible for the set of plant species that became the 'industry standard'. *Calceolaria, Lobelia, Pelargonium, Petunia, Salvia* and *Verbena* – tender exotics from South America and South Africa – favoured for their bright flowers and the range of colours. Moreover, they were easy to hybridise and propagate, so by the 1850s there was a spectrum of six colours: blue, pink, purple, scarlet, white and yellow, available in myriad tints and tones.[19]

Scale

Bedding displays were made on all scales. Reference has been made to the vast numbers of plants employed at two of the Rothschild residences (see page 117), and even more extravagant was Wimbledon House where 60,000 plants were crammed into the two hundred or so oval, round and moon-shaped beds, each about 15ft (4.57m) in diameter. At the more modest end of the scale, however, were residences such as Thornham Hall (Suffolk) where, during the 1850s, the plants list numbered a mere 16,000, mainly cupheas, felicias, gaillardias, gazanias and lantanas which were distributed throughout about 150 beds.[20]

In the early 1850s the mantle of bedding-king passed to Donald Beaton (1802–63) who had been head gardener at Shrubland Park. Beaton was clearly a delightful chap, for David T. Fish who entered the service of Sir Philip Broke at nearby Broke Hall in 1845, was insistent when writing some thirty years later, that 'it must be recorded to the honour of his memory, that from the time of my entry into Suffolk until his death he treated me as a father, and delighted to pour his rich stores of knowledge and fertilising streams of practice into the young man who was all ear to listen and afterwards to learn. If James Dodds and his staff of assistants [at Scone Palace] had some hand in hammering the school-boy into a shapely workman, Robert Fish and Donald Beaton finished the horticultural man

Bedding was all about numbers and intricacy. Published in The Gardeners' Chronicle *in 1871, this parterre at Castle Ashby was 220sq ft, the pattern was picked out in clipped box, and the beds were filled with 20,000 flowering plants.*

for his best work.' As early as 1851 Beaton, whose career as a writer had allowed him to retire at the age of fifty, had so formalised bedding that according to Stuart 'he thought that every parterre had to contain different heights of plants in different shades, but only in three shades and three heights. This only gave nine beds, or groups of nine, still with one sort of plant in one bed.' [21]

Shading and ribbon borders

Other head gardeners had also been developing new approaches to bedding. One of the most prolific and original was John Fleming who, from the moment of his appointment at Trentham, demonstrated exactly how valuable a head gardener's comprehensive education was. The site near Stoke was cold and exposed and the ground itself was also most uncongenial. Fleming's first task before he could begin to plant was to install an extensive drainage system laid at a depth of 6ft (1.83m), and to improve the soil using vast quantities of ash and manure. Fleming also created a 12-acre (4.86ha) arboretum beyond the flower garden. It was the vast terraces designed by Charles Barry, however, that provided Fleming with the perfect canvas for his new approach to bedding. Trentham was the apogee of the bedding fashion, and one of the main reasons why the gardens became 'a byword for innovation on a heroic scale, the testing ground for ideas that were to filter into advanced practice a decade later'.

As so often can be the stimulus for innovation, it was friendly professional rivalry, between Fleming and Beaton, that drove forward the evolution of bedding. Both worked extensively on the proper use of colour theory within the schemes, the effects of plant height and habit, the numbers of plants used to achieve an effect, and both were always striving for novelty. And two innovations emerged simultaneously at Trentham and Shrubland Park (or so Beaton claimed) and both were valuable tools by which the formal garden could be extended into the wider landscape.

Shading was a planting technique by which adjacent groups or rows had similar flower colours so that the rows seemed to blend seamlessly together and thus blur into one another and the distance. The following is an example of Fleming's conception at its finest.

Two beds, divided by a gravel walk, in a direct line 200 yards [182.88m] long, slope gently towards the river; each, about 9 feet [2.74m] wide, is planted with flowers to represent the colours of the rainbow. The left side also contains a succession of circular raised beds, with festoons of roses; and a background of hollyhocks tower up in front of a well-trimmed, thick hedge of evergreens, shaded in turn by forest trees and others.

However, it was the ribbon border which received greater approbation. As the name suggests this was a long narrow border which was

occupied with three continuous lines of colour extending their whole length. The first on each side of the walk is blue; the second yellow; and the third, on one side, is scarlet, and on the other, white. The following are the plants employed on one side: - *Nemophila insignis*, for blue; *Calceolaria rugosa*, for yellow; and the Frogmore geranium, for scarlet.[22]

Spring bedding

When the Duke of Buckingham relocated to Cliveden, Fleming went with him, and here he planted the 3½-acre (1.42ha) parterre on Barry's terrace between 1851 and 1853. The triangular beds were edged with clipped privet and spruce, and partly filled with azaleas and rhododendrons with spaces left for hollyhocks, gladioli and foxgloves as well as summer and spring bedding. The spring bedding show alone used over 20,000 plants, as well as nearly 10,000 tulips, and it was this latter scheme which demonstrated another of Fleming's innovations, the twice-annual bedding system. Once the main summer display of tender plants was over, Fleming planted the beds with bulbs and biennials that overwintered *in situ* and provided a spring flower show as a forerunner of the summer show. Fleming published his thoughts in *Spring and Winter Gardening* (1864) in which he classified plants according to their uses in the beds:

1 Edging – frequently a double line of dwarf plants using two different subjects.
2 Groundwork – the main plants massed through the bed.
3 Interplant – a second plant mixed in smaller numbers through the bed with the groundwork.
4 Dot plants – large plants or plants of striking character used in small numbers.

Fleming was not the only head gardener striving to extend the flowering season. William Ingram (1820–94), appointed head gardener to the Duke of Rutland at Belvoir Castle (Leicestershire) in 1853, 'won for himself a foremost position amongst his fellow horticulturists' and earned a reputation 'in the development of spring gardening, which has become so deservedly popular in many quarters'. It is debatable as to whom was the more innovative, Fleming or Ingram, but Ingram often receives more credit for his approach and was more novel than Fleming. Rather than simply filling the formal beds on a terrace, Ingram planted his spring-flowering subjects in huge drifts in informally shaped curvaceous beds that wound themselves through the dells and glades of the Spring Garden.

This 1873 drawing by Mrs Ingram, wife of the head gardener, shows the Duchess's garden at Belvoir Castle and the pattern of sinuous and curvaceous beds designed by her husband and filled with a display of spring flowering plants.

Spring bedding was part of Ingram's wider-reaching master plan to 'endeavour to remove an acknowledged blemish in our gardening practice' – and instead to 'give interest to the gardens by gathering together all kinds of plants of horticultural value, rather than to depend upon the attraction afforded by the more limited number that brighten our parterres for a short season'. To this end, and lamenting 'the banishment of the fine old herbaceous plants' which he termed 'unsuited for the blaze of a parterre, which yet shed a light of beauty on rocky ledges or shady nooks' Ingram reinstated perennials as 'a labour of love', and in addition collected together as many hardy shrubs and plants as were suitable, and filled every bed as soon as the summer flowers were over.[23]

Subtropical bedding

Bright-flowered tender annuals had dominated the bedding scene for about three decades when John Gibson (1815–75) decided to take a different approach. Gibson, who had begun his career under his father at Eaton

The portrait of William Ingram of Belvoir Castle accompanying his biography published on 13 March 1875. William was one of the great 'British Gardeners' featured in the series carried by The Gardeners' Chronicle.

Hall near Congleton (Cheshire), was apprenticed to Joseph Paxton at Chatsworth in 1832, rising to foreman of the exotic plant department (see page 173). He left Chatsworth after seventeen years to become superintendent of Victoria Park (which included Greenwich Park) in London. In 1855 Gibson laid out Battersea Park, becoming superintendent there two years later. In 1864 he decided to experiment. Many new tender exotic plants had been arriving over the previous decades and what these lacked in bright flowers they more than made up for with striking foliage and form. Using such plants Gibson created a new attraction – he studded an irregularly shaped lawn with tree ferns, planted eye-catching specimens such as palms, bananas, *Montanoa bipinnatifida* and *Wigandia caracasana*, as well as formal beds of *Solanum* and *Canna*. Thus was born subtropical bedding. This style evolved with time as many of the tender subjects were replaced with hardy ones of similarly exotic form.

Carpet bedding

It was at Cliveden, but with a return to tender plants, that Fleming made his last great innovation. Perhaps inspired by Gibson's work with plants noted for their foliage rather than their flowers, Fleming 'down-sized' and turned his attentions to those members of the group that were dwarf. These low-growing foliage plants he planted in patterns and clipped into an even surface. In 1868 *The Gardeners' Chronicle* suggested it be called 'carpet-bedding' when they reported on the H S monogram (Harriet Sutherland) that Fleming had picked out in different coloured *Arabis*, echeverias, sedums and sempervivums. The esteemed periodical enthused that the low-growing plants and clipped foliage formed a surface as smooth and even as a Turkish carpet, and suggested that everyone try it next year.[24]

PLANT BREEDING

The culture and cultivation of plants, and plant breeding were the two major areas in the science of horticulture explored by head gardeners; both came together in the arena of the Horticultural Show.

The first edition of Williams' *The Orchid-Growers Manual* (1852) contained 'a brief description of upwards of Two Hundred and Sixty Orchidaceous Plants'. By the time the sixth edition appeared in 1885, the number had risen to upward of 2,000. Such figures confirm the huge number of new plants that became available to garden-owners during the nineteenth century. Many new introductions from abroad were sold by nurseries, while many new hybrids, especially tender annuals and vegetables, were bred and sold as seed by seedsmen, for example Suttons of Reading and Thompson and Morgan to name just two (established in 1806 and 1855 respectively). However, if the genetics behind the process were not understood, hybridising techniques constantly improved, and many new resulting ornamental and edible hybrids were also created by head gardeners.

No doubt Thomas Foster was tickled pink when he read in *The Florist* in 1853 that Beningbrough Hall (York) had 'attained considerable celebrity under his control'. However, Foster, who remained in his post for nearly forty years, was most famous for raising two of the century's most popular grape varieties –Foster's Seedling and Lady Downe's Seedling (both 1835). The latter, named for his employer, remains in cultivation. Other times new varieties were named for the garden, such as the Ecklinville apple, the Bryanston Gage and the Penrhyn Seedling melon. In the vegetable garden, a retired head gardener, Robert Fenn, made the greatest impact raising a blight-resistant potato. Amongst his many new varieties was International Kidney, now better known as Jersey Royal. Other popular introductions were Douglas' Tender and True Cucumber, the Nuneham Park onion, and Chou de Burghley, raised by Richard Gilbert. All these individuals and their varieties made a valuable contribution to the range of and quality of crops grown in the kitchen garden.

However, one garden stands out as a particularly fertile source of new plants – Frogmore. In January 1838 a Treasury Commission was set up to investigate the expenditure on, and the poor state of, the royal gardens. One of the subsequent recommendations was to centralise the production of edible crops and flowers required by the various royal households at Frogmore and to build a new, larger kitchen garden there. The estimated cost was a staggering £30,000 but it was calculated that this would quickly be offset by the savings made as a result of the Lord Steward no longer being required to buy in fruit and vegetables, a cost that was running at an even more staggering £110,000 per annum. The management of the gardens, and probably their design, were the responsibility of Thomas Ingram (*d.*1872), aided no doubt by the always-interested Prince Albert. Everything about the garden was on a grand scale. Work began in December

The royal walled garden at Frogmore showing the head gardener's house and range of glasshouses either side. The illustration appeared in Charles McIntosh's The Book of the Garden *(1853) when the house was occupied by Thomas Ingram.*

135

As an ex-head gardener Benjamin Williams became successful both as a nurseryman and author, and although this advertisement for his Victoria and Paradise Nursery shows the Camellia House, he was best known for his orchids.

1841 on the original design which was to cover an area of 31 acres (12.56ha) and boast twenty-five forcing houses. However, it was quickly realised that the open ground was too small and it was enlarged, mainly for the production of vegetables, and by 1849 the garden covered 55 acres (22.26ha) and the cost had risen to £45,000. *The Florist* reported in 1854 that the iron trellis against which the pears and apples were trained was upwards of a mile (1.6km) long and that the vast range of fruit houses annually produced between two and three tons of grapes, and 800 dozen of each apricots, peaches and nectarines. But the produce was not just spectacular for its quantity, but also its quality. Of the fruits Ingram exhibited at Shows held by the Royal Horticultural Society, Dr John Lindley of *The Gardeners' Chronicle* was to comment 'These are Royal fruits, and Mr Ingram deserves to be a Royal gardener'.

And if such skills were not enough, Ingram was also a dab hand at breeding plants. In his years of active service a constant stream of new cultivars emerged from the Frogmore Gardens – Frogmore scarlet-fleshed

Novelty was a must for every garden of note, and while some head gardeners did breed new varieties, it was often easier to purchase them from specialist seedsmen, who also supplied the more 'everyday' flowers and vegetables.

melon, Frogmore Prolific apple, Frogmore Bigarreau cherry, Golden Frogmore peach and Late Frogmore pine (a strawberry). And even though this was not an ornamental garden, Ingram also developed ornamentals – several new rose varieties, including 'Miss Ingram', *Begonia* 'Ingrami', and *Pelargonium* 'Frogmore Scarlet' which was widely used in summer bedding displays.[25] Other popular bedding plants raised by head gardeners included the Belvoir wallflowers, the Trentham Rose pelargonium, and the variegated-leaved pelargoniums of which 'Mrs Pollock', bred by Peter Grieve at Culford Hall (Suffolk), remains widely grown.

Certain head gardeners dedicated themselves to a particular genus. Edwin Beckett, head gardener to Vicary Gibbs at Aldenham House (Hertfordshire), was responsible for much early work on improving the Michaelmas daisy, while James Douglas made great headway in developing Malmaison Carnations. Andrew Turnbull of Bothwell Castle, on the other hand, was a particularly successful breeder of heaths (*Erica* spp.) raising a number of new cultivars that received public approbation, including 'Erica Marnockiana, E. Jacksoni, E. Austiniana, E.

Turnbulli [and] E. Bothwelliana alba, &c.'.[26] Others tackled a wide range of subjects.

Particularly floriferous was Anthony Parsons (*b*.1810), whose passion for flowers was aroused from his 'very earliest days' when 'the delight at the purchase of a Pelargonium called Commander-in-Chief . . . determined me in my future career'. Appointed head gardener at Ponder's End in 1833, Parsons exhibited in many different classes, including pineapples, grapes and roses at the Chiswick and the metropolitan shows with great success. But it was his venture into 'the improvement of various florists' flowers' that brought his greatest achievements. An early creation was 'the Dahlia known as Metropolitan Wonder', after which he 'introduced to the floricultural world' great numbers of pansies which were distributed though seedsmen. Parsons also created 'Verbena Enfield Scarlet' and followed this with 'considerable success in raising new varieties of Petunias. Later on I made Hollyhocks my chief study, with very satisfactory results – letting out, through Mr Chater, twelve fine varieties in one season, 1851.' Parsons moved to Danesbury the same year, and here began to experiment with 'Achimenes, in which I have been eminently successful, having obtained among others Mauve Queen, Aurora, Williamsii, and Fire-fly, which are not yet approached by the production of any other raiser'.[27]

But developing a reputation as a breeder of tender annuals was not sufficient for John Wills (1832–95) who occupied two headships including Oulton Park (Cheshire). For when he moved to London in 1867 Willis invented a new profession – that of a floral decorator, or florist. Working first for the Ashburton Park Nursery in Chelsea and later establishing his own business in Onslow Crescent in 1872, Wills' creations were in great demand. Within two years he was undertaking commissions for the royal family, and later in the decade for King Leopold II at Laeken in Belgium. Often on a large scale and featuring foliage plants and palms, one of Wills' specialties was the creation of floral landscapes, often on a geographical theme. One display for the ballroom of the Royal Horticultural Society in the 1870s featured scenery from the Arctic to the tropics; and for the reception at Charing Cross Station to celebrate the return from Berlin of Lord Beaconsfield in May 1878, he transformed the whole platform into a Palm Grove. According to Wills it was not unusual for the cost for a single event in Belgrave Square to be £1,500; and for the Mansion House Ball in 1874 held in honour of the Duke and Duchess of York, he supplied two tons of ivy and 2,000 blooms of Maréchal Niel roses.[28]

PLANT NUTRITION AND SOIL SCIENCE

Be they new varieties or old faithfuls, plants all respond best to proper care, and an area of constant investigation was how to most successfully cultivate plants. Plant nutrition was of particular interest, and while Sir Humphry Davy's *Elements of Agricultural Chemistry* (1813) remained the standard text for the next fifty years, widespread qualitative and quantitative experimentation resulted in a constant stream of revelations explaining the hows and whys of plant nutrition. By 1841 the Highland and Agricultural Society of Scotland was evaluating the application rates of various fertiliser types including farmyard manures, bone and fish compost, sodium nitrate, ammonium sulphate, ammonium chloride, aqua ammonia, guano, urine, gypsum and others. However, the most significant advances in the effects of inorganic fertilisers and organic manures on nutrition and yield were made by Sir John Bennett Lawes, who established the Rothamsted Experiment Station in the grounds of his estate near Harpenden (Hertfordshire) in 1843. His work is continued on the same site to this day by Rothamsted Research. Much of Lawes's wealth came from the commercial exploitation of his patented process for combining sulphuric acid and finely ground phosphate to produce the first man-made fertiliser – superphosphate. In 1842 he built his first factory for the manufacture of a product that became the world's leading phosphate fertiliser for over a century.

Experimentation and research into plant nutrition were topics very close to the heart of a head gardener. It was the consequence of the unpleasant experience 'liquoring' camellias with closet sewerage whilst a foreman at the Royal Exotic Nursery that stimulated David Fish's later interest in plant nutrition. His observations that the camellia foliage was much darker as a result of the 'rich food that had been given them in their liquor' led to his study of 'the sewage question' and to the conclusion, though rather a novel one at that time, that the only possible solution of it was the 'conversion of dead matter into living, and to change poison into food, through the ministry of plants and the cleansing agency of the earth'. Fish's observations of the 'sanitary powers of plants and the ability of the earth to deal with the residuum of lire, labour, combustion, decomposition' had been 'practised, tested, and proved sufficient' for nearly a quarter-of-a-century at the time of his writing in 1875. Among the more recent applications of the abilities of plants to cleanse are the use of reedbeds for the ecological treatment of water, plants tolerant of high levels of pollutants such as heavy

David Taylor Fish, who together with his younger brother Robert, was one of the most influential head gardeners of the era. As well as pursuing his interest in plant nutrition, David also wrote extensively in the horticultural press.

metals or poor soil conditions used to colonise spoil heaps created as a result of mining activities, while the common spider plant (*Chlorophytum comosum*) is a boon to any office for it possesses an ability to remove from the air formaldehyde, a carcinogen often released from new carpets.

Soil science rather than simply nutrition was a topic dear to the heart of William Ingram, who was an accomplished amateur geologist. His favourite study was 'the distribution of soils, their varied character, derivation, and influence on vegetation'. However, Ingram was also interested in meteorology, and for over a quarter-of-a-century 'conducted a series of observations ... which may some day be of use. Local rainfall is a matter that should always be ascertained, especially as the rainfall varies in cultivated districts from 15 to 50 inches [38.10 to 127cm].' [29]

CULTIVATION

As all the periodicals attested to, every single new plant hybrid or introduction was the subject of comment and debate on how best to raise it. Of the ornamentals, great attention was paid to Cockscomb (*Celosia* spp). and in the kitchen garden, the cultivation of the perfect vine must have consumed almost as many column inches as hours spent in the vinery growing the perfect bunch. William Miller experimented with some success using both bottom heat and deep cultivation in vine borders and also published research into vine extension and 'the root fungus question'. However, the 'grape king' was roundly acknowledged to be Archibald Fowler (who also wrote for *The Gardeners' Chronicle*), who experimented with the soil conditions desired by, and root run propensity of, the old and new vines at Castle Kennedy. When a foreman there, George Johnston was so impressed with Fowler's vines that he admitted years later that 'I have a strong impression that I have never seen anything since to surpass them'. The success of Fowler's experiments was measured by the fact he was 'a most successful exhibitor for many years' on several occasions, exhibiting bunches of remarkable size, notable amongst these, a bunch of 'White Nice, weighing 17 lb. 2 oz. [8.23kg]; exhibited in Edinburgh in 1867'.[30]

HORTICULTURAL SHOWS

It was one thing to have a glowing report about your garden published in a periodical, but it was quite another to go head-to-head with your peers and to exhibit. For it was in the arena of the Horticultural Shows where the playing field was level, no quarter given, and the judging impartial that a head gardener was tested to the limit and able to demonstrate his merit. For here, on the exhibition table and on display for all to see, was the evidence of his abilities to raise plants or crops to the very highest standard.

Exhibits and shows became particularly popular in the second half of the century and were held at all levels, from the local village event up through the city and county level, to national and international stages. Thomas Foster regularly won at the York Horticultural Society Shows; in April 1835 he took prizes for cucumbers, kidney beans, potatoes and strawberries – all out-of-season and thus forced under glass. In August he added apricots, black and white grapes, nectarines, peaches and pineapples to his tally; and September three types of *Dahlia* – 'striped', 'dark scarlet' and 'globe' took the honours.

National shows really meant those held in London by both the Royal Horticultural and Royal Botanic Societies. These shows were held throughout the year and, like the Chelsea Flower Show today, were a fixture in the social calendar. There was more than pride at stake – a win would bring some prize money, recognition and maybe even gratitude from one's employer. One of the most successful exhibitors of the age was George Johnston, 'whose name has often been found well up amongst the prize winners at great horticultural gatherings'. Johnston began to exhibit fruit in 1868, and within seven years had won over £300 in prize money 'chiefly for large general collections of fruit, and for Figs, Grapes, Melons and Peaches', while his Pineapples won for him the certificate of the Royal Horticultural Society. Another fruit expert was William Miller, who 'during the years 1867, 1868, 1869, at the Royal Botanic Gardens, Regent's Park . . . carried off successively the gold medals for collection soft fruit'.[31]

That especial Victorian passion – orchids – was always a highlight of any show, and brought success to John Webster (*b*.1814), head gardener between 1838 and 1850 to the Hon. Mrs Huskisson at Eartham (Sussex). Mrs Huskisson was a 'great admirer of Orchids' and thus Webster developed not only a fine collection, but also skill in their cultivation, managing to get 'that shy flowering Orchid, *Renanthera coccinea*, to produce fine large flower-spikes for a number of years in succession'. This plant won Webster several medals, including two Silver Banksian Medals from the Horticultural Society in 1844 and 1846, and he also won a Gold Banksian Medal for six orchids shown at Chiswick in 1847.[32]

To win First Prize was desirous, but to the very successful exhibitor came another accolade – to be invited to judge. At a regional level Mr Fraser, the head gardener at Red Castle (Ross-shire), was 'justly looked upon as one of the best judges and cultivators of fruits, especially Grapes and pot Figs, in that part of the country'. Anthony Parsons, whose achievements and 'uncompromising and unswerving integrity' were recognised by his peers and 'his services are much sought for and appreciated as a censor at the metropolitan exhibitions' was asked to judge. Another was William Ingram, who when his 'pen was not . . . employed for the "Doctor," as we admiringly called Dr. Lindley' writing for *The Gardeners' Chronicle*, he was to be found judging at Chiswick with his old friends Spencer and Frost 'in the palmy days of flower shows, when Mrs. Lawrence and Lady Antrobus were rival exhibitors'.[33]

THE INTERNATIONAL HORTICULTURAL EXHIBITION

One of the greatest shows of the century was the International Horticultural Exhibition and Congress, hosted at the Royal Horticultural Society's gardens in Kensington in late May 1866. The tented enclosure covered some 563 by about 300ft (171.60 by 91.44m) and the interior was divided into 'seven similar and equal parallel aisles, running the whole length of the area' contained exhibits and plants from across the world. Variety and beauty met the eye everywhere; and 'nowhere was there any conspicuous violation of order, taste, or due subordination of parts and colours' and unlike the Chelsea Show these days 'nowhere was there any symptom of crowding amongst the throngs of admirers'.

The setting included grass slopes, covered with 'the choicest and rarest plants' including superb *Nepenthes* from Borneo, and a highlight of the Show was a collection of Japanese lilies. But 'the most conspicuous features were the Orchids'.

There were numerous classes within which head gardeners and their employers could compete – the List of Awards published in *The Gardeners' Chronicle* ran to nearly two pages of tiny print. And although many categories were won by nurserymen – 'Six new plants introduced into Europe' went to Monsieur John Linden of Brussels with *Anthurium regale, Cyanophylum spectandum, Hilodendron lindeni, Maranta lindeni, Bigonia ornata* and *Dichorisandra musaica* – head gardeners more than kept their own. First in 'Stove and Greenhouse Plants' went to Thomas Baines, head gardener to H. Micholls of Bowden near Manchester for a collection of sixteen 'magnificient' plants including *Franciscea confertiflora, Acrophyllum venosum* and *Genetyllis tulipifera*. Other classes for ornamental plants included Hardy Deciduous Shrubs in Flower Roses, Orchids Florists' Flowers, Azaleas, Rhododendrons, Cape Heaths, Ferns, Palms, Cycads and of course, Orchids. In the fruit division, James Barnes of Bicton took first for his Smooth Cayenne Pineapples, Mr Turner won '3 bunches of Muscat of Alexandra' (Mr Fowler second) and also a second for his Peaches (Grosse Mignonne). Pineapples and Grapes caused the most excitement with other classes including Melons, Peaches and Nectarines, Raspberries, Bananas, Figs, Strawberries, Cherries. In the Vegetable Division there were categories for Salading, Cucumber, Potatoes, Asparagus, Cabbages, Broccoli, Rhubarb. One disappointment for the correspondent was the exhibition of garden designs – or lack of it, for as it was noted, no professional would draw up a plan for a 20-acre (8.09ha) garden for a mere £10 prize money.[34]

However, not all shared the general enthusiasm for the ways shows were conducted. Writing some twenty-three years earlier Barnes of Bicton decried the system of exhibiting that focused on the 'production of certain articles' or specimens on the grounds and noted that it very rarely properly rewarded 'either skill or industry' of the gardener. Moreover, Barnes stated 'with confidence' that some of the leading exhibitors of the time did not grow their exhibits but scoured 'the country over in search of them, to the no small satisfaction of the nurserymen from whom they are purchased'. This he asserted put the gardener at a grave disadvantage, and thus discouraged them from exhibiting. This unfairness Barnes considered compounded by the 'respectable men' who were chosen as judges, but were often 'totally incapable of estimating the merit of the articles for want of practical knowledge'. In his view exhibitions had degenerated 'into something like horse-racing'.

Yet Barnes did not reject wholly the awarding of prizes 'for single productions' but argued that regulations should ensure that the exhibit had been grown by the exhibitor. Better still, he considered, would be a shift in emphasis to a competition in which the whole garden was considered by a committee of practical gardeners. This peer group would examine everything from 'the fruits and vegetables which he raises, to see whether they are of good kinds, well grown, healthy, and without insects or diseases . . . the order and beauty of his flower-gardens, pleasure-grounds, walks . . . in short, every thing under his care, from the stoke-holes of the furnaces, and root-cellar, fruit-room, onion-loft, and tool-house, to the botanic stoves and conservatories'. Only then, and if he excelled in 'the greatest number of things, taking his place altogether' would he be worthy of a prize. Barnes was convinced that were such an holistic approach to be adopted, it would provide a greater stimulus to improving gardening standards 'than the present mode of giving premiums for fine specimens, which are generally either produced by gardeners to the neglect of almost every thing else under their charge, or purchased by their employers in the spirit of gambling'. However, Barnes' suggestions fell on deaf ears and either under pressure from his employer, or perhaps being an eminently practical man and deciding to join them if he couldn't beat them, he continued to exhibit – and on the show table, he did beat them.[35]

Far harsher criticism was poured on the people and organisations who ran the shows. At a Council Meeting of the Royal Horticultural Society held on 25 May 1875 the President, Lord Bury, and the Treasurer, had 'indulged in such an unwarrantable attack upon gentlemen who allow their plants to be exhibited at the Society's shows, and the gardeners who show them'. This accusation was made in the strongest terms by Thomas Baines (1823–95), who went on to add that 'nothing less than sheer ignorance of the relative position that the Society holds to horticulture at the present time, or a disposition to wreck the ship they are incapable of steering' could have inspired the pair to speak as they had. Baines, who had been head gardener at Rowdon (Cheshire) for twenty years before moving to Southgate House near London, pointed out that the Society's 'sphere or usefulness in the advancement and promotion of horticulture' had become much narrower than it once had been. Two reasons were cited, plant hunting had been taken over by commercial nurseries, and the cramped area of the Society's Chiswick garden as an experimental grounds was no match for 'every well appointed private establishment' which was 'more or less an experimental garden', and which produced results far more relevant and conclusive for its own immediate locality than 'anything of a similar nature, however well carried out, in a distant place'. As a result Baines claimed, as far as the promotion of practical horticulture was concerned, the Society had 'little scope except through the influence of its exhibitions'. The two Council members had insulted both those gentlemen who permitted their plants to be shown and those head gardeners who did the growing, exactly the two groups 'who virtually make these exhibitions'. Amongst the slurs was a claim that those head gardeners who regularly exhibited – 'rabid prizemen' as the Treasurer called them – did so only to secure prize money; while their employers were deeply offended by Lord Bury's insinuations that many gentlemen only exhibited because of an immodest and conceited desire to win, and that they paid part of their gardeners' wages from the prize money (money which was generally considered to be the sacrosanct right of the gardener).

Baines held that none of these accusations were true, for comparatively few head gardeners could grow plants 'up to the high point of excellence required for exhibition at the present day' and were paid well anyway. And in a counter-offensive he accused the Society of ill-treatment of those winning head gardeners whom the Council had accused of 'pressing' in an 'indecent manner' to get their prize money – money that the tardy Society was withholding (the matter eventually went to the County Court). Baines further accused the Society of another dishonourable act, citing that this same group of creditors contained seven of the nine recipients of the Lindley Medal, the Society's highest award for cultural skill. This had been instigated a decade previously, yet, Baines curtly noted, not one of the men had received their medals. Of the employers Baines was adamant that they were not glory seekers but gentlemen who 'disinterestedly contribute so much towards the support of the principal horticultural societies throughout the country' by allowing the transportation of, and considerable risk to, valuable plants 'so that they may be enjoyed by the public at the exhibitions'.[36]

TECHNOLOGICAL ADVANCES

Head gardeners adapted the advances made in other industries but they also invented some cunning solutions to problems and challenges within their own field. We have seen that tender plant culture became immensely fashionable and that the garden writer Loudon made two notable advances in the design of the greenhouse – the ridge-and-furrow roofing design and the flexible iron glazing bar. Lucas Chance's 1832 pioneering process for the manufacture of cylinder (rather than blown) glass was a development in an unrelated field that had a significant impact on glasshouse design. Not only was the glass cheaper but the panes were also larger, thus allowing improved light transmission into the house. This advance, combined with the repeal of a second, Victorian glass tax in 1838 which resulted in glass prices dropping by 80 per cent, were two major fillips for the glasshouse industry. When it came to heating glasshouses, some head gardeners attempted to design their own coal-fired boilers, but most of the development work was carried out by engineering companies. In the first half of the century the pros-and-cons of hot water versus steam as the medium of heat transportation was much debated by gardeners. Controllable heat was a major advance, and head gardeners spent much time and effort devising heating regimes for various plants and plant groups, often sharing their advice and findings in the pages of the horticultural press. As a result of the feedback given through the pages of the gardening periodicals hot-water systems gained the upper hand.

Many head gardeners designed their own ranges of glass – mention has been made of Fleming at Cliveden and Ingram at Frogmore, but in these instances they laid out the grounds with manufactured glasshouses they bought in. How Paxton advanced glasshouse design we shall explore in the next chapter, but another inventive glasshouse architect was John Halliday. As head gardener at Scone Palace in the 1860s he erected a very successful but somewhat unusual peach and fig house. With a roof frame manufactured entirely from cast iron, its form was an 'elliptical quadrant, 8 feet 4 inches wide and 15 feet 9 inches high [2.51 by 4.80m], furnished with planted-out trees on the back wall, and otherwise furnished with trees in pots'.[37]

The new gardens Archibald Fowler laid out at Glamis Castle for the Earl of Strathmore included 'kitchen and flower gardens, with all the glasshouses and many miles of drives, as well as extensive additions to the lawns and shrubberies'. According to George Johnston who implemented the plans, Fowler designed the 'construction, heating, ventilation, and general plan of the glass-houses' which were 'the most complete and efficient character'. The forcing houses received special praise from *The Gardeners' Chronicle*, which stated that they were 'some of the most perfect and complete we have ever fallen in with'. The magazine also noted that in 1843 Fowler was the inventor of 'the travelling apparatus for delivering the grass from mowing machines' the 'right to patent and use of which he later made over to Shanks of Arbroath'.[38]

At Trentham Fleming had the constant problem of moss and weeds smothering the gravel paths. With his hand-weeding bill running at between £80 and £100 per annum (£8–£12 per acre/0.4ha) and determined to 'extirpate the evil in a wholesale manner', Fleming invented a weeding machine in 1849, which he exhibited at the Great Exhibition two years later. With its tall smoke stack and looking not dissimilar to Stephenson's *Rocket*, the contraption comprised a coal-fired boiler and hot-water tank, front-mounted spray bar, and pulling handle, all mounted on four metal wheels. Into the tank went 30 gallons (136.38 litres) of water and 60lb (27.21kg) of salt, and the liquid was brought to the boil. Then a valve was opened and the machine pulled by one man sprayed the boiling saline on to the weeds and moss. One fill would cover 80 to 85 square yards (66.89 to 71.07sq m), and over the year the machine reduced weeding costs to £1 4s an acre (0.40ha).[39]

However, perhaps the most famous contraption invented by a head gardener was developed by William Barron (1800–91) who was head gardener to the Earls of Harrington at Elvaston Castle (Derbyshire) between 1830

It may look like a sledgehammer to crack a nut, but John Fleming's weeding machine, which sprayed boiling saline onto gravel paths, was efficacious and cost-effective. Using it he was able to slash his hand-weeding bill by up to 90 per cent.

and 1865. Barron, who had served his apprenticeship at Edinburgh Botanic Garden and helped plant the new conservatory at Syon House, was responsible for the design and planting of the garden for the fourth Duke. The Duke, who had shocked society by living openly with his mistress, an actress, had retired with his, by now, wife to Elvaston where the couple lived very reclusively. Although the subject of a lengthy description by Robert Glendinning published as a series of articles in *The Gardeners' Chronicle* in late 1849 and early 1850, the gardens remained almost a secret until the Duke's death in 1851, and when 'discovered' they caused a sensation.

Barron's first job was to drain and trench the site and improve the soil before planting could begin in 1835.

However, it was the four gardens inspired by the Earl's own love life and designed by Barron that caught the Victorian imagination. Drawing on diverse garden historical inspirations from home and abroad, and redolent with themes of chivalry and chastity, they were a shrine to romantic love. The Alhambra Garden featured a summerhouse of oriental style with the garden laid out in the oriental scroll style, the walks paved with octagonal tiles, and making a focal point, a statue of the Earl kneeling before his wife. Immediately under the south front of the house was the *Mont Plaisir* garden, Barron's interpretation of a seventeenth-century French garden by the designer Daniel Morot. Inside the enclosing yew hedge wound covered walks, with 'windows' cut into the walls. Garden of Fairstar had a Moorish style ironwork bower and the Fountain Garden featured a shell grotto set within a rockery, featuring a golden statue of Queen Eleanor. A fifth garden, the Garden of Three Sisters, was laid out by the Earl's three sisters in an old-fashioned style of geometric beds and filled with scented plants including honeysuckle and roses.

The gardens as a whole were renowned for their trees, and the pinetum was particularly impressive, boasting nearly every conifer that would survive the climate. In 1852 Barron published *The British Winter Garden* which focused on conifers as providers of winter colour and the practicalities of transplanting trees. It was to accomplish the latter that Barron invented and became famous for a method of and machinery for successfully lifting, transporting and transplanting trees of all sizes, and especially very large ones.[40]

Working on the principle that the most successful way to transplant any plant is to keep as large a mass of undisturbed soil around its roots as possible, Barron simply applied it to bigger plants. To move the vast root ball that accompanied a mature tree, Barron invented a lifting mechanism and a vehicle which could accommodate and support the size and weight of a mature tree. Using this method Barron moved over 10,000 large trees, some from further than 30 miles (48.23km) distant, and in 1842 began successfully moving trees in all seasons and without prior preparation, although he preferred not to move when in leaf. Glendinning described the procedure for moving a tree once its root ball had been excavated:

A platform of planks was formed under the tree to be removed, the whole resting on two central poles; this done, the carriage (which was constructed with six wheels and two strongly trussed beams, the ends of which rest in the bolster of each axle, and so arranged as to be easily taken to pieces (the axles being 19 feet [5.79m] apart), was placed one beam on each side of the tree. The entire mass was then raised, by means of a principal screw, and suspended in strong chains under the beams. Thus placed, except in high winds or very rough roads, the load will ride without a gye [*sic*] rope. All the trees at Elvaston have been carried upright, the same as they grew; and in this way a Lombardy Poplar, above 70 feet [21.33m] high, weighing with the ball more than 12 tons, was carried a great distance. For the moving of smaller trees, a three-wheeled machine with a roller at each end,

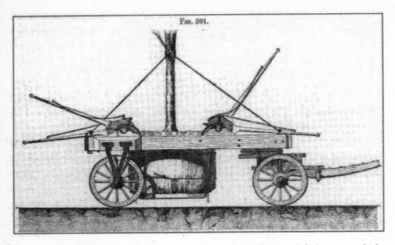

William Barron's patented tree transporter was basically a modified wagon which enabled him to lift and securely move mature trees that were then transplanted into the · garden at Elvaston Castle, thus creating an 'instant landscape'.

and having a lever for raising and lowering the plants (which can be done in five minutes when ready), is found useful.[41]

Sadly, the fifth Duke suffered from the extravagances of his predecessor and the gardens were hard hit by financial restraints. Eventually Barron decided to leave Elvaston and established a business as nurseryman and landscape designer. Abbey Park in Leicester was his most significant commission, but his greatest coup came in 1880 when he successfully moved, amid much controversy, the 1,000-year-old yew in Buckfast Abbey churchyard to a new home where it would not damage the church.

Having explored how a head gardener rose to his position and some of the contributions made to the nineteenth-century garden by head gardeners in general, let us look more closely at the life and works of two in particular. Sir Joseph Paxton, the century's most famous head gardener, who set new standards in garden design; and James Barnes, one of the century's finest horticultural practitioners.

CHAPTER 7

◆◀◆▶◆

Paxton of Chatsworth

For each profession every era throws up a superstar. For the category 'head gardener of the nineteenth century' this man, without a shadow of doubt, was Sir Joseph Paxton (1803–65). He was a skilled horticulturist, had a keen artistic eye and significant engineering skills. Enterprising, affable and kind, Paxton was a workaholic who was loyal and down-to-earth, but who regularly demonstrated an independence of spirit. As his obituary in *The Times* on 9 June 1865 put it, Paxton 'rose from the ranks to be the greatest gardener of his time, the founder of a new style of architecture, and a man of genius, who devoted it to objects in the highest and noblest sense popular'. His work transforming Chatsworth into the century's most famous and influential garden alone would have been sufficient to earn him this crown. However, Paxton also gained international fame as the designer of the Crystal Palace, the great glass structure four times the size of St Peter's Basilica in Rome that housed the Great Exhibition of 1851. The inspiration for this iconic structure came from a plant he grew and experiments into glasshouse design that he conducted at Chatsworth.

Joseph Paxton made two significant contributions to the development of the Victorian garden. In the realm of garden design he irrefutably proved with his ornamental gardens at Chatsworth that art and nature could co-exist happily side-by-side, the one complementing the other. Paxton's achievements were lauded in the horticultural press (although more widely after his death); but perhaps more importantly for the dissemination of his triumphs to a wider audience, the gardens were open to an eager public, which flocked in, went home, and aped Paxton's theories, styles and creations.

This wider public also avidly purchased Paxton's other great contribution. The Great Exhibition stimulated a great interest in glass structures – thousands who visited his Crystal Palace went home wanting their own miniature version. Thus Paxton kick-started a fashion for conservatory and/ or glasshouse ownership; and he was happy to oblige the eager purchasers. In

June 1859 Paxton launched his 'Hothouses for the Million', a catchy marketing phrase for the mass-produced range of the flat-pack conservatories and glasshouses. Advertised widely in the horticultural press, this lucrative business was efficiently run by Paxton's secretary Samuel Hereman from his London office near Pall Mall East.

Joseph Paxton was born in Milton Bryant near Woburn (Bedfordshire) in 1803, the eighth of nine children of William, a farm labourer, and Ann. His early life seems to have been a generally unhappy one: his father died when Joseph was seven, and the experience of living in the household of an elder brother was so unpleasant that Joseph ran away. However, at the age of thirteen, he went to work for his eldest brother William, who was superintendent and bailiff to Sir Gregory Page Turner at Battlesdon Park (Bedfordshire). In December 1816 William took out the second of two leases of land on the estate. Covering 2½ acres (1.01ha), the plot encompassed most of the productive gardens – kitchen garden, fruit garden, orchard and nursery (not included were the hothouses and plants); and here Joseph undertook his apprenticeship. After a couple of years Joseph moved to Woodhall near Walton (Hertfordshire), where he worked for about three years under the well-respected William Griffin, head gardener to Samuel Smith. Griffin was also an early subscriber to the (Royal) Horticultural Society Gardens in Chiswick and may have been a great inspiration to Paxton. For, after a further stint of a couple of years back at Battlesdon, on 13 November 1823, Joseph joined the Horticultural Society's garden as a labourer.

After only a year at Chiswick, Paxton was promoted to foreman in charge of the arboretum, and his weekly wage rose from 14 to 18 shillings. However, on 22 April 1826 he abruptly resigned his position. The twenty-three-year-old Paxton had met the thirty-six-year-old William George Spencer Cavendish, sixth Duke of Devonshire (1790–1858) in the Chiswick garden (which was on land rented from the Duke's estate). It was an encounter that changed the lives of both men. The Duke, impressed by Paxton's self-confidence, horticultural knowledge, passion, patience and good manners – apparently Paxton had made the effort to speak loudly enough so that the Duke, who was slightly deaf, could hear – acted on an impulse. He offered Paxton the position of head gardener at Chatsworth on a salary of £65 and with a cottage. On 8 May 1826 Paxton (rapidly promoted through the ranks of the Horticultural Society from mere garden foreman to Fellow) travelled north to his new job. His

Glass structures were the fashion in the second half of the nineteenth century. Joseph Paxton, who began the fashion, provided a whole range of flat-pack greenhouses, while other manufacturers provided more ornate alternatives. This 1,260 sq ft (117m²) model cost £700.

account of his arrival sums up his excitement, remarkable energy and confidence:

> I left London by the Comet Coach for Chesterfield; arrived at Chatsworth at 4.30 a.m. in the morning of the ninth of May 1826. As no person was to be seen at that early hour, I got over the greenhouse gate by the old covered way, explored the pleasure grounds and looked round the outside of the house. I then went down to the kitchen gardens, scaled the outside wall and saw the whole of the place, set the men to work there at six o'clock; then returned to Chatsworth and got Thomas Weldon to play me the water works and afterwards went to breakfast with poor dear Mrs Gregory and her niece. The latter fell in love with me and I with her, and thus completed my first morning's work at Chatsworth before nine o'clock.

Nine months after they met, Joseph married the twenty-six-year-old Sarah Bown (1800–71) on 20 February 1827, and no doubt the dowry of £5,000 provided by her mill-owner father came as a pleasant surprise. Sarah, who had a strong personality, proved to be the perfect wife for Joseph. Supportive of him in all his works and frequent absences, she not only offered him succour and wise council, but she also proved herself to be a sensible, intelligent and adept manager, overseeing the financial management of the gardens when Joseph was away.

ORNAMENTAL GROUNDS

The day after Paxton headed north from London, the Duke left for Russia and the coronation of Tsar Nicholas I, who became a firm friend, and remained away from Chatsworth for the next six months. Upon his return, he discovered that Paxton had been busy putting the gardens into order. And there was much work to do. The previous Duke and his wilful wife, Georgiana, had preferred life at court to that in the country, so that by the mid-1820s the gardens were both wholly out of fashion and quite run down. But the Duke, who, up until this point had shown only a modicum of interest in gardening – following his inheritance in 1811, he had added a new parterre in front of the stone-built greenhouse and initiated a forestation programme which saw over two million new trees planted – was now swept along on a Paxtonian wave of enthusiasm, and quickly developed a passion for gardening. Over the coming three decades the two men together created the century's greatest garden.

It took a generation of hard work to fully develop the style that was uniquely Paxton's, and the early phases of his work can be summed up in one word – consolidation. In 1832 he restored the stone-built greenhouse of 1697, converting it in the process into a hothouse; and in front, and to form an appropriate setting, he designed a new parterre. The process of extending and re-aligning the Cascade perpendicular to the house began in 1833 and took a decade to complete. Paxton also planted Monkey puzzles, cedars and laurels in large number, and on the long terrace placed clipped Portuguese laurel in tubs to imitate citrus. With Jeffrey Wyatt (later Wyattville, 1766–1840), the Duke's architect who added a new north wing to the house, Paxton discussed and modified the design for the new orangery.

In 1831, Loudon visited Chatsworth for the first time and his published report was critical of the ornamental gardens. Not specifically Paxton's contributions, but what Loudon saw as the peculiar combination of remnants of earlier incarnations of the gardens, in particular the seventeenth-century formal and eighteenth-century informal. In fact, the canvas that Paxton inherited contained the remnants of three previous gardens. The South Lawn was a relic of a sixteenth-century formal garden, while the Western Terrace and Cascade were remains of the substantive formal garden laid out in the late 1690s. Beyond was the informal eighteenth-century landscape by Brown. Loudon's 'hint' to Paxton was for a massive reorganisation to separate the two elements, and making use of the existing terraces, it would have been straightforward for Paxton to have simply slotted in an Italianate garden. Indeed, the Western Terrace was laid out by Wyatt with a formal parterre. But importantly, this aspect of the garden, while impressive when looked down on from within the house, is not especially visible from within the wider garden.

Paxton was stung by Loudon's criticism and published a rebuke in his own magazine *The Horticultural Register* ridiculing Loudon's suggestions, and on the ground, did the opposite. Working sympathetically with remnants of earlier incarnations into which he inserted the new, Paxton set about creating a garden in which he deliberately arrayed the natural and the unnatural, the formal and informal in a series of striking juxtapositions. Yet although startling and surprising, his arrangements were not jarring, for with great skill (and aided by the indigenous topography)

Paxton managed to square the circle and to harmonise and unite art and nature, and in so doing developed a style which brought him most renown as a designer and influencer of fashions. This harmony was recognised in 1857 by 'J.H.C.', who used the example of the flow of water through the garden to demonstrate this balanced blend:

> Here Nature and Art revel in luxuriance, and, blended together by a nice combination of both, produce a grand and imposing effect. From the summit of a richly-wooded hill, some hundreds of feet in height, and nearly a quarter of a mile distant, commences this succession of sparkling falls, and terminates immediately at the feet of the visitor. Falling first over natural rocks and projections for a considerable distance, the water is then conducted by an artificial aqueduct of several arches of great height to form a fine fall, and it again appears at a distance below in all directions, both internal and external, from a curious temple…[and] forming in front of it two jets of spray…the water…descends, for about 300 yards, a succession of steps in a perfect river…No lover of the beautiful in Nature or Art can leave these falls without a lively impression of their picturesque beauty and happy effect. [1]

PINETUM

In 1829, the Duke, by now and by his own admission 'bit by gardening', promoted Paxton to 'Gardener and Woodsman' and raised his salary to £226, which included an allowance for finding and keeping a horse. However, this was pocket change compared with the £2,000 that the Duke spent on the gardens that same year. Much of the money was spent on their first major new project – the transformation of 8 acres (3.24ha) of the southern park into a pinetum (a scientific collection of conifers). In all, Paxton managed to procure over fifty taxa of conifer – quite some achievement given that China and Japan remained closed to Western plant hunters, and David Douglas, the first plant hunter to explore the Pacific North West of America had returned from his first adventure just two years earlier. Indeed, it was seedlings of Douglas' most famous discovery and the one that bears his name – the Douglas Fir (*Pseudotsuga menziesii*) that Paxton personally transported from London, nurturing them in his hat.

The pinetum was an especially early example and it created a fashion amongst the gardening glitterati – notable examples were made at Bicton (see page 200), Biddulph Grange, Bowood and Elvaston Castle – not only because it was art and nature combined, but also because a pinetum was a garden feature that could be filled with expensive novelty. The influx of new conifers begun by Douglas continued through the century as the Himalayas (*Cedrus deodara*, 1831), North Africa (*Cedrus atlantica, c.*1840) and the Americas (the reintroduction of *Araucaria araucana*, 1843, from the south and *Sequoiadendron giganteum*, 1853, from the north) yielded up treasures. Then, a treasure trove of new conifers arrived when the plant hunters managed to secure access into China (*Cupressus funebris*, 1849) and later, Japan (*Pinus thunbergii*, 1852). And, of course, conifers were not restricted to a pinetum, they were also eagerly added to existing arboreta and used to ornament native woodlands and, especially in their juvenile form, formal gardens.

It was the shared experience of planning and making the pinetum which marked the strengthening of the friendship between the Duke and Paxton. Together they greatly enjoyed developing the garden, and out of their professional relationship developed a deep and mutual friendship built on trust, respect, shared aims and an enjoyment of each other's company that was to last until the Duke's death. In 1833 the Duke took Paxton on the first of their three garden tours they made together. On this occasion the destinations were some of Britain's finest gardens, but the following April Paxton received a summons from the Duke, who was then in Florence, to meet him in Paris and together they visited a number of gardens including Versailles and St Cloud. On their last trip together, a seven-month Grand Tour that began in late 1838, the same year that the Duke was elected President of the Horticultural Society, he and Paxton visited Switzerland, Italy and Turkey. For a man of the Duke's standing to travel in the same coach with his head gardener and to treat him as a trusted companion rather than an employee was an early and bold statement of how their close friendship crossed both social boundaries and the employer-employee arrangement. With time, Paxton also became the Duke's confidential advisor, and it was he, who in 1844 devised a means of negating his friend's debt of nearly £1 million by arranging the sale of two of his Yorkshire estates to the railway entrepreneur George Hudson.

ARBORETUM

The Duke and Paxton entertained noted botanists at Chatsworth, and corresponded with other renowned worshippers of Flora. No doubt it was the constant revelation of just how diverse and interesting the realm of botany was, combined with the Duke's competitive spirit and bottomless resources, that egged both men on to create an arboretum on a far grander scale that the pinetum. Eighty acres (32.39ha) of woodland and park either side of the existing walk that formed a circuit of the pleasure grounds was allocated. In January 1835 work began – the timber harvested while clearing the site more than paying for the arboretum – and the project was complete within a remarkable six months. Paxton wrote to Loudon of the new arboretum in June, providing a plan of the layout and arrangement of the trees. This was the largest collection of trees in Europe, some 1,670 taxa of 75 orders, planted not by geographical origin but according to the Natural System devised by the French botanist Antoine Laurent de Jussieu (1748–1836) – much of whose system remains in use today.[2]

Both the pinetum and the arboretum were early examples of how Paxton managed to so successfully integrate art and nature. By their nature, collections were scientific and educational, the positioning of the trees within the groupings was artistic, and the two features slotted perfectly into the naturally wooded site at a suitable distance to the south and east of the house.

THE GREAT STOVE

While the arboretum project had been executed in a mere six months, the next of their great schemes in the ornamental garden took six years to plan and complete. This was Paxton's greatest achievement at Chatsworth, and sadly, the one element that no longer exists.

In its day, the Great Stove, erected between 1836 and 1841 at a cost of £36,000 was the world's largest glasshouse. The 'footprint' of the building was ¾-acre (0.30ha) and was covered with 52,287 square feet (4,857.46sq m) of glass. The individual panes were 3 feet 9 inches (114.30cm) in length and 6 inches (15.24cm) wide, and the glazing was carried out by Mr Drake of Edgware Road in London, at a bargain price of 16 pence per square foot. The panes were secured to the frame with

24,560 moulded sash bars, equivalent to about 40 miles (64.37km) in length and were fabricated by a steam-powered cutting machine invented by Paxton and for which the Society of Arts awarded him their silver medal in 1840. The million or so cubic feet (28,317cu m) of enclosed interior was heated by 7 miles (11.27km) of 4-inch (10.16cm) pipe carrying hot water from eight boilers. The heating system was so ingenious that within the glasshouse a temperature gradient was maintained, one end enjoying sub-tropical heat the other a cooler, temperate warmth. To maintain the attractiveness of the building within its setting, the boilers were housed in the basement and the chimneys were carried in a tunnel up the side of the hill to the distance of nearly a furlong (201.17m) – a technique that also prevented the smuts falling back onto the glass. The coal, of which the boilers consumed a tonne a day, was transported to the subterranean boilers by an underground tramway.

The world record for the structure was held by Paxton and the Duke until the title passed to the Palm House at Kew, which was built between 1844 and 1848 by Richard Turner to a design by Decimus Burton. In fact, at the outset of the Great Stove project, the Duke, a little apprehensive at the magnitude of what was proposed, had called on Burton to keep a watching brief. However, the concept and its actualisation, was Paxton's alone. After a year or so of careful thought, planning, seeking of advice and experimentation, Blanche, Countess of Burlington laid the foundation stone on 29 September 1836. The completed, and by this point weather-tested Great Stove, made it to the second page of the first issue of *The Gardeners' Chronicle*, which appeared on 2 January 1841. Of 'striking novelty and beauty of appearance' Paxton's 'entirely new mode of Glazing' was deemed 'a great superiority to every other method', indeed it was 'the most perfect system of Horticultural Glazing that has yet been devised'.

The design, which retained heat and transmitted light better than anything before it, and was also structurally sound, having passed with flying colours all the 'various trials to which every alteration of season and temperature can subject it', was a hybrid. Paxton had adapted Loudon's ridge-and-furrow concept to a curvilinear structure with a double curve, and used both metal and wood for the frame. To the top of the first curve the frame was cast iron, which supported the wooden ribs above that held the ridge-and-furrow glazing of the second curve.[3] But more than simply a triumph of glasshouse architecture, Paxton was supremely successful in positioning such a large and artistic structure – for the Great Stove was a very attractive work of art in its own right – within the landscape. The effect of his artistic/natural contrast and balance became even more theatrical in subsequent years with the construction of the immense rockworks (see page 166).

To fill the vast interior space, Paxton was given free rein to spend lavishly. He and the Duke were also the fortunate recipients of generous largesse from many well-wishers and keen horticulturists. Baron Hugel who, according to Loudon, had gathered together one of Europe's finest plant collections at his residence of Hietzing near Vienna, sent the Duke many of his prize specimens. From closer to home came a collection from Wimbledon House, and from Walton-on-Thames, the residence of Lady Tankerville, a collection of large palms. Their safe removal and transportation Paxton oversaw himself, and an earlier experience of transporting and transplanting overly large specimens no doubt bolstered his confidence. A decade earlier Paxton had lifted and transported an 8-tonne weeping ash with a canopy diameter of 28ft (8.53m) and root run of 37ft (11.28m) the 28 miles (45.06km) from Derby to Chatsworth. Here it was installed as the centrepiece of the new north forecourt and thrived. Now he had to move a number of palms, the largest of which weighed 12 tonnes and required a special wagon drawn by eleven horses and the removal of turnpike gates along the route to Chatsworth; and in order to remove the entire contingent of palms, the conservatory at Walton had to be demolished. Robert Bowie (*b*.1817), later head gardener at Chillingham to the Earl of Chillingham, recalled the event which occurred while he was a journeyman at Walton-on-Thames.

In the summer of 1840 I assisted at the taking up and packing of them, which at that time was considered rather a hazardous undertaking. Many gardeners came from a considerable distance to see the operations when we were busy with them. Mr Paxton was most particular in having every root saved, in order that their removal might be successful. We were a long time over the job; they were, however, well worth taking every pains with, for they were really splendid plants, and afterwards did well. Some time after they had been got safely to their destination, Mr Paxton returned to Walton to settle accounts. After giving us young men (there were three of us) very handsome presents in money, he also presented each of us with a copy of his *Botanical Dictionary*, which at that time I valued highly, and often afterwards consulted when uncertain as to the correct spelling of names.[4]

The ground plan within the Great Stove was described by *The Gardeners' Chronicle* as 'very simple' with a 'central nave and two side aisles' and a gallery running round the building between 'the main structure and the lantern' with the broad walk running the length of the building from end to end between the pair of end doors. In the centre, a smaller path, called 'the *Musa* Avenue', crossed the broad walk at right angles. Almost all the plants were planted out in beds, thus 'unsightly tubs and contrivances for raising this or lowering that specimen' were 'dispensed with'. Care was taken to ensure that the soils within the beds were specially mixed to suit the requirements of the plants; and the roots of the larger and vigorous specimens were contained so that their less energetic neighbours were not out-competed.

The plant collection was arranged not along botanical lines as in the arboretum, but by geographical origin. The sense of the exotic was further heightened by the tropical birds flying hither and thither, and the glittering mineralogical specimens. To get a full sense of the wonder and size of the Great Stove, the visitor ascended to a wrought-iron gallery and platform, reached by a staircase in one corner, which Paxton subsequently hid with rockwork, and which in 1875 was 'laved at the base by a serpentine streamlet of water'. Once fully planted, the building and its contents were roundly celebrated and marvelled at. The King of Saxony called it 'a tropical scene with a glass sky'. A highlight of the visit by Queen Victoria in 1843 was an after-dark drive in an open carriage through the structure, specially illuminated for the occasion with 12,000 oil lamps placed along the ribs. Two years later when Charles Darwin visited this miniature floral world, he wrote that he was 'transported with delight . . . the water part is more wonderfully like tropical nature than I could have conceived possible. Art beats nature altogether there.'[5]

With the passing of years the collection matured and the effect of a tropical paradise became even more spectacular. A decade after its completion, Mrs S.C. Hall gave a potted and excited summary, breathlessly exclaiming that the Great Stove was

filled with the rarest Exotics from all parts of the globe from farthest Ind', from China, from the Himalayas, from Mexico; here you see the rich banana, Eschol's grape, hanging in ripe profusion beneath the shadow of immense paper-like leaves; the feathery cocoa-palm, with its head peering almost to the lofty arched roof; the farfamed silk cotton-tree, supplying a sheet of cream-coloured blossoms, at a season when all outward vegetable gaiety is on the wane; the singular milk-tree of the Caraccas; the fragrant cinnamon and cassia – with thousands of other rare and little known species of both flowers and fruits.[6]

A more thorough description of the contents was not given in the horticultural press while Paxton was in charge. But in 1875, when the garden was under Thomas Speed, *The Gardeners' Chronicle* offered this tour:

if we suppose the visitor entering by the door nearest to the mansion, and passing first round the aisles and then up the centre, we shall be enabled to indicate, in something like order, some of the more prominent objects of interest. First of all, after feasting on the grand vista of the central avenue, the hanging baskets before alluded to will attract attention, not only from their dimensions, but from their beauty, richness and variety of furnishing. A Dicksonia, one of the first imported, is one of the first plants that demands notice. Near it is a group of giant Agaves, looking grander and finer here, in all probability, than in their native country, where no fostering care prevents them from injury and disfigurement. The side 4 stages at the time of our last visit were largely occupied with Epiphyllums...From this side walk a view is obtained of a remarkable plant of *Renanthera coccinea*, one of the features of Chatsworth. It is attached to a birch stump, and is now as high as the top of the column near which it is placed; it has bloomed for six years in succession, the remains of the old inflorescences being left on the plant to satisfy the doubts of the incredulous: Crinums, including the deliciously scented *C. Elphinstoni*, occupy the foreground, while in the background Beaucarneas, Dracænas and arborescent Yuccas rear aloft their long leafy tresses. A glorious mass of Bamboo, with leaves of richest green, the secret of which was rendered patent to nose and eye at the time of our visit, in the shape of copious applications of rich manure, forms an arch over one end of the central avenue, passing by which we come to masses of Sugar-cane, to a Cinnamon bush, with its tender unfolding leaves of a lovely pink colour. Near here is a fine specimen of the Looking-glass tree, *Heritiera macrophylla*; and then crossing the end of the *Musa* transept we come to a clear pool bordered with Colocasias and

Papyrus, Richardias and Pontederias, and other aquatic plants, and backed up by a giant rocky mass all overgrown with countless Begonias and seedling Ferns, Dicksonias and Adiantums chiefly, and between whose crevices noble specimens of Monstera, with their grand foliage, entwine themselves, and, as it were, bind the stones together. Near here is placed a rugged branch of many arms, thickset with Elk's-horn Fern – a striking picture in itself. Having now completed the circuit of the house, we may pass up the central avenue, noticing on the left fine specimens of Palms; including *Phoenix dactylfera, Sabal, Corypha australis*, about 50 feet [15.24 m] in height; *Chamrerops Griffithii, Arenga saccharifera*, and *Ceroxylon andicola. Dracæna Draco* and *Araucaria brasiliensis* are also represented by large specimens.

On the opposite side is one of the finest plants of *Latania borbonica* in the kingdom, and near it are good examples of *Sabal Blackburniana, Corypha umbraculifera, Borassus flabelliformis*, and *Seaforthia elegans*; the last-named was bearing its beautiful clusters of lilac flowers at the time of our visit... *Hedychium Gardnerianum*...we observed... be also fruiting in the conservatory here, where it has not previously been known to fruit. Access to the gallery is obtained by a stone staircase in the rockery, and from it may be obtained a splendid bird's-eye view of the house and its contents. The symmetrical forms of the *Ceroxylon* and other Palms may, from this vantage ground, be seen to great perfection, and as each plant has room to develope [*sic*] itself, the magnificence of the prospect may readily be imagined.[7]

ROCKWORK

In his *Handbook* to the garden, the Duke enthused that 'in the autumn of 1842 there was not a single stone in these parts, you will now find a labyrinth of rocky walks. You would be surprised to see the structure of which the foundations were then laid. I charge you to take notice of several features of this new work; of the old copper willow tree re-appearing after a long eclipse, the Queen's Rock, Prince Albert's and the Duke of Wellington's last removed and grandest of all. The spirit of some Druid seems to animate Mr Paxton in these bulky removals.'

What, in 1875 *The Gardeners' Chronicle* was to call 'the most extensive and most ambitious rock-garden made by the hands of man that is known to us', Paxton began in 1843 and took four years to complete. The construction of the massive rockworks also required he invent machinery with which to manoeuvre and accurately position the enormous boulders. Later, Paxton was generous in lending this machinery. William Adam recounted in his *The Gem of the Peak* (5th edn, 1845), that the 'necessary apparatus' used to move 'a block of stone weighing 50 tons', a part of Rowtor Rocks, a rockwork feature in the nearby village of Birchover, was 'obtained from Chatsworth'.[8]

Rockeries had been a fashionable garden feature since the days of Repton who, for example, created a rugged rock feature at Welbeck Abbey (Nottinghamshire) in 1789. Loudon, writing in 1834, was of the opinion that the cultivation of alpines was the proper purpose of a rockery, while the grouping of rocks in order to create an ornamental feature fell into three categories. First there was Repton's 'imitate nature', second there was the 'contrast' and third, the 'scale model'. The 'contrast' was just that – a very natural rock feature juxtaposed with a very unnatural feature such as a bedding display or hothouse. An early example of the scale model was to be found at Hoole House (Cheshire), the home of Lady Broughton, where in the 1820s at the end of her lawn she placed her mini-Savoie and the valley of Chamonix, which rose four times the height of a man and used quartz and spar to imitate ice and glaciers.

However, always one to innovate, Paxton developed his own approach which was in essence a hybrid between the contrast category and the scale model. Convinced that large rockworks should be part theatre – the visitor should encounter them unexpectedly – and should be given an appropriate setting away from the formality of the flower garden, Paxton took advantage of the natural hillside and the result was stupendous. Immense, dramatic and improbable, the rockwork – covering over 6 acres (2.43ha) – conjured up by Paxton was influenced by his travels through the Alps and the striking local scenery. He made use of brownish gritstone from the abandoned quarry workings at nearby Dob Edge, and his method of cantilevering boulders increased their visual impact most dramatically.

One of the first constructions was the Strid or 'Bolton stride', a large-scale imitation of a feature near the Duke's estate at Bolton Abbey (Yorkshire), where a stream in a chasm was crossed by stepping stones. Paxton, assimilated the unnatural amidst the natural – a 60ft (18.29m) hollow laid out as a straight walk with a formal staircase at either end. Excavating, moving, adjusting and cementing the vast boulders continued apace, pools were lined and water courses were laid. The result was part nature, part art, a tortuous and massive assemblage of deep ravines, tall cliffs and craggy outcrops, pierced by walks, arches and 'viewing windows' and ascended by flights of steps with balustrades of Irish yew.

One of the last features to be made was the dramatic Wellington Rock, which is linked to the equally theatrical Strid by the water running through. The waterfall pouring over the Wellington Rock into the pool at its base flows into a stream and over another waterfall into the Strid. The water is gravity fed from the hilltop reservoirs (as are all the waterworks) and the upper part of its descent was a 150ft (45.72m) fall from the faux-ruined aqueduct. Work on this started in the summer of 1839 and was inspired by the one the Duke had seen during his visit to Wilhelmshohe garden in Cassel, Germany.

Another device Paxton used to unite the various elements and to blend his massive man-made feature into the natural environment was to plant the nooks and crannies between the rocks. Paxton's planting approach was that 'all the vegetation which accompanies an extensive rockery should be subordinate to it, and be merely sufficient and so disposed as to give relief and diversity to it'. Thus much of the rockwork was planted with drifts of plants, of amongst others, *Berberis darwinii*, rhododendrons, *Cotoneaster*, wild currants and bilberries – and the effect has been called an early example of ground-cover planting. Where the rocks met the water, nature met art as Paxton planted tender plants such as *Amaryllis*, *Lobelia*, *Pelargonium* and *Zinnia*. Yet it was an approach that drew some criticism. *The Gardeners' Chronicle* suggested that the 'alpine and rock plants' were not 'in such numbers or diversity as might be looked for; truly there is room for representatives of the whole flora of Switzerland or the Pyrenees'.

But minor gripes aside, it was roundly agreed that Paxton more than exceeded his own expectations – Mrs Hall for one was enraptured by the result. Paxton probably would not have welcomed her assertion that his construction appeared like 'mimic Alpine scenery', but she was absolutely correct in her analysis that Paxton had achieved a believable illusion of the pseudo-natural because 'Art has been most triumphant; the rocks which have all been brought hither are so skilfully combined, so richly clad in mosses, so luxuriantly covered with heather, so judiciously based with ferns and water-plants, that you move among, or beside, them, in rare delight at the sudden change which transports you from trim parterres to the utmost wildness of natural beauty.'

Almost twenty-five years later the effect of passing this way was even more dramatic and theatrical for not only had the rockwork and its plants had time to mature, but the Great Stove had also been erected, so that the visitor now passed 'abruptly from smooth dressed garden to this picturesquely undulating spot, with its rocking stones, nicely poised stone doors, and other surprises, not forgetting the "water tree" so fascinating to the Sheffielders; and again, still more surprising, you pass under a rocky arch, and find yourself suddenly face to face with the great conservatory – a grand structure, so cleverly hidden that you would scarce suspect its existence were it not for an occasional glint between the trees'. The original Willow Tree Fountain had been made in 1693 and had fallen into disrepair, so Paxton had a new one fashioned from 8,000 pieces of copper and brass producing 800 jets and hid this artificial feature away amongst his naturalistic rockwork – yet another successful juxtaposition.[9]

The great rockwork, together with those rockeries created at Pencarrow (Cornwall, from 1834) and Elvaston Castle near Derby (from 1838) set fashions for natural-looking rockery for the second half of the century, although with time there developed a greater emphasis on direct imitation of the laws of geology, particularly in terms of the alignment of the strata and the arrangement of the different-sized rocks.

One of the reasons why Chatsworth became such an influential and inspirational garden for the general public was that the Duke opened his gates to the hoi polloi who came to see for themselves. Numbers of visitors rose significantly as a result of the laying of the railway line from Ambergate (which owed much to Paxton's persistent and persuasive lobbying) and the new railway station at Rowsley which became operational in June 1849 and was a mere 3 miles (4.8km) from Chatsworth. And when Thomas Cook added Chatsworth to his tour company's itinerary, it became England's most visited country house. Of the many marvels that day-trippers gazed at and were amazed by, the Rockwork and the Great Stove were the highlights. Many took the ideas home, intent on re-creating their own mini-realm where art and nature co-existed. Sadly, though, and in a similar way to Loudon's Gardenesque, Paxton's unification of art and nature was mauled and misrepresented by those neither blessed with Paxton's resources of site and funds, nor his talent. Thus arose many imitations of Chatsworth in which exactly the opposite was the result – art and nature were juxtaposed with eye-watering disharmony and the theatrical became as to street mime.

EMPEROR FOUNTAIN – 1844

Great theatrical waterworks had always been a feature of the gardens, and Paxton stuck to the score. When Princess Victoria and her mother, the Duchess of Kent, visited in October 1832, Paxton designed and presented his first *coup de théâtre*. After dinner, all the waterworks in the park were illuminated with coloured Bengal lights. The thirteen-year-old princess was enchanted and even the Duke had never seen anything like it, as the fountains glowed red, then blue, the Cascade appeared like a river of fire, and finally, rockets shot up in all directions. When Victoria made her return visit as Queen, she and husband Albert were treated to even more spectacular illuminations. At nine o'clock, the Cascade was lit with white, blue and then red Bengal lights, while lamps illuminated the other water-works and 3,000 Russian lamps hung in the trees. An hour later the sky was illuminated with a spectacular fireworks show.[10]

A year later, in 1844, just as Paxton's Great Stove was about to lose its title as the world's largest glasshouse, Paxton earned himself his second world record, engineering the world's tallest gravity-fed fountain. The Duke had been impressed by both the 190ft (57.91m) and 120ft (36.58m) jets he had seen respectively at Wilhelmshohe in Cassel and Peterhof in Russia. So, when he heard that his friend Tsar Nicholas was to visit Britain (and, he expected, Chatsworth) he asked Paxton to build the largest. Thus was con-ceived the Emperor Fountain, and what Paxton engineered was a single jet rising from the centre of the canal in front of the southern façade of the house to a height of 296ft (90.22m) 'thus overtopping in its airy grace the highest trees in its vicinity. It is difficult to imagine anything more beauti-ful in its way than this simple jet. Of course, its noble proportions have much to do with the effect, but setting them aside, what a contrast does it present, in its elegant simplicity'. The immense water pressures and volumes needed to play the fountain required Paxton to experiment extensively and to dig a new reservoir of 8 acres (3.24ha), elevated some 350ft (106.68m) above the garden and hidden in the hills. The reservoir required the excava-tion of 100,000 cubic yards (76,500cu m) of earth and enjoyed an average depth of 7ft (2.13m). It was filled by rainwater and natural run-off from the moor that was collected by a 2½-mile-long conduit. From the reservoir over 200 tons of iron pipes were laid to bring the water to the fountain head – no wonder the Duke apprehensively wrote in his diary 'I walked up with Paxton to see the new reservoir, half frightened by the immense work'. Then, in June 1844, the fountain unfinished, word came that the Tsar had arrived early and unexpectedly in London. To the Duke's disappointment (and perhaps Paxton's secret relief) he did not venture north. The fountain was completed later that summer and, with only 2ft (0.91m) of water in the reservoir, it was inaugurated. The Duke, in his diary, excitedly wrote 'it is a glorious success. The most imaginative object and a new glory of Chatsworth. O Paxton!'[11]

KITCHEN GARDEN

Yet it was not just the great displays of ornament open to public scrutiny where Paxton was hard at work improving. Situated three-quarters-of-a-mile (1.21km) from the house, was the kitchen garden whose walls enclosed about 12 acres (4.86ha), divided into four compartments, with a wide slip all round. Within the boundary was also situated the gardener's residence, which in due course Paxton developed into a substantial stone structure. Within the protective walls, where the edible harvest was safe from grabbing fingers, and some of the Duke's most prized plants were cosseted away from accidental harm or deliberate theft by eager or dishonest visitors, Paxton celebrated many more innovations and triumphs.

The kitchen garden of a nobleman of such standing and wealth as the Duke, was, of course, expected to grow great quantities of produce to the highest standard. However, when Paxton arrived, and in the Duke's words 'At the kitchen-garden he found four pine-houses, bad; two vineries, which contained eight bunches of grapes; two good peach houses, and a few cucumber frames. There were no houses at all for plants, and there was nowhere a plant of later introduction than about the year 1800. There were eight rhododendrons, and not one camellia . . . In a very short time a great change appeared in pleasure-ground and garden: vegetables, of which there had been none, fruit in perfection, and flowers. The twelve men with brooms in their hands on the lawn began to sweep, the labourers to work with activity.'

So Paxton set to work to improve, and when Loudon made a second visit in May 1839, he was unstinting in with his praise of the kitchen garden. Here was 'much to be learned by the young gardener; and, indeed, we do not know a better school for young gardeners in the kingdom'. The forcing and cropping were organised so that the harvest would coincide with the autumn months when the Duke was in residence, but 'notwithstanding this, we saw ripe grapes, peaches, and cherries in pots'. Most gardeners kept the latter cool throughout blossom-set but Paxton discovered that a high temperature 'even to 70°F [21°C], greatly preferable'. He also discovered that washing peach trees with a mixture of lime and water, which was routinely carried out in autumn 'for the purpose of destroying insects', also helped to ripen the wood 'or at least to fit it for standing the frost of winter, by extracting part of the moisture from it'.

The interior of one of the peach houses at Chatsworth in 1875. The mature trees were trained to take maximum advantage of the incoming sunlight, while simultaneously providing shade for the tender plants grown in pots beneath them.

Although far from a complete list of what was grown, the following gives an indication of the quantity and some of the ingenious cultivation methods devised by Paxton. In 1839 he was forcing 3,000 strawberry plants, the same number as a later head gardener, Thomas Speed did in 1875. Therefore it is reasonable to assume that similar figures for Speed's harvest were also achieved by Paxton – 300 pineapples, bunches of grapes up to 4lb (1.81kg), 2,000 plants of Snow's Winter White Broccoli, 12,000 Williams' Matchless Red and Turner's Incomparable Dwarf White celery, 6,000 endive, an acre (0.40ha) of asparagus, a quarter-of-an-acre (0.10ha) of rhubarb, an immense quantity of seakale, kidney beans for ten months out of the twelve 'being obtained from pot plants', 2,000 Brussels sprouts, and of mushrooms, 'a generally abundant supply is kept up without intermission'.

Paxton was also a pioneer in growing and fruiting the banana. How the banana came to Chatsworth was recounted by William Fawcett in 1921 and re-told by Reynolds. In 1826 Charles Telfair, who was resident in Mauritius, obtained the plant from southern China; and sent two plants to a friend of his in England, a Mr Barclay of Burryhill (*sic*). Upon Barclay's death the bananas were offered for sale by the nursery of Messrs Young in Epsom, and in the late 1820s Paxton had purchased one of two plants for £10. Paxton housed this dwarf banana in a greenhouse at a temperature of 65–85°F (18–29°C) and grew it in a mixture of well-rotted manure and rich loam kept wet. It first flowered in November 1835. The following May over a hundred fruits were ripening, and the following year Paxton named the banana *Musa cavendishii*, which is now technically called *Musa* (AAA group) 'Dwarf Cavendish'.[12]

GLASSHOUSES

As he more than proved with the Great Stove, Paxton became an expert and innovative glasshouse architect. But he began his experiments and developed his expertise within the privacy of the walled gardens.

When Loudon published the generally critical account of his first visit in 1831, one area where he gave praise was the kitchen garden. Here twenty-two men worked and Paxton, who had 'greatly improved' it, had raised an 'extensive range of wooden forcing-houses'. Loudon was somewhat surprised at the choice of material, being convinced that the future of glasshouse design was 'metallic' houses. On this occasion, Loudon was proved wrong and, erected in the style Loudon had invented but Paxton perfected using the ridge-and-furrow, the wooden houses were certainly less expensive than their metal counterparts, and proved to be particularly adaptable. However, as the Great Stove demonstrated, used on a grand scale wood had the disadvantage that considerable labour was required to maintain the paintwork to a standard that the wood beneath did not rot. One of Paxton's early developments, his device for covering 'frames, pits, or low houses' at night-time provided a level of insulation more than that afforded by 'mats or boards' and was far less grand. The contraption which he devised required minimal effort to cover and uncover and was basically a 'thatched roof of somewhat larger dimensions than the frame, pit, or house to be covered, resting on side walls, and independent of those which support the glass; the lower edge or base of this roof slides on a railway, which extends at either or at both ends of the house, so as to afford space: for the roof to stand on in the day time, or when it is not wanted'.

Within the kitchen garden Paxton erected glasshouses for both orna-mentals and productive crops, and by 1857 there was an extensive range of the latter. This was a necessity because the poor climate – in the seven years to 1875 the garden always suffered a late May frost – meant that wall fruit performed disappointingly. As well as pits for pineapples and a melon ground, the glass used for forcing edible crops included a strawberry house, mushroom house, cucumber house, peach house, fig houses and several vineries – the whole vinery range being 249ft (75.90m) long and subdi-vided into eight bays. Each bays was planted with a single cultivar, so one house was entirely filled with the Canon Hall muscat, 'a favourite grape with Mr. Paxton, another with Hamburgh grapes, others with the common muscat, and with Frontignan, and so on'. Paxton also applied the same principle of grouping to 'the fruit trees on the walls', and he 'trained each tree or plant of the same kind into nearly the same size and shape', and this approach allowed him tight control over what was grown, 'even the number of bunches of grapes that each vine is to bear, or dozens of fruit that are to be allowed to remain on each wall tree after thinning, are predetermined by Mr Paxton the preceding autumn or winter, according to the strength of the tree and the ripeness of the wood; and instructions are given accord-ingly to the foremen of that department'. But it was the glasshouses Paxton designed for the ornamentals, and the plants themselves, that drew the most attention and for which he was justly famous.[13]

ORCHID HOUSES

The first tropical orchid flowered in Britain in 1731, by 1760 twenty-four tender species were in cultivation, and in the following sixty-six years before Paxton's arrival at Chatsworth, 154 genera had been classified. Of the thousands of exotic plants that arrived in Britain in the nineteenth century, orchids were treasured above all others by employers and head gardeners alike. To the garden-owner they were the ultimate horticultural status symbol – as rare and expensive as they were diverse and beautiful. To the head gardener, successful cultivation of these delicate and demanding treasures was a demonstration of one's prowess as a horticulturist, and to manage an extensive collection was a statement that one was head gardener to an establishment of wealth and taste.

With his love of status symbols, his ambitious and acquisitive nature, his over-riding desire to be and to have the best of the best, and with vast reserves of cash at his disposal, the Duke of Devonshire was a perfect candidate to become an orchid-oholic. He took his initial step along the road of addiction in 1833 when he became fascinated with his first orchid purchase *Oncidium papilo*, the butterfly orchid, which had cost him £100. From that moment on, the Duke wanted more, and so one of Paxton's first experimental glasshouses, erected in 1834, was an orchid house. Consisting of fifteen bays of a wooden construction supported on sixteen slender cast-iron columns, it was described as 'one of the earliest of Paxton's ridge-and-furrow erections . . . of wood and glass . . . This house has no doors, but the side sashes slide in double grooves, so that entry and exit are easy. It is nearly 100 feet [30.48m] in length by 26 feet [7.93m] in breadth, 13 feet 6 inches [4.12m] in the lowest and 15 feet [4.57m] in the highest part of the back wall, while in front the height is respectively 8 feet 6 inches and 10 feet [2.59 and 3.05m].'

The orchid collection at Chatsworth, thanks to the Duke's passion, grew quickly and received nationwide approbation. By 1857 it was so large that the original house became too small to house the collection and had been superseded by a range of three orchid houses, each dedicated to a collection of orchids from a specific geographic location. 'J H C of Alton' provides a useful inventory of the contents of each of the East Indian House, South American House and Mexican House (all plant names as given then). In the Indian House 'the lover of Epiphytes and aerial cultivation may drink his fill. The whole or greater part of the plants in this house are suspended in baskets'. Particularly fine were the vandas, saccolabiums and aerides. Notable specimens included 'the beautiful little *Saccolabium miniatum*', 'the miniature *Phalænopsis rosea*', the 'curious-flowered *Angræcum eburneum*', the '*Phalænopsis*-like-leaved *Trichoglottis pallens*' and 'most striking' the *Phalænopsis amabilis* and *P. grandiflora*. The South American House boasted 'two immense plants or *Dendrobium Paxtoni*, one of which numbers over one hundred of its large and brilliant spikes of pendulous bloom, and is truly a magnificent object', together with a 'choice collection' of dendrobiums. Of the cattleyas it was considered of the *Cattleya labiata* that 'we might travel from the Channel to the Tweed without meeting with a more noble or interesting specimen'. Of the fine collection of oncidiums the finest was *O. amplicatum major*, a specimen of which had that year produced 'thirty distinct blooms'. The house also was home to a Stag's-horn Fern 'some four feet in width' and two 'fine' *Nepenthes distillatoria*. The Mexican House contained some remarkably fine plants of '*Dendrobium nobile, intermedium, moniliforme*', together with a 'good general collection of Stanhopeas in flower', *Cyrtochilum maculatum, Sophronitis cernua, S. grandiflora, S. violacea*, the 'sweet-scented' *Epidendrum fragrans*, 'the curious' *Cypripedium insignis*, and 'the sombre-coloured' together with a 'number of Australian and North American Pitcher plants'.[14]

PLANT HUNTING

We have met John Gibson, who was Superintendent of Battersea Park and pioneer of subtropical bedding (see page 132), but earlier in life, as an undergardener of two year's experience he was rapidly elevated by Paxton to the lofty position of the Duke's personal orchid hunter. In February 1835, and knowing of the Duke's budding passion for orchids, James Bateman (1811–97), already a hopelessly addicted orchid-nut, and subsequently creator of the nineteenth century's second most influential garden, Biddulph Grange (from 1849), wrote to the Duke. Bateman begged to inform his Grace that a friend of his, the Rev. John Huntley of Kimbolton (Cambridgeshire), was proposing to sell his orchid collection due to an unfortunate change of financial circumstances. This collection had taken Huntley more than twenty years to accumulate, and Bateman assured his Grace that it was especially fine – containing over 200 species, many of which were very rare. However, Bateman added the rider that Huntley would only agree to sell the collection as a complete lot. Paxton was duly dispatched to confirm Bateman's claim, and to negotiate with Huntley.

Paxton was very impressed by the collection, which he discovered comprised some 300 plants. Accordingly the price was high – £500, so high in fact that despite a touch of professional avarice, he tried (but failed) to dissuade the Duke from making the purchase. The money paid and the orchids safely ensconced at Chatsworth, the collection pushed the Duke over the edge into absolute addiction. In March he instructed Paxton to send a plant hunter to India with the express purpose of gathering as many new orchid species as possible for his collection. Thus Gibson now embarked on an intensive crash-course in orchid cultivation and identification before embarking in late September with the party belonging to Lord Auckland, a friend of the Duke who was travelling to take up his post as Governor General.

Orchids, however, were not Gibson's only goal. He was also under specific instruction to procure and return with a live specimen of a tree discovered in Burma some nine years previously by Nathaniel Wallich. This was the fabled *Amherstia nobilis*, which was named for Lady Sarah Amherst (1801–76) the wife of William Pitt Amherst, the Governor General of Bengal, who collected plants in Asia in the early nineteenth century. With its long inflorescences of stunning yellow and scarlet, it outshone every tree in cultivation in Britain – and gave many an orchid a run for its money in terms of pure exuberance. As yet, though, no specimen had made it back to Britain alive, and to be the first to introduce and to flower the *Amherstia* was exactly the type of one-upmanship challenge in which the Duke and his right-hand man revelled.

After an outward bound voyage lasting six-and-a-half months, Gibson set out from Calcutta for the Khasia Hills in Assam, a destination which, while wet and dangerous, was also a goldmine for an orchid-hunter. When Gibson finally set sail back to England on 3 March 1837, he could sit smugly in his cabin, proud in the knowledge that the fruits of his strenuous labours amounted to a haul of over 1,000 tender exotics, of which 300, including 100 orchids, were new to science. The latter included *Coelogyne gardneriana*, *Dendrobium devonianum*, *D. gibsonii* and *Thunia alba*. He was also responsible for introducing *Rhododendron formosum*.

Also in his cabin were two *Amherstia* plants which he had secured, not from the jungles of Burma, but the elegant setting of the botanic garden in Calcutta, and which spent the entire four-month journey by his side! The plants that Gibson returned with – not least the *Amherstia* – caused a wave of excitement within the horticultural world, and were worth a fortune. For his hardships endured while collecting, and his skill displayed nurturing them safely home alive, Gibson was rewarded with promotion to foreman of the exotic plant department![15]

The *Amherstia* was described as 'one of the most superb objects imaginable, with large pinnate leaves, and large scentless flowers, of a bright vermilion colour, diversified with three yellow spots, and disposed in gigantic ovate pendulous branches', and Paxton was desperate to be the first to flower this wonder. The plants so carefully nurtured on their journey to their new home were now given pride of place in their own greenhouse erected within the kitchen garden for their express cultivation. With a curved roof the polygonal greenhouse was climate-controlled to as closely as possible imitate that of their natural habitat. As *The Gardeners' Chronicle* delightfully put it 'planted out in the centre of the house, one might almost imagine the plant conscious of the consideration paid to it'. On the shelves around the perimeter of the house, there was by 1875, a fine collection of Pitcher plants 'which thrive in the damp moist heat, which is maintained in imitation of the climate of Martaban. The Pitchers serve as veritable insect-traps, and from one we saw the half-decayed body of a gigantic cockroach extracted. Dracænas, Crotons, Marantas and other heat-loving plants, find a congenial home in this house. Here, too, is a fine example of the lattice-leaf plant, *Ouvirandra fenestralis* [grown] to great perfection... Some of the leaves we found to measure 12 inches in length and 6 inches in width.' But unbeknownst to him, Paxton was in a race to be the first to flower the *Amherstia*. And this was perhaps the only occasion on which he came second. The winner was Mrs Louisa Lawrence of Ealing Park, whose tree blossomed in late March 1849.[16]

The accomplishments and successes that the Duke craved, and upon the achievement of which Paxton thrived, did not come cheap. According to Paxton, the total expended on the garden in the decade to 1840 was in the region of £10,000, and between 1830 and 1835 alone, Paxton racked up a bill of over £2,500 on seed, plants and trees, and spent a further £3,049 building and maintaining new glasshouses. From 1836 to 1840 glasshouse expenditure totalled £5,704 excluding the cost of the Great Stove.[17]

But it was not just a financial cost that Paxton and the Duke had to bear, for the garden also cost the lives of two Chatsworth plant hunters. The success of Gibson's twenty-month expedition amply demonstrated the potential rewards to be reaped from sending one's own plant hunter to collect rarities. Buoyed up by their success, Paxton and the Duke now looked to their next adventure – to capitalise on the work begun in western America by David Douglas. Douglas had died only three years previously, and the exciting new conifers which he had introduced were still rare, expensive and very desirable. Paxton and the Duke decided to send out two plant

The Amherstia House was designed by Paxton specifically to house the rare Amherstia nobilis *brought back from India by the Duke's own plant hunter, John Gibson, in 1837. To the left are Pitcher plants (*Nepenthes spp.*) from Borneo.*

hunters to California and the Pacific North West to bring back seed of what Douglas had already introduced and, it was hoped, to discover many more new species. Gibson's trip had also revealed just how expensive such an undertaking could be, and so perhaps encouraged by the fiscally prudent Paxton, another similarity between their plan and the Douglas trips was the method of funding – by a consortium who would share the cost and the bounty. Paxton wrote to potential members in November 1837, and soon had a list of twenty-four who would each contribute £50. On 20 March 1838 the ill-fated pair of Peter Banks and Robert Wallace, two under-gardeners at Chatsworth, set off. The pair were to be away for three years, during which time they were to be paid £1 4s each per week (£54 per annum). The two men were also to keep account of their expenses, and were to beware of bears and women.

However, in May 1839 tragic news reached Paxton. Letters dated 7 November 1838 arrived to inform a stunned Paxton that in late October the boat carrying his two plant hunters down the Columbia River had struck a rock in rapids near the appropriately named Dalles des Morts and both men had drowned. Paxton mourned both men and the loss of the potential harvest they could have made, but he also felt guilty for sending them across land, rather than by sea via Cape Horn, as had been recommended by John Lindley.[18]

THE VICTORIA HOUSE

Within the confines of the ornamental garden Paxton constructed a range of glass called the Conservative Wall in 1848. Running for a distance of 340ft (103.63m) and erected against the south-facing garden wall, it rises up the slope in a series of steps or bays about 27ft (8.23m) in length, and about 18ft (5.49m) high. Paxton planted it with a wide collection of shrubs, of which camellias were the prized specimens, and which still bloom today. However, his last glasshouse erected within the confines of the kitchen garden a year later was also Paxton's last great contribution to the garden, and appropriately, it also achieved a first. In July 1849 – the same year that Paxton became agent for the Chatsworth estate on a salary of £500 per annum – he embarked on another challenge as a result of a letter from his friend William Hooker. Hooker was the first Director of the Royal Botanic Garden, Kew, and had been hard at work for eight years re-establishing

Kew as the world's foremost botanic garden. His position came about as a direct result of the Government commission set up 1838, whose members included Paxton, in order to survey and assess the generally poor state of the royal gardens, and to make recommendations (see also page 135). One of these was to take Kew under Governmental control and to appoint a Director.

Hooker's letter explained that he had, after several unsuccessful attempts, succeeded in germinating seed of the 'Royal Water Lily', *Victoria regia* (*Victoria amazonica*). According to an article in *The Gardeners' Chronicle* in 1850, this remarkable plant had been discovered in Bolivia by the Czech botanist Tadeas Haenke (1761–1817) in about 1801. It was first introduced into Britain by Thomas Bridges who brought back seed in 1846. Two plants were raised at Kew, but both died, and subsequent cultivation of roots brought back from the Upper Essequibo in Guyana also failed. Hooker had succeeded, however, with seed sent back by Dr Hugh Rodie and Mr Luckie of George Town, Demerara in small phials filled with pure water. The first of four batches arrived on 28 February 1849, and by 23 March half a dozen seedlings were thriving. By the summer their number stood at upwards of fifty, half of which Hooker distributed among 'the principal cultivators of rare plants', which, of course included Paxton.

Just as the *Amherstia* had been honoured with its own glasshouse, so, too was the Royal waterlily. But more immediately, Paxton travelled to London to collect the seedlings on 3 August 1849, his forty-sixth birthday. With four leaves only 6in (15cm) in diameter this precious specimen was carefully nurtured in a temporary home – a large square tank that Paxton had built in the space of three weeks, complete with water heated to an appropriate Amazonian temperature. The waterlily thrived – the leaves reaching 4ft (1.22m) in diameter by early October, and on 1 November a flower bud appeared. A week later, on the evening of 8 November, the bud burst. At almost a foot (30cm) in diameter the bloom opened white and faded to pink over the coming three days. For the second time in a little over seven months the Queen was presented with a remarkable flower. Whereas Mrs Lawrence had sent her *Amherstia* to the palace, Paxton presented his water lily bloom in person. Ever generous, Hooker travelled to Chatsworth to marvel at Paxton's success. Not so Mrs Lawrence, who cried off, citing a sore throat. Public interest was phenomenal, and in a stunt worthy of a modern tabloid, Paxton's youngest child, seven-and-a-half-year-old Annie, was stood on a tin tray (to spread her weight) and put on the leaf, thus creating an image which still causes wonderment today. Paxton reported in early February the following year that the plant had just developed its fifty-fifth leaf and twenty-fifth flower bud – but possibly owing to the low light levels of winter, growth was reduced – the leaves down to about 2ft (0.61m) in diameter from a peak of 15ft (43.57m), and the flowers from 11 to 7in (27.94 to 17.78cm).

Meanwhile the specially designed Victoria House took four months to complete, cost about £800 and was inaugurated in April 1850. Taking the form of a large glass box with a framework of four thin, wrought-iron beams supporting the roof and braced by eight cast-iron columns, hollow in order to take rainwater from the roof, this structure was the first of Paxton's to have a completely flat ridge-and-furrow roof. As such, it was the ultimate development of his structural experimentation with glass. At just over 60ft (18.29m) long, by 47ft (14.33m) broad and 12ft (3.66m) high, the centre was occupied by a large central circular tank, which was 33ft (10.06m) in

Perhaps the most iconic garden image of the century. Paxton's youngest daughter Annie standing on the giant leaf of the Royal waterlily (Victoria amazonica) which first flowered in Britain at Chatsworth on 8 November 1849.

diameter, with a smaller one within it some 15ft (4.57m) across and 4 to 5ft (1.22 to 1.52m) in depth. Within the house were a further eight smaller tanks for other aquatic treasures. The main tank was mounted on four wheels on which it rotated thus mimicking the sluggish movement of its native river habitat, and the heating pipes running through the house and embedded in the soil within the tank warmed the air and water to the appropriate temperature of between 80 and 90°F (27–32°C). The water lily was offered for sale in 1851 by Knight and Perry of the Royal Exotic Nursery who in an advert placed in *The Gardeners' Chronicle* on 22 May that year stated that a good aquatic house could be erected for about £500 – that being the sum they had paid for theirs. By 1857 Paxton had got cultivation down to a fine art, with the young plant usually placed in the tank in the middle of April and flowering in very early July. In autumn and winter the tanks were filled with camellias, azaleas and other greenhouse plants.[19]

THE GARDEN COMPLETE AND LIFE OUTSIDE CHATSWORTH

Now, twenty-four years after he had arrived at Chatsworth, Paxton's transformations of the garden were complete. The kitchen garden was running like a finely tuned machine, producing the highest-quality edibles both outdoors and from the forcing houses. Here too, the results of Paxton's experiments into glasshouse design were standing solid and filled with countless horticultural treasures. Beyond the walls, the Great Stove nestled amongst the woods of the pinetum and offered a striking contrast with the nearby massive rockworks. All that was needed now was time to allow the garden to mature.

From about 1840 onwards Paxton had taken on an ever-increasing range of outside interests and projects, and from about 1850 his career veered away from Chatsworth, although he remained in his position and ensured the quality of the gardens never slipped. His three main spheres of interest and activity were publishing, garden design and architecture.

Publishing

Paxton's first foray into the world of periodical publishing had been his *Horticultural Register and General Magazine*, which started in July 1831 and copied much from Loudon's *The Gardener's Magazine*. For five years until its closure, it was Loudon's first direct competitor, and partly because it was cheaper, Loudon's circulation fell quite dramatically. Paxton's second foray into the world of periodical publication was the launch in 1834 of *Paxton's Magazine of Botany and Register of Flowering Plants* which ran until 1849. However, his most successful venture was *The Gardeners' Chronicle*, which began in 1841 and published weekly, co-founded with William Bradbury and two prominent members of the Horticultural Society – Sir Charles Wentworth Dilke (proprietor and editor of *The Athenaeum*), and John Lindley, Professor of Botany at University College, London. When *The Gardener's Magazine* closed in 1843, *The Gardeners' Chronicle* became its natural and very successful successor, and by 1851, weekly domestic circulation stood at about 6,500, with numerous foreign subscribers. In comparison *The Observer* and *The Economist* sold 6,230 and 3,826 respectively. Surprisingly, perhaps, Paxton published only two books – *The Cultivation of the Dahlia* (1838) and *The Pocket Botanical Dictionary* (1840) with which he was assisted by Lindley.

Garden design

Paxton carried out a number of garden designs for private clients and he also devised a number of public parks of which Birkenhead Park (1843) is the most famous. The first municipal park expressly designed for the free recreation of local residents, it quickly became known as 'the people's park', and the design was implemented by one of Paxton's apprentices at Chatsworth, Edward Kemp (1817–91) who went on to establish a career as a garden designer, penning the very popular *How to Lay Out a Small Garden* (1850). Paxton's other great public design was for the gardens surrounding the new home for the Crystal Palace at Sydenham. Paxton's enormous terraced water gardens, which were superintended by another former apprentice, Edward Milner (1819–84), later himself a famous landscape designer in his own right, set out to rival Versailles. The 12,000 jets, cascades and fountains consumed 12,000 gallons of water a minute, and just as King Louis XIV's garden almost bankrupted France, so Paxton's extravagance cast a permanent blight over the financial success (or lack of it) of the Crystal Palace Company. However, Paxton seems to have avoided any blame, even to the extent of being granted a lifelong lease of a sizeable house, Rockhills, on the Sydenham site.

Architecture

Paxton's first venture into the world of architecture was in 1837 with the rebuilding of most of the cottages in Edensor village, part of the Chatsworth estate. The self-taught Paxton rebuilt the Duke's Irish property of Lismore Castle (County Cork) from 1849, and in the 1850s designed a number of large country houses, most notably Mentmore (Buckinghamshire) for Baron Mayer Amschel de Rothschild, and Château de Ferrières near Paris for Baron James de Rothschild. But he is best remembered as the architect of the Crystal Palace for the Great Exhibition of 1851; he famously doodled the concept for this huge glasshouse on a piece of blotting paper while bored in a meeting on 11 June 1850. The design concept fittingly came from Chatsworth, for as Paxton revealed in a lecture to the Society of Arts in 1850, it had been the 'natural feat of engineering' of the *Victoria amazonica* leaf that had inspired his design of the glasshouse within which it was housed, and which in essence was the forerunner of the Crystal Palace (so named by Douglas Jerrold in *Punch*).

The Great Exhibition turned in a profit of more than £186,000, but despite receiving fortune and fame – £5,000, a knighthood and election three years later as Member of Parliament for Coventry, Paxton remained in his post at Chatsworth until the Duke's death in 1858. His patron and friend died on 18 January, and the reading of the Duke's will revealed the dire state of his finances. Significant economies would have to be made at Chatsworth, and Paxton, who had drawn up a proposal for sweeping redundancies and savings, resigned on 27 January 1858 rather than implement them. The seventh Duke gave him his house on the estate for life, and the next year (and unexpectedly) settled £500 a year on him. Moreover, as the 1875 article from *The Gardeners' Chronicle* amply demonstrates, the gardens were kept up.

Let us finish with a speech given by Charles Dickens, who was the guest of honour at the Annual Dinner of The Gardeners' Benevolent Institution held on 9 June 1851:

> I have risen to propose to you the health of a gentleman who is a great gardener, and not only a great gardener but a great man – the growth of a fine Saxon root cultivated up with a power of intellect to a plant that is at this time the talk of the civilized world – I allude, of course, to my friend the chairman of the day. I took occasion to say at a public assembly hard-

by, a month or two ago, in speaking of that wonderful building Mr Paxton has designed for the Great Exhibition in Hyde Park, that it ought to have fallen down, but that it refused to do so. We were told that the glass ought to have been all broken, the gutters all choked up, and the building flooded, and that the roof and sides ought to have been blown away; in short that everything ought to have done what everything obstinately persisted in not doing. Earth, air, fire, and water all appear to have conspired together in Mr Paxton's favour – all have conspired together to one result, which, when the present generation is dust, will be an enduring temple to his honour, and to the energy, the talent, and the resources of Englishmen.

"But," said a gentleman to me the other day, "no doubt Mr Paxton is a great man, but there is one objection to him that you can never get over, that is, he is a gardener." Now that is our case to-night, that he is a gardener, and we are extremely proud of it. This is a great age, with all its faults, when a man by the power of his own genius and good sense can scale such a daring height as Mr Paxton has reached, and composedly place his form on the top. This is a great age, when a man impressed with a useful idea can carry out his project without being imprisoned, or thumb-screwed, or persecuted in any form. I can well understand that you, to whom the genius, the intelligence, the industry, and the achievements of our friend are well known, should be anxious to do him honour by placing him in the position he occupies to-night; and I assure you, you have conferred great gratification on one of his friends, in permitting him to have the opportunity of proposing his health, which that friend now does most cordially and with all the honours.[20]

CHAPTER 8

───◆•◆•◆───

Barnes of Bicton

The Florist's pseudonymous correspondent 'O P' encapsulated it perfectly in 1857 'Few gardens have gained greater celebrity than those at Bicton. The extensive collections of plants, together with the favoured climate of that locality, have frequently been the subject of comment in gardening periodicals.'[1] The man who created all this was James Barnes, the eldest of five brothers, all of whom entered the family profession.

James was born in Farnham (Surrey), where his father was head gardener at Willey House. Soon after James's birth, his father moved to the Rev. Onslow at Ripley, and became manager of Mr Lassam's nursery in Witley. In 1814 Barnes senior entered the service of Henry Gill of Eashing House in Godalming, and here, the eight-year-old James who since the age of five, had been 'chiefly employed in weeding walks and nursery seed-beds, and in bird scaring', became fully employed. When the octogenarian Gill died, the property passed to his daughter and her husband, Mr Frankland, and the couple set about a vigorous programme of renovation and expansion. The mansion was enlarged, and 'entirely new gardens, with pleasure-grounds, shrubberies, and plantations formed, and also a new park from the adjacent farm lands' were created under the superintendence of Barnes senior. James was to work as an apprentice under his father on these improvements until 1818.

THE EARLY DAYS

Then, one frosty February morning, James, aged a mere twelve, 'wishing to go to London, to see the gardening wonders he had heard of as being carried out there' set off, and walking through several snow storms arrived 'soon after noon in Chelsea, in time to seek for work' and that very afternoon was engaged 'for the next day by Mr Moore, of the King's Road'. At this time, the land from Sloane Square to Fulham was occupied by florists, nurserymen and market gardeners who sold at the Covent Garden market. Moore was a noted cultivator of cucumbers and mushrooms, and 'a good grower too of Grapes, Pines, and Melons, and a forcer of all early fruits and flowering plants'. James worked for four years with the Moores.

Growing cucumbers

Barnes then moved to the other side of London, to Mr Stone of Peckham, as a 'framer', in charge of '1000 lights of framing, 2600 hand and bell glasses for growing Cucumbers, Melons, early Potatoes, &c., forcing Asparagus and Sea-kale in an extensive way, and fourteen acres [5.67ha] of beautiful ground for vegetable-growing'.

After a few years, and deciding he could learn no more, Barnes took a position as superintendent of the forcing department for a market gardener at Bermondsey, 'a very extensive grower of grapes, peaches, pines, strawberries, mushrooms, and all kinds of salads, fruits, and vegetables'. Two years later he rose to be superintendent in overall charge of 40 acres (16.18ha) of market garden at Greenwich, with 'some 2000 lights of framing, 5000 hand-glasses ... and extensive crops of all outdoor vegetables in season'. Barnes recalled that in the decade after his arrival in London, the cucumber was one of the population's favourite, and thus most widely grown vegetables. Indeed, so popular was it, that each spring Barnes had under his charge up to '6000 hand and bell-glasses, all covering cucumber plants on the ridging-out system' and '1600 frame-lights covering frame cucumbers' – taking an average of four feet (1.22m) per light gives a total of 6,400 linear feet (1.95km). The method of cultivation was, in early spring, to transplant out the cauliflowers and lettuces, which had been over-wintered in the frames, and while some frames were used to force asparagus, seakale, early potatoes and herbs, most notably, mint, tarragon, sweet basil, sweet marjoram, the majority were used to grow cucumbers on hotbeds. Frame-grown cucumbers were harvested from 'about the middle of April', and those grown under hand- and bell-glasses from the beginning of June. In this way Barnes could harvest 'above 8 tons of Cucumbers...in one day'. In fact Barnes so perfected his skill of forcing early-frame cucumbers that he could regularly cut 'by the end or middle of January and with these I took many 1st prizes at the Chelsea, Battersea, Tottenham, Windsor, and other Cucumber clubs or shows, as they were then called, and which held meetings from about February 25 until March

Growing cucumbers was a passion of James Barnes, and something he was particularly good at. However, he tended to grow them in a frame on a hotbed rather than in a glasshouse.

8 or 10 each spring'. Barnes also experimented with breeding cucumbers, his greatest success being 'Man of Kent'. Named by the Horticultural Society, from whom he also received a medal, this variety won Barnes 'almost or quite every 1ˢᵗ class prize offered at all the shows at that time held about London'.

Barnes' twelve years of market gardening taught him the different methods of sowing and growing all manner of crops 'from the commonest vegetable and salad to the most rare and expensive fruits' and this knowledge was to prove invaluable in later life. It also taught him what hard work was. Barnes wryly commented that he 'could sleep as well riding on the top of a load all through London to Covent Garden as I now can on a bed, and have done so many times; and sometimes then what little sleep I did get was on the pavement in the old market, amongst vegetables, and before the business of the market began' – around 6am. Later, as a head gardener, Barnes was very industrious – to the point of working himself to exhaustion, and he also demanded the same of his staff. So when he paid tribute to the class of market gardener (two-thirds of whom he recalled were Irish) who 'work harder, and to have more hardships to contend with, than any other class of men I have ever met with', he knew what he was talking about.

Barnes also highlighted the high-risk nature of the market gardening business: production costs were expensive – he put the average cost for 'working one acre of ground under the spade, reckoning the rent, taxes, manure, horses, &c., and getting the produce to market' at £50 per annum, and market gardeners were also at risk from heavy losses.[2]

Perhaps the hard work and associated stress of running a market garden were a contributory factor to the character of Barnes' last employer in London, 'an irritable, intemperate man'. So displeasing did Barnes find his situation that after staying 'through two forcing seasons', he moved on and changed horticultural tack, superintending the forming of the extensive pleasure grounds at Beulah Spa in Norwood (Surrey). Here, John Davidson Smith had bought the manor in the 1820s, and in 1831 opened a briefly fashionable pleasure resort, with the spa buildings designed by Decimus Burton, and a mineral spring in the coppice as the centrepiece of his pleasure grounds.[3] Once Beulah Spa was completed, Barnes was engaged by Mr Hall Dare of Cranford House in Great Ilford (Essex) to replace George Mills, who was moving to Gunnersbury Park in London. Here Barnes remained as head gardener for four years until the death of his employer. A further five were spent at Chislehurst (Kent) as head gardener to Sir Herbert Jenner, before in 1839 and aged thirty-three, he was engaged by Lord Rolle of Bicton.

WORKING AT BICTON

So began a headship that lasted nearly three decades and which brought garden, gardener and employer great repute and many plaudits, but which was to eventually end in acrimony and dispute. An early indication of his employer's mindset was evident soon after his arrival. Barnes claimed to have established if not the first, then one of the first cottagers' and cottage garden exhibitions in Kent in the 1830s. Giving good garden seeds to the cottagers, together with information on how to sow them, and how to grow fruits, flowers and vegetables, 'It was truly astonishing how attentive and industrious the cottagers became, and what splendid things

Barnes' portrait as it appeared in The Gardeners' Chronicle *on 24 November 1874.*
This was over five years after he had resigned from Bicton and made legal history by
successfully suing his former employer for libel.

they produced. Everything about the locality became improved, and the local nobility and gentry soon saw the improvement, and subscribed to support the society, while the exhibition day became quite an enjoyable holiday, as well as affording a profitable sight.' However, when he mentioned his achievement and offered to assist 'in every possible way . . . for the improvement of the poor, wretchedly-managed households and gardens of the surrounding dilapidated, neglected-looking villages', Lord and Lady Rolle behaved in a way very different to the nobility of Kent. Barnes was met with a 'flat denial, with the intimation that these folks knew too much already'.[4]

Barnes' personal experience of the less-than-humane side of Lady Rolle's character came in 1869, and that May he resigned as a result of it. His reason for departing was the shoddy treatment he received from the widow (Lord Rolle had died in 1842) while 'in the midst of severe affliction, brought on by over-exertion and unremitting labour'. A short time before his resignation the sixty-two-year-old Barnes, who throughout his career had been blessed with rugged good health, 'broke down' as a result of overwork. For, although the head gardener of a garden whose nationwide reputation he had established, he was working '18 to 20 hours daily' with 'sudden exposure to many varying temperatures, and constant changes from agricultural duties to every branch of horticultural practice, including floriculture, arboriculture, &c.'

By this point there was so much bad blood between the protagonists that soon after Barnes' resignation the widow Rolle accused her former employee of leaving the gardens in disorder. Barnes, who always prided himself on keeping an orderly garden and more than amply demonstrated through his own actions and the approbation received from his peers that he was one of the finest head gardeners in the realm, felt not only that his former employer was displaying an inexcusable level of ingratitude, but, more importantly, she was impeaching his impeccable reputation.

Barnes, always a determined man of action and assured self-belief, sued for libel – and won, receiving £200 in damages. The case became 'a matter of legal history', but the verdict certainly rankled with her Ladyship, for reading the 1871 description of the garden published in the *Journal of Horticulture* – anonymously, and given the notoriety the case had generated, one could say with great disloyalty to head gardeners in general and Barnes specifically, the reader is left with the impression of pharaonic expurgation.

Gone were the plaudits such as those from Loudon, who in 1842 reported in glowing terms that 'we do not think we ever before saw culture, order, and neatness carried to such a high degree of perfection, in so many departments, and on so large a scale, and all by the care and superintendence of one man. From the commonest kitchen crop in the open garden, and the mushrooms in the sheds, up to the pine-apples, the heaths, and the Orchidaceæ, every thing seemed to be alike healthy and vigorous. We could not help noticing the evenness of the crops of cabbages, cauliflowers, savoys, &c. in the kitchen-garden; and the extraordinary vigour and beauty of the pines, heaths, hothouse plants, chrysanthemums, &c., in the houses; and nothing could exceed the neatness of the lawn, the walks, and the flower-beds.'

No hint of the praise given some sixteen years later by Barnes' distinguished peer, Robert Fish, who finished his 'long gossip about Bicton' by expressing great pleasure in 'shaking hands with and receiving kindness from, a gardener, from whose practice, as embodied in his writings, I had previously derived much instruction and advantage'.[5] Instead, it was Mr Glendinning, Barnes' predecessor (who himself had left the gardens to Barnes in a poor state) who was named as the major driving force behind the garden; and while not named, Barnes' reputation was dragged through the mud by inference. The reader is told that when Mr Begbie succeeded to the head-gardenership he found that as a result of 'year after year of deaths...allowed to occur in the Pinetum unnoticed', no less than 900 specimens were now missing. And that the victim of this neglect, the maligned Lady Rolle, would not allow the labels, 'marking where they stood and recording their names, to be removed, but they remain as a record of neglect'.

More vitriol follows. The vines, of which Barnes was a passionate and extremely successful cultivator 'could not have been in a satisfactory state in 1869, neither are they at the present time' and as for the orange trees 'once the pride of Bicton, are now in a sad picture'. Yet, even if the accusations were true, and given Barnes' professionalism and more pertinently the verdict, they clearly were not, the account does not say much for Begbie's skills. For in comparison, within two years of his arrival Barnes had turned around the neglect he inherited from Glendinning.[6]

The truth of the matter was that 'Barnes of Bicton' as he became affectionately and respectfully known within the horticultural profession, possessed phenomenal skills as both a cultivator and as a manager. Examples of his successes were manifold: he grew a Queen pineapple to a whopping 8¼lb (3.74kg) bred a new and very popular white strawberry called 'Bicton Pine', and raised the shrub named by Dr Lindley as *Colletia bictonensis* (now *C. paradoxa*, syn. *C. cruciata*). The stock of the strawberry Lady Rolle sold to Messrs Knight & Perry of the Royal Exotic Nursery in Chelsea, and that of the shrub to Messrs. Veitch & Son of the Exeter Nursery for £100. Barnes was also the first in the country to produce viable seed of the dioecious Monkey puzzle – he had both a female and male tree growing in the garden (the cones weighed up to 8lb). So successful was his conifer cultivation that on one occasion he was able to exhibit at a Royal Botanic Society Show in Regent's Park a 'collection of about 100 species and varieties of Conifer that were coning in the Bicton arboretum'.

WRITING: THE PEN AND THE DIBBER

Indeed, so respected was Barnes' work as a head gardener that to work under him carried a great cachet when applying for later positions. Many of the most successful and capable of the next generation of head gardeners learned their trade under him, including J. Taplin, who succeeded Paxton at Chatsworth. However, Barnes, unlike Paxton, was as prolific with his pen as he was successful with his dibber. As well as co-writing with George W. Johnson the definitive 'The Pine Apple. Its Culture, Uses and History', which appeared as the June and July issues of *The Gardener's Monthly* in 1847, and *Asparagus Culture* (1870) with William Robinson, Barnes was a regular contributor to many periodicals.

In the early 1840s Loudon visited Bicton, and it was in response to a request from the great man that Barnes addressed a series of twenty-four letters to *The Gardener's Magazine*. Although not a complete guide to every operation carried out in the garden – to do that would have required something the size of Loudon's *Encyclopædia* – the over 40,000 words penned by Barnes between 27 September 1842 and 16 January 1843, focused primarily on specific contents of his garden and the practicalities of cultivating a selection of plant and crops. Refreshing as much for their candid honesty as their practicalities and realities, Barnes' epistles provide a unique insight into how one of the country's most successful and respected head gardeners managed and cultivated some of the parts of his larger domain.

THE PLEASURE GARDENS

The ornamental gardens, glasshouses and kitchen gardens at Bicton were detached from the house at a distance of 0.4 miles (0.64km) to the south east; and by the century's standards the pleasure grounds were neither large nor designed to the latest styles. They were, however, nationally renowned for being, what in modern parlance we would call a 'plantsman's garden'. Barnes' letters are from a time before the sheltered Cornish valley gardens such as Penjerrick, Glendurgan, Trebah and Heligan had risen to their plant-filled zenith, and before the plant hunters had brought back copious quantities of new treasures from China and Japan. Indeed, it was not until a month after Barnes penned his final letter that Robert Fortune (1812–80) set sail for China on his first great plant-hunting expedition. Yet what made the gardens so special was the enormous diversity of rare and unusual plants cultivated to the highest standards both indoors and out – where the munificent climate helped them to reach enviable proportions. For the purposes of this discussion the gardens are broken down into the various departments.

Ornamental glasshouses

Set at the top of a south-west-facing slope and forming a concave terminus to the twin, 230ft (70.10m) long walls that enclosed the Flower Garden (now the Italian Garden) along its western and eastern boundaries was a modest array of seven greenhouses dedicated to the tender ornamental collections. Either side of the classically inspired temple and an integral part of the complex (which bore a remarkable resemblance to Miller's 'blueprint at the Chelsea Physic Garden – see page 36) was a pair of what Barnes called conservatories.

Constructed of stone, each of the pair measured 'about 40 ft. [12.09m] long, 18 ft. high [5.49m], and 18 ft. [5.49m]wide', and inside, the flowering display was changed seasonally. When Loudon visited on 19 and 20 September they were filled with pelargoniums, fuchsias, balsams, globe amaranthus (*Gomphrena globosa*), *Primula sinensis*, *Achimenes coccinea* and

Looking up the slope of the Flower Garden, bound either side by a tall wall, to the range of ornamental glasshouses. Behind these was Barnes' walled garden – the powerhouse of his floral and vegetal empire.

14 different varieties of cockscombs (*Celosia cristata*). The autumn show was of specimen shrubs, many of them large, including 'a row of large orange trees, banksias, many varieties of acacias' and the 'very rare' *Swammerdamia antennana*.

The citrus were housed in the Orange and Camellia House, which was home to a collection of neglected orange trees that required Barnes' remedial care, and to the collection of camellias that he subsequently gathered – he lists fifty-three types. He potted the camellias in a mix of 'loam and heath soil in equal quantities, stones, and river sand, one barrow of rotten dung to eight of the above mixture, well mixed up together as roughly as possible'. He gave them 'a good soaking of manured water (a solution of cow and sheep dung, soot, lime, nitrate of soda – see page 226), two or three times in the season'.[7]

NEW HOLLAND HOUSE AND NATURE'S TEACHINGS

The New Holland House, 47ft (14.33m) long, 16ft (4.88m) wide and 14ft (4.27m) high, and with a 2ft 10in (0.86m) Portland stone-topped table running down the centre of the building and a shelf of the same stone around the perimeter, was home to a geographical collection of plants. Barnes considered the Australian flora 'the most lovely and interesting tribe of plants ever introduced into this country . . . and which generally come into flower at a very convenient season of the year'. And their successful cultivation was another area in which Barnes excelled, and his 'noble collection' always contained 'something new and interesting'. His published list of 'a few out of the collection' numbers 154, including ten banskias, and in addition to remarkable specimens of *Chorozema varium* (*Chorizema varium*) and *Pimelea decussata*, Barnes was particularly proud of his *Lechenaultia biloba*. This 'very valuable plant which has been said by many cultivators of plants to be a bad ugly grower', was charmed by Barnes in to growing perfectly. Using as compost a mix of charcoal, stones, a little sand, and some heath mould 'all jumbled together in lumps as large as bricks broken into about six or eight pieces', in two years and from a cutting he had a specimen '1 ft. 3in. high [0.38m] . . . and 7 ft. 9 in. [2.36m] in circumference, thick with shoots . . . I have counted 500 blooms open on the plant all at one time. If there is one plant in the house more beautiful than another, it is this plant. If £100 were offered for a fellow plant to it, it could not be got.'[8]

POTTING

Much of Barnes' success as a cultivator can be attributed to the fact that he was a careful and thoughtful studier of nature who applied his observations to his cultural techniques. Thus those plants in his care were patiently accorded the conditions that they desired in order to thrive. This 'do as nature does' approach was no more evident than in the way he approached potting. Loudon had clearly been surprised by the 'very rough manner I potted every thing' but in explanation Barnes wrote 'I consider that we ought to assist nature' going on to add that with the exception of plants such as 'balsams, chrysanthemums, pelargoniums, and plants of that description' he did not mix soil up beforehand. Rather, he handled and potted plants 'according to their constitution'. Citing New Holland (Australian) plants as an example, Barnes pointed out the foolishness of treating them as one simply because they came from the same geographical region. Rhetorically he asked 'do you not think it would appear ridiculous of me, if I were going to fresh pot my New Holland plants, if I were to say to one or more of my men, "Get so much heath mould, so much sand, so much loam, and mix all well together, for we will pot the New Holland plants to-day"; or to the boy, "Get the pots all ready crocked?" Do you think these plants would require all potting at the same time, and in the same soil? I think I hear you say, No. Some of these plants make their growth at a very different season from what others do; some are natives of high hills, others are natives of swamps and valleys; some grow amongst flints, stones, chalk, limestone, sandy places, loam, and rotten vegetable earth: therefore, do you not think I should be wrong in attempting to pot them all at one time, all in one mixture, because they all came from New Holland? Now this is precisely my system all through . . . which is, to take the opportunity of potting each plant at any season when it wants it, and not to return home and pot a house full of plants because I saw my neighbour do his yesterday.'⁹

CHARCOAL

One of Barnes' pet topics was his obsessive promotion of charcoal as a 'purifier of all things', using it widely as an essential component of potting compost and to 'sweeten' water. Of the introduction of charcoal into general use, Loudon enthusiastically wrote that it was a 'new and important feature, apparently of great importance, for which the horticultural world is indebted to Mr Barnes'. It was in his first letter to Loudon that he shared the secret of his discovery. It had been in 1829 or 1830 and when at Beulah Spa he had been 'rummaging about the woods for loamy mould'. He came across an area where charcoal burners had been working. Noticing how 'wonderfully strong' the plants in the vicinity were, he took a basketful of charcoal back to the garden and experimented with it 'amongst my cucumber soil. I found it improved them in strength and colour, so that I began to try it with other soft-growing plants; and thus I have continued using it, when I could succeed in getting it, with hundreds, I might say thousands, of plants under pot culture and with great success.' In his assertion that charcoal is a purifier he was absolutely correct – activated charcoal does adsorb particles to its surface, and that is why it is used in so many types of filter, including deodorising shoe inserts.[10]

CAPE HEATHS

Barnes also found the Cape Heaths to be in a particularly sorry state upon his arrival, but within three years they too had been rejuvenated. He applied his own method of revivication and potting to these notoriously difficult group of plants; the latter again inspired by the natural growing conditions of heaths. Accordingly, his compost mix imitated these, and rather than sifted soil he used 'stones, pebbles, knobbly flints, charcoal and a portion of sand, with sods of fibrous tough heath soil merely taking the hatchet and chopping off the furze, heath, bushes, &c., and giving the sod a chop or two'. In addition to this very free-draining compost, to keep the plants in peak condition Barnes ensured that they were placed in 'a healthy airy situation', watered with 'pure water' (using charcoal to purify it if necessary), 'syringed often on a fine morning' and always he kept the heath-house 'well washed and cleansed', assured of the fact that 'no plant that I am acquainted with enjoys cleanliness more than heaths do'. This collection was housed in the span-roofed Heath House, which was the same dimensions as the New Holland House. Barnes' list of 'a few' ericas inhabitants ran to ninety-eight species and cultivars. The quality of the plants and the success of his rejuvenation programme spoke for themselves. The one specimen of which Barnes was particularly proud was *Erica metulæflora*, which at 3½ft (1.07m) tall and with a spread of 10ft 2in (3.10m) put forth over 2,000 heads of flowers in 1842, but which, two years previously, had been 'as tall as I am, scraggy, naked-stemmed'. However, the prize specimen was *Erica massoni*, which received glowing praise from two head gardeners, James Cruickshank and Thomas Bray, who visited Barnes in August and October 1843 respectively. Cruickshank wrote of the heath, which measured 2½ft (0.76m) tall and with a spread of 8ft 7in (2.62m) that it was 'such a splendid specimen that I do not think there is the like of it ... in the United Kingdom', while Bray gushed that the 'extraordinary specimen (was) truly grand, with upwards of 300 heads of its beautiful wax-like flowers expanded. It is worth going any distance to see.'[11]

ORCHIDS

Collecting orchids was not only a highly addictive, but also a highly expensive pastime. Yet no self-respecting garden of the era was without them, and Bicton was no exception. The Orchideous (*sic*) and Stove House, built to the same dimensions and internal layout as the New Holland and Heath houses, was 'crowded with plants to overflowing'. Barnes offered a list of 150 stove plants and another of naming 'a few' of the orchids – 139 varieties from 46 genera. This latter collection, while not in the same league as the one being gathered at Chatsworth at the same time, was nonetheless a notable and valuable one. To put it into context, when Williams published his *The Orchid-Growers Manual* in 1852 he listed 'upwards of two hundred and sixty orchidaceous plants', thus to have well in excess of half the total a full decade before was no mean feat. Barnes again waxed lyrical on the benefits of charcoal added to the potting mixture, and somewhat smugly suggests that it 'does not require a quarter of the care and attention to cultivate the orchideous plants that many persons use'. Recognition of his 'natural' approach to plant care was made by *The Florist* in 1857, and about *Renanthera coccinea* in particular. This was a notoriously obstreperous orchid 'which seldom flowers under ordinary cultivation'. Barnes, however, had had great success with flowering it 'annually for many years ... we believe the secret of his success with this plant is in adhering to the laws of nature, by giving it seasons of growth, maturation, and rest with native regularity'.[12]

PALM HOUSE

The last of the ornamental glasshouses to be mentioned was also the earliest to be erected at Bicton in the nineteenth century, and was by far the most attractive. The Palm House, which stands just to the west of the Flower Garden walls, was built in *c.*1820 by W & D Bailey of Holborn, to whom Loudon had given his inventive principle of the curvilinear glasshouse, and it remains one of the most handsome extant glasshouses of the era. With its bulbous curves and overlapping panes of scalloped glass – over 18,000 in total – it is 58ft (17.68m) long, 34ft (10.36m) wide and 33ft (10.06m) high, and Barnes filled it with a wide collection of different tender specimens, many of which were especially large. All were grown in a compost composed of 'loam, charcoal, stones, and sand, with occasionally a little manured water'. In 1842, of particular note were the *Cycas revoluta*, a native of Japan and which boasted a head of 700 fruits, and a *Doryanthes excelsa* from Australia with a 16ft (4.88m) tall flowering spike. The aforementioned Bray, who was head gardener to E.B. Lousada of Peak House in nearby Sidmouth and regular visitor to Bicton, waxed lyrical about the 'noble and interesting plants' he observed during his tour of the Palm House, being particularly impressed by the four varieties of *Musa* (bananas) which were all in flower. For while Barnes noted the fruit was generally (but incorrectly) considered inedible, with his usual attention to detail he discovered that they were delicious if the fruit were left to ripen fully on the plant and were neither harvested nor eaten with a knife – for this spoilt the flavour.[13]

THE FLOWER GARDEN

With its walls cloaked with *Magnolia grandiflora exoniensis* (*Magnolia grandiflora* 'Exmouth') 'with hundreds of blossoms out daily', the Flower Garden, legend had it, was designed by André le Nôtre (see page 14). Barnes gave little information about the bedding displays, and only obliquely does he refer to the large numbers of plants that graced the beds cut in the lawn, noting that the pots in which the plants had been grown prior to bedding out, and before they were required again in spring, he used in the autumn months for growing his chrysanthemum cuttings. Thankfully, Fish writing in *The Cottage Gardener and Country Gentleman* in 1858 was more forthcoming.

At a time when the bedding craze was at its peak, with 'pastry cutter' beds carved out of lawns and made on terraces, and filled with flowering displays designed on the principle, the gaudier and more clashing the colour scheme, the better – Fish remarked that Barnes' Flower Garden 'was a pleasant change from the fashionable-grouped flower gardens'. Barnes' novel approach was to integrate 'little groups of bedding plants' between and around the collection of specimen trees and masses of shrubs. In spring, when many of the permanent residents bloomed (*Aloysia citridora, Magnolia fuscata* and masses of camellias caught the eye of 'O P' writing in 1857 in *The Florist*), the beds were filled with 'blooming bulbs, Primroses, Polyanthus. Violets, &c., and in summer with traditional tender bedding plants'. The effect, according to Fish, was most pleasing, for 'instead of blazes of colour, without a sufficiency of light and shade, there was a great variety of outline and form, arising from the naturally diversified mode of growth and foliage presented by the numerous trees and shrubs'.

With the walls providing additional shelter to what was already a naturally mild climate, Barnes was able to grow outside many trees and shrubs that would have required a greenhouse elsewhere in the country. His list of some of the many notable specimen trees and shrubs from around the world that studded the Flower Garden included collections of camellias, clematis, escallonias and rhododendrons. The gathering of the latter featured, amongst many others, flowering specimens of the Himalayan species *R. arboretum* (introduced in *c.*1810), and two introductions by the plant hunter George Don – *R. campanulatum* (1825) and *R. barbatum* (1829). From Australia and topping 22ft (6.71m), the *Leptospermum baccatum* was particularly impressive, as were the several large *Wisteria chinensis* (*Wisteria sinensis*), first introduced from China in 1816 by John Reeves. And from the Americas two notable conifers: at 25ft (7.62m) and no more than sixteen years old was a specimen Douglas fir, while originating from Chile was an 11ft (3.35m) *Araucaria imbricata* (*Araucaria araucana*). The latter must have been grown from the first batch of seed brought to Britain by Archibald Menzies in 1797, for it was not until 1844 that William Lobb re-introduced it in bulk when plant hunting for the Veitch and Son Nursery, based at nearby Exeter.[14]

AMERICAN GARDEN AND ROCKERY

The Rockery and adjacent American Garden were both begun in the 1830s by Glendinning and completed by Barnes, who was responsible for the planting and for adding the Shell House to the Rockery in 1845. One especially attractive design element of the Rockery was the way in which the water appeared out of the top of a centrally positioned pyramid of rocks and trickled down the edifice, giving the effect of a 'weeping pillar'. It was as practical as it was attractive, for a system of pipes and valves enabled Barnes to water the entire Rockery at once. Fish, who admired the water feature, called this a 'rock or block' garden and noted it was 'chiefly graced with Ferns, small Alpines and other fine-leaved plants'. Barnes himself was particularly proud of the berberis, ribes and *Cunninghamia sinensis* (*Cunninghamia lanceolata*) another early introduction from China, this time by William Kerr in 1804, while Fish commented on two bamboos – *Arundinaria falacta* and *A. Himalaya* (*sic*).

The Rockery plant collection was complemented by that in the American Garden. The original concept of the American Garden, which dated back to the second half of the eighteenth century, was an area dedicated to a geographically inspired collection of plants. However, since many North American plants were ericaceous, over time the definition of an American Garden had broadened to include this group of plants. Hence, the example at Bicton, which was at its peak between April and July, was filled with a diversity of acid-loving shrubs, nineteen sorts of *Magnolia* and thirty *Crataegus*, 'Ghent and other azaleas' and a 'rich collection of the rarest rhododendrons' most of which originated from the Nepalese Himalayas, and of which Barnes lists thirty-nine varieties 'and many others'. In a letter dated 11 February 1843 'W' of Exeter excitedly reported that the especially fine camellias and rhododendrons had flowered 'beautifully all the winter', and in the American Garden 'a large plant of *Rhododendron Nobleanum* . . . had on Christmas day above 200 heads of bloom fully expanded'. *Rhododendron Nobleanum* (*sic*) is now classified as *Rhododendron* Nobleanum Group, a hybrid of *R. arboreum* and *R. caucasicum* which was raised by Anthony Waterer of Knap Hill Nursery in *c*.1832.[15]

PINETUM AND ARBORETUM

According to Loudon, the wider ornamental grounds were laid out by William S. Gilpin, while Robert Glendinning created the lake and islands, which were home to a collection of 'all kinds of aquatic birds and fowls…which are never permitted to be shot'. When Barnes arrived, this area of the garden was already famed for its collection of 'noble trees' both native and foreign. Barnes was particularly impressed by a fine 'Lucombe oak 68ft [20.73m] tall and with a trunk circumference of 8ft 8in, [2.64m]' and the 'largest ash I ever saw, measuring 85ft [25.91m] high, 12ft [3.66m] in circumference'.

Loudon also asserted that the arboretum was made and maintained under the supervision of Veitch and Son 'who are taking all measures to have the plants correctly named, and all the blanks and deficiencies supplied'. He adds that trees were carefully planted 'on raised hills of prepared soil, and carefully staked and mulched, where . . . necessary', with 'six men constantly employed mowing the grass, and mulching the dug circles round the plants . . . destroying weeds as soon as they appear; and removing dead leaves, suckers from grafted plants, insects, decayed blossoms, &c.' The trees were arranged according to the 'Natural System, beginning near the house with the Clematideæ, and ending at the entrance to the walled flower-garden with the Juniperinæ'.[16]

A grass walk wound through the collection and was flanked with rhododendrons and other shrubs – Fish reported that Barnes confided to him that during one of his first years at Bicton he had planted more than 30,000 rhododendrons besides these paths. Loudon insisted 'Nothing can be more perfect than the style in which every part of this arboretum is kept'. Connected to the arboretum thus making it part of the tour was a menagerie 'containing a rich collection of birds, monkeys, and various other foreign animals'. By 1857 the extensive collection of Coniferæ in the pinetum, which eventually covered 36 acres (14.57 ha) and contained more than 3,000 taxa, had gained a national reputation for excellence, 'with many specimens of the rarer kinds . . . equalled by few in this country'. Indeed 'O P' writing in *The Florist* considered that 'the collection is one of the most complete we have witnessed, and for a lover of the family there is ample to repay the trouble of a long journey'.[17]

KITCHEN GARDEN

While Barnes' letters to Loudon make clear the pride and sense of achievement he feels in his accomplishments within the ornamental grounds, his emphasis is slanted towards the productive gardens, which suggests this was the aspect of his work from which he derived the most pleasure – perhaps not surprisingly, knowing his background. According to Robert Fish writing in 1858, the kitchen garden was 'to the lover of good culture, and to the young gardener . . . the most important feature at Bicton'. But as early as 1843, within four years of his arrival, Thomas Bray commented that 'from the mushroom to the pineapple, it far exceeds all that I have ever seen'; and according to 'W' the kitchen garden was looking wonderful, with:

> peach, apricot, and pear blossoms on the walls and within the glasshouses
> and pits there were excellent pine-apples here, and a good succession
> coming on. I think I never before saw such a show of pine-apples, at this
> season of the year, as are now coming on here. The peach-house presents a
> splendid assemblage of blossoms, and the fruit seemingly setting well. Mr
> Barnes' new potatoes are thoroughly ripe, and he has a good crop.
> Mushrooms, cucumbers, French beans, asparagus, &c., have been very
> abundant all through the winter, and still continue so [and] Mr Barnes has
> grapes as large as marrow fat peas.[18]

Such accounts by visitors, and a glance at Barnes' 'Vegetable, Fruit and Flower List' reveal just what a diversity of edible crops he produced in the kitchen gardens. Yet the list, while impressive in its diversity and quantities produced, tells nothing about how the crops were grown. Thankfully, though, in his series of articles for Loudon, Barnes lets the reader in on some of the secrets of his successes, and it is fascinating to see how, in an age when pesticides were rudimentary and the biology of plant nutrition not fully understood, a top head gardener produced crops of such calibre. In Barnes' own words we shall read how he cultivated some of his crops – see Appendix A for Barnes' tips on cultivating vegetables – but one of the elements that makes this personal account of his productive realm so interesting is the 'behind the scenes' detail.

BEHIND THE SCENES IN THE GARDEN

Barnes describes some of the realities and practicalities of what went on just over the wall from the beauties of the Flower Garden – the 'everyday' work carried out in the 'everyday' structures that was taken for granted and generally did not make it to the pages of the gardening press. Within the sanctum of the walled garden, Barnes' 'Back Sheds' comprised a shed running the whole length of the back of the Palm House, which acted as a store for large flower-pots and 'string stretched out going through the process of painting' – it was painted green to be less noticeable when used in the garden. Two store rooms contained baskets, hampers, flower-pots, wire, trellis, new tools, charcoal dust, bone dust and soot; and running along the back of the two vineries was a long, open shed filled with old sugar hogsheads, packing tubs and cement casks storing the different loams, heath- and leaf-mould, and different types of dungs and sands. The open sides were shelved to enable the 'drying and sweetening different soils on in the winter; as it faces the north it answers two purposes, first by sweetening the soil, then by keeping the snow from blowing all over the shed'. Finishing the collection of utilitarian buildings were a shed at the back of the stove in which tubs and boxes filled with 'pebbles of different sizes, broken stones, and broken potsherds of all sizes' were stored, the tool-shed and, of course, the potting shed.

In his first communiqué to Loudon, a sign perhaps of how important he considered it, Barnes talks at length about his potting bench, 'it being the manufactory of all the hothouse business; that is to say, sowing, propagating, and potting in all its stages, from the seedling to the mature plant'. The bench had a surface of Portland stone and was supported on walls of the same, which divided the space beneath into bins in which the separate sorts of 'mould or soil' were stored. Around the bench were the tools of this particular trade, and their diversity reveals how specific each potting task was – the exact combination of the ingredients dependent on the plant itself. On the bench were 'sods of heath mould and of different kinds of loam, leaf mould, &c.', while on the side benches were 'pots filled with four different sizes of pebbles, from the size of a grain of wheat to the size of the palm of the hand; four different sizes of broken freestone; four different sizes of charcoal (considering the pot of charcoal dust one of them); four different sorts of sand; two sorts of bone, one of half-inch size, the other of dust; four different sizes of broken pots for draining, potsherds of sizes for putting over the hole of any sized pot; a basket of moss, one of soot, and another of rotten cow-dung; a hammer, choppers for cutting sods of mould, &c., pincers, potting-sticks, sieves of different sizes; wire of sizes for making trellises of all kinds for training plants; flower-stakes of all sizes made by the men in wet weather, and painted green; green string of all sizes for tying and training plants, also painted by the men'.

Adjoining the potting shed Barnes had a small greenhouse which he called the propagating house. Within were nurtured the sown seeds and struck cuttings, together with the products of grafting and 'inarching'. Once again, Barnes employed charcoal in quantity in the compost mix – some cuttings and seeds being struck or sown 'wholly in charcoal'. An indication of Barnes' productivity was that from a stock of a 100 or so varieties of *Chrysanthemum*, he annually produced over 1,000 plants using a system that gave him four successions of plants and a flowering period from mid-October until the following February. For additional out-of-season flower colour he also produced winter-flowering pelargoniums, cinerarias, Guernsey lilies, camellias and *Primula sinensis*.[19]

Within the walled garden was the expected range of glasshouses, pits and frames and the open ground. Fish noted that at Bicton 'no forcing is done with fire heat', rather that the 'brick pits, for Melons, &c., (were) heated by linings, and these are boarded over for neatness'. In addition, Fish noted there were many wood pits, earth pits and turf pits 'in the outside slips, for protecting and forwarding all sorts of things' as well as 'a good number of frames, or boxes, set on dung beds . . . the safest and most economical, where a fair amount of fermenting material can be procured at first'.[20]

PINEAPPLE

In the eighteenth and nineteenth centuries the pineapple was considered the most delicious of all fruits, and a head gardener's reputation was directly proportional to his skill at cultivating it. The pineapple, which is native to tropical South America, was introduced into England from Barbados in 1657 and its cultivation was a subject that aroused much strong opinion, caused head gardeners no end of strife, and became a very popular topic for discussion in books and magazines. The famous painting by Danckerts, supposedly showing the Royal gardener John Rose presenting to Charles II the first pineapple cultivated in England, must have been painted between 1668, when the artist first arrived in England, and 1677 when Rose died. However, it is unlikely that this was a pineapple grown in Britain, although their successful culture was a matter of record by 1693, for on 14 October that year Tilleman Bobart (son of Jacob senior, the first Keeper of the Oxford Botanic Garden) penned a letter describing his visit to George London at Hampton Court Palace. Here Bobart was shown 'a very fine Ananas near Ripe in the stove which is to be presented to ye Queen in few dayes'.[21]

Philip Miller devoted two pages of his *dictionary* to the 'Ananas' and the eighteenth century's first great pineapple raiser was Henry Telende, head gardener to Sir Matthew Decker at Pembroke House on Richmond Green in London. Here, in 1722, according to John Macky, the garden contained 'stove-houses, which are always kept in an equal heat for his Citrons, and other Indian plants, with Gardeners brought from foreign Countries to manage them'. A Dutchman, Telende probably learned his pineapple cultivation technique from Piter de la Cour at Leiden Botanic Gardens – the latter certainly sent pineapple plants to Telende, who grew forty or so pineapple plants that regularly fruited. Telende's cultivation technique was described by Dr Bradley in his *General Treatise of Husbandry and Gardening* (1724), and like Barnes, a great part of his success was due to his sensitivity to the needs of plants. A five foot deep, brick-lined pit was filled with filled with a foot-thick layer of fresh horse dung, covered with a thicker layer of tanners bark. Pineapples were propagated by suckers or the crown of leaves, then once established the potted plants were transplanted into a succession house (a type of hotbed). From February to October, the pots were set into the pit which was covered with a glass frame; and if it was a very cold winter, to a hotbed within a stove house with glass walls and roof. Telende also ensured the water he gave his pines was the same temperature as the soil.

Later in the century Telende's cultivator's crown passed to William Speechly (1734?–1819) who trained at Milton Abbey (Dorset) and Castle Howard before becoming head gardener first to Sir William St Quintin at Harpham (Yorkshire) and subsequently the third Duke of Portland at Welbeck (Nottinghamshire). In the 1770s following a fact-finding trip to Holland, Speechly designed and erected the new pine and grape stove, which became so famous. In 1779 he published *Treatise on the culture of the pine apple and the management of the hot-house*, which together with his *A treatise on the culture of the vine, &c.* (1790) were the century's most significant publications on the cultivation of the century's most desired fruits and which provided benchmarks for subsequent cultural improvements. Several publications on pineapples appeared during the first half of the nineteenth century, but it was Barnes' contribution which rationalised the debate.

Barnes was arguably the nineteenth century's premier pineapple grower. In 1839 he took possession of a large pine-pit 'nearly the length of the orange-house', and in the 1840s, he regularly grew Queen pines 'weighing more than 2½ or 3lb' (1.13 to 1.36kg) which, when exhibited at the 'grand exhibition at Chiswick' were considered 'an enormous weight' and so unusual that one exhibit was stolen 'and found its way to Bow Street'. When Thomas Bray visited in October 1842 he commented in almost awed tones of Barnes' prowess as a pineapple cultivator, citing a mighty 'Queen Pine' of 6lb 2oz. (2.78 kg) in weight, a length of 11 inches (27.94 cm), and a circumference of 18 inches (45.72 cm, but adding 'these are not singular, nor any novelty here.' Barnes' record was 8 ¼ lbs (3.74 kg)![22] Yet, despite his promise to, and amid much anticipation by, readers, Barnes was not able to publish his advice in *The Gardener's Magazine*, for following Loudon's death, the periodical ceased publication in 1843. However, the man who had such success in this arena and rationalised pineapple cultivation did pass on his knowledge through 'The Pine Apple. Its Culture, Uses and History' (see page 191).

Barnes' new pine pit, which was in use by 1857, enabled him to provide and control all the essentials for growing pineapples – 'a thorough command of the root temperature [as well as an] abundance of light, heat, and ventilation'. It was 80ft (24.38m) in length and 16ft (4.88m) wide – sufficient to take seven rows of large plants, and being span-roofed, the plants were accessible on both sides. It was divided into four or five compartments which were provided with bottom heat from hot-water pipes, and the valve system enabled separate temperature control for each bay. The hot-water pipes were laid in a chamber covered by slates, and on top of the slates was placed about two feet depth of leaves, into which the potted plants were plunged. This technique avoided 'the fluctuating evil of the common leaf bed' and 'the injurious effects of lifting large plants in and out of the pits', while simultaneously saving a great deal of labour.[23]

GLASSHOUSE FRUIT

When he arrived at Bicton, the range of glasshouses restricted Barnes in what he knew he could achieve. In addition to two peach-houses with which Barnes was dissatisfied, believing that the trees were too far from the glass to fruit early, he had two vineries. This number was a great disappointment to Barnes, who was fonder of the 'beautiful vine' than any fruit plant, because, 'the kinder you treat it, the more it will do for you'. He wistfully wished there were more, for in his opinion such 'noble gardens' as Bicton should have had vineries 'from which grapes could be had every day in the year'. Grapes could also be a good money-maker, for a previous employer and from a £70 vinery Barnes had raised a crop that fetched 'more than 240 guineas' at market. Although he passed no further comment on his techniques, Barnes was recognised as a noted cultivator of the vine, a fact attested to by Thomas Bray who said of the vinery in 1842, that it 'far surpasses everything grown in the way of grapes'.

However, Barnes was as persistent as he was persuasive, and in about 1854 he was granted 'an excellent' new range of glass 244ft (74.37m) long by 20ft (6.10m) wide and about 12ft (3.66m) high at back and 5ft (1.52m) at the front. Because of the mild climate in that part of Devon, the range was unheated except for a couple of portable small stoves, and it was divided into three bays: vines and peach trees occupying either end, with figs in the centre.

Barnes had his own system of managing the peach trees: as soon as the fruit was gathered, they were carefully examined 'and any superfluous wood removed at once'. In addition, those trees which had made too strong growth received 'a severe root-pruning' and less severe pruning was meted out to 'less luxuriant' growers. Using this process, growth was 'effectively checked, and however strong is always well-matured. The consequence is that the trees are furnished with excellent bearing wood, without the least symptom of gum or canker, which are the results of over-growth, and the precursor of premature decay.'

The figs, which previously had been wall-grown outside, were planted against the back wall of the house and trained down the roof towards the front on a 'strong iron trellis' so that they were all above the head. The floor was pitched from side to side, and the roots were confined to about two feet in depth and little more than a yard in width. This technique provided a double crop as well as abundant 'standing room . . . for early Cauliflower, early Potatoes in pots, and moderately early Strawberries and French Beans'.[24]

PESTS AND DISEASES

Pests and diseases have always been a problem to gardeners, especially inside the frames, pits and greenhouses where the result of an infestation were as noxious as some of the so-called cures: bunches of grapes 'shanked, cankered, and mildewed', a 'house of fruiting pines . . . covered with scale and coccus of all kinds' or the stench of 'black and yellow sulphur, black soap, and many other fetid drugs'.

In France it had been recognised as early as 1809 that nicotine killed aphids and its use was developed both in the form of a smoke or a wash to control insects. Another French development, this time from the 1840s, was the application of lime sulphur as a fungicide to tackle grape vine powdery. Thus, when Barnes was writing he was working in a generally pre-efficacious pesticide era, for it was not until about 1850 two important natural insecticides were introduced. Rotenone is found naturally in the roots of the derris plant (a climbing leguminous species native to South East Asia), and pyrethrum in the flower heads of a species of *Chrysanthemum*. Not surprisingly, given Barnes' ability for meticulous observation and lateral deduction, much of his pest-control regime was based around the rigorous application of his principle that prevention is better than cure. Asserting 'dirtiness is the parent of all disease', he was a stickler for hygiene, ensuring that within the houses a strict regime was maintained; his 'grand secret' for prevention, to whit, 'to sweep, brush, and mop; to use pure water and pure soil, with a proper drainage'.

Barnes did not use 'blue vitriol in manured liquid to keep the smell away' nor 'poisonous drugs to kill vermin and cure diseases'. To remove 'vermin' from already-infected plants Barnes recommended syringing the plants with 'clean hot water from 140° to 150° Fahrenheit [60–65.5°C]'. A handful of moss was placed over the soil in the pot and covered with a circular cloth collar tied round the pot rim to prevent hot water reaching the soil and scorching the roots. The pot was placed at an angle propped between two bricks in a 'V' shape, and the syringing process repeated at intervals until the plan became 'clean and healthy'. If the plant was in 'a growing state' Barnes recommended the syringing be done outside so that the steam could escape and minimise the risk of scalding foliage. And it was not just the edibles that suffered. When he arrived, the collection of ericas was suffering a rampant infection of mildew. It was 1846 before it was discovered that a fungus *caused* disease rather than being the *effect* of another pathogen (this discovery was made about potato blight, which incidentally, Barnes was one of the first to describe). However, Barnes was absolutely correct in his succinct assertion that the circumstances that precipitated an outbreak of mildew were 'drought and poverty; dry at bottom, foggy and damp at top'. The cure? 'Sulphur dusted on them in a proper manner' and then proper cultivation in order to prevent another outbreak.[25]

OUTDOOR FRUIT

As well as forced in the range of glasshouses, peaches were also cultivated outside, the kitchen garden walls 'furnished with well-trained trees of nearly all the most approved varieties of Peaches, Pears, Plums, &c. The walks are also flanked by Pear trees, either as espalier or on circular trainers; this latter system of training Pear trees, of which the fruit keeps only a short time when ripe, is perhaps the most profitable that can be adopted, for by this means a greater number of trees can be grown in a given space; by making a judicious selection, a better supply of fruit can be obtained than would be from larger trees.'

Barnes also grew many types of apples, sometimes against the odds. In 1857 the orchard presented 'a striking contrast to those in the neighbourhood, and in fact to every one I have had an opportunity of seeing during the past summer'. It seems that that year had seen a particularly bad infestation of aphids but Barnes' home remedy, which he had practised 'for many seasons' had done the trick again. For three or four weeks from the time that the trees commenced to blossom, Barnes was in the habit of piling 'large quantities of combustible refuse; such as old saw-dust, weeds,

Vegetable, Fruit, and Flower List, for the Week ending Saturday Sept. 25. 1842.

Sept.	19	20	21	22	23	24	25
Mushrooms - dish	1				1		
French Beans -		1	1	1	1		1
Warwick Peas -			1				
Early Frame Peas				1			
Long Pod Beans -		1					
Windsor Beans -					1		
Cauliflowers -	1	1	1		1		1
Artichokes -				1			
Cape Broccoli -	1		1			1	1
Cabbage -	1	1	1	1	1	1	1
Greens or Coleworts					1		
Turnips -	1	1	1	1	1	1	1
Carrots -	1	1	1	1	1	1	1
Potatoes -	1	1	1	1	1	1	1
Vegetable Marrow -		1				1	
Spinach -			1		1		
Silver Beet -	1						
Cucumbers for Stewing - dish		3				5	
Peas -			1			
Lettuce -		1				1
Endive -			1			1
Red Cabbage -					1	
White Celery -		1			1	
Tomatoes -			1			
Horseradish - dish				1			1
Onions -	1	1	1	1	1	1	1
Shallots -		1			1	
Leeks -	1			1		
Garlic -			1			
Parsley, Curled, bun.	1	1	1	1	1	1	1
Sweet Marjoram -		1			1	
Sweet Basil -			1			1
Fennel -				1		
Tarragon -	1			1		
Green Mint -			1			
Chervil -	1	1		1	1	1	1
Sorrel -			1		1	
Winter Savory -	1					
Chives -				1		
Pennyroyal -				1		
Salad for Servants.							
Cucumbers - dish	1		1		1		1
Lettuce -	1	1	1	1	1	1	1
Radishes -		1		1		1	
Picklings.							
Gherkin Cucumbers				200			
Onions, silver-skinned - peck		1					
Red Cabbage doz.					1		
Capsicums -			200				
Chillies -				200			
Green Tomatoes doz.	6						
Ripe Tomatoes for Sauce - doz.				7			
Cut Flowers, basket	1			1			

Sept.	19	20	21	22	23	24	25
Dahlias - doz.	4			4			
Magnolia Flowers -	2			2			
Plants for baskets in front hall -	26			14			
Salad sent in for Table.							
Cucumbers - dish	1	1	1	1	1	1	1
Lettuce -	1	1	1	1	1	1	1
Radishes -	1	1	1	1	1	1	1
Celery -		1		1		1	
Endive -		1		1			
Red Beet -	1						
Mustard and Cress		1				1	
American Cress -				1			1
For Preserving.							
Orange Flowers qt.		10					
Magnolia Flow. doz.		3					
Figs - doz.				2			
Grapes - basket		1					
Guava Fruit - doz.			8				
Damsons - qt.		8					
Apples for Jelly, bush.				2			
Kitchen Fruit.							
Apples - peck	2			2			
Waste Peaches -		9					
Plums - qt.				1			
Cherries - lb.		1½					
Currants -	1			1			
Raspberries -	1				1		
Pears for stewing dz.		2					
Apples for roasting				2			
Table Fruit.							
Pine-apples							
Brown Sugar-loaf	1						
Queen -			1				
Otaheite -					1		
Cycas revolùta -	9				7		
Mùsa Cavendishii -		7		7	7		
Guava Fruit -		9		9			
Black Hamburg Grapes - lb.	1	1	1	1	1	1	1
Sweetwater, Dutch	1		1		1		
Muscat of Alexandria	1		1		1		
Peaches, Malta -	4		5		5		
Figs - dish	1	1	1	1	1	1	1
Cherries -	1		1		1		
Keen's seedl. Strawberries	1		1	1		1	
Red Currants -	1	1	1	1	1	1	1
White ditto -	1	1	1	1	1	1	1
Apples -	1	1	1	1	1	1	1
Pears -	1	1	1	1	1	1	1
Walnuts -	1	1	1	1	1	1	1
Melons -	1	10	1		1		
Impératrice Plums			1	1	1		
Ice -							

An example of Barnes' weekly list. The list informed both kitchen and employer what had been harvested, and provided Barnes with a reference source as well as a 'paper-trail' were he accused of not supplying certain items!

Taking full advantage of the gentle climate of south Devon, Barnes was able to grow fruits both outside and under glass using only minimal extra heat. Wall-grown fruit trees were trained to maximise cropping area. These are cordons.

tree-leaves, small sticks, &c.' at various spots in the orchard and letting the fires smoke away slowly. To repel another pest that wrought havoc – the gooseberry caterpillar, Barnes discovered that a mix of fresh, dry soot and wood ash applied when the weather was damp so that it adhered to the plants not only cured the pest problem but also cleansed fruit trees and bushes of moss and lichen.[26]

THE OPEN GROUND

While Fish was 'rather surprised' at the 'smallness' of the open ground, he was more than impressed at how Barnes remedied this potential drawback by his methods of 'close and rotation cropping'. It was noted in Chapter 1 that the mediæval system of cultivating the open space used raised beds with trenches between them, and Barnes used a variation of this, but without retaining the soil behind some sort of edging, which 'O.P.' writing in *The Florist* called a 'peculiar' system of working, but which Fish, having used a similar technique, could attest to its advantage.

Barnes divided most of the open ground into 'ridges, running north and south, 12ft [3.66m] wide at the base, and raised from fifteen to twenty-four inches [38.10 to 60.96cm] in the centre'. The ridges provided a protection to each side alternately, and since 'surface and rather deep-soil stirring are much insisted on' the wide ridges enabled the soil to be cultivated without treading the ground – the gardeners walked in the valley between the ridges. The advantages of this system were also evident to O.P., who recognised that for crops 'of Lettuce, Spinach, Onions, &c., that are expected to withstand the severity of the winter, the situation is much more favourable than the level surface would be; while the great depth of soil effectually prevents summer crops from suffering during dry weather'. The proof was in the growing, and O.P. was impressed with the ridges on which he had 'seen Cauliflowers, Cabbage, &c., planted so thickly that the surface was literally paved'.[27]

However, to sustain such intensive cultivation the soil had to be constantly maintained in peak condition, and here again Barnes had to start almost from scratch. When he arrived, he discovered that the kitchen garden that had been created on 'an artificial level . . .well supplied with water all the year round, from a beautiful stream which runs through it [and had been] formed at an immense expense, having thousands of loads of loam to make the borders, &c.' was in a pitiful state, and infested with weeds, slugs and snails, and other 'vermin'. Weeding he cured with his favourite tool – the goose-necked hoe together with proper soil cultivation, and eradicating slugs and snails he achieved using an approach as organic as it was effective. For six weeks and on a daily basis he deposited tablespoons of 'fresh grains from the brew house' every few feet, both 'inside and out', then, every evening Barnes patrolled the piles, dusting the molluscs, which had gathered 'like bees when swarmed', with fresh quick-lime. The corpses were gathered up the following morning and buried. To prevent further infestation he grubbed up the box hedges and edged the paths with cobbles set on end, which created, in Fish's opinion, 'very clean and comfortable' walks.[28] Soil improvement required drastic remedial measures. In the winter of 1842–43 Barnes brought in and trenched into the borders '500 cubic yards, equal to as many cart-loads, of marl and loam'. From then on, it was a continual and gradual process. Barnes made it a 'standing rule to return as much as possible of the refuse of vegetables back to the ground again, by trenching down cabbage leaves, broccoli stumps, pea haulm, and all such articles, in a green state. The benefit to the soil is great, and the saving of labour considerable; for I have seen much time lost in clearing a piece of ground of the vegetable rubbish on its surface, previously to trenching.' Yet, even nineteen years later, he was still improving. Fish reported that he increased the depth and fertility, by loosening 'more and more of the subsoil every year, and adding what fresh soil can be obtained from the neighbourhood, and the refuse from potting benches, &c.'[29]

TOOLS AND STAFF

We have seen in an earlier chapter how, upon his arrival, Barnes had to knock his staff into shape (see page 98); but he also had to educate them in some pretty rudimentary horticultural skills. But first he had to improve upon the poor collection of tools, the 'most paltry I ever met with', which amounted to 'a spade the length of my hand, and two long-handled spades, so worn that there was no fear of the men over-fatiguing themselves by lifting too great a weight; one two-pronged fork, with a broken handle; one old drain-hoe; and two old Dutch hoes'. Educating by example, Barnes just about succeeded with that revolutionary invention and modern marvel, the potato fork, but when it came to his crane-necked hoes (he had a set of varying sizes), he 'could not persuade any of them to use them, for . . . my hoes appeared to them the most ridiculous things imaginable.'[30]

From the illustration in *The Gardener's Magazine* ridiculous was certainly a word that could be used to describe Barnes' design for a besom used for 'sweeping up grass walks, &c.', which rather than the traditional conical shape was fan-shaped with a maximum width of 4ft (1.22m). Barnes called this a 'hen and chicken broom', the besom was composed of 'broomlets' of twigs wired together with brass wire with the 'broomlet' with the longest twigs in the middle. The brooms were made of three different lengths, depending on the weather and whether the work was light or hard. Given that Barnes did nothing without a good reason, we can assume that his odd-shaped sweeper worked effectively.[31]

ART. V. *Bicton Gardens, their Culture and Management, in a Series of Letters to the Conductor.* By JAMES BARNES, Gardener to the Right Honourable Lady Rolle.

(Continued from p. 436.)

LETTER XIX. *Crane-necked Short-handled Hoes.*

I NOW give you an account of the different uses I make of my little crane-necked hoes. (*fig.* 108.)

Nos. 1. and 2.,

Fig. 108. *Crane-necked Hoes.*

in *fig.* 109., I use for cutting and thinning out all kinds of vegetable crops to their final distance, such as carrots, early turnips, parsneps, onions, lettuce, &c.; and for stirring the surface amongst any growing crops, where there is not room for a larger hoe.

Nos. 3. and 4., in *fig.* 109., are for the same purpose, the first time of thinning; and for hoeing such crops as do not require to be made so thin, as well as among all kinds of plants that are pricked out, such as celery, cauliflowers, broccoli, cabbage, &c.

Nos. 5. and 6., in *fig.* 110., I use for all kinds of seed beds;

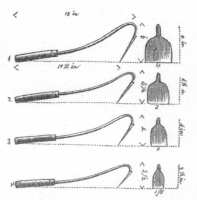

Fig. 109. *Elevations of Crane-necked Hoes.*

for radishes, carrots, &c., in frames and pits; for small seedlings just pricked out in frames, pits, under hand-glasses, or in hooped beds; amongst peas in rows, when they first come up; or any other small crop where there is not room for wider hoes, and the surface requires breaking. I make it a rule never to have any hand-weeding done, except in the gravel walks; as I am well convinced there is much mischief done by incautious and thoughtless people weeding amongst crops.

Nos. 7. and 8., in *fig.* 110., I use for stirring the surface of potted plants, seed-pans, &c. No. 8., with a sort of pointed

K K 2

Barnes' favourite tool – the crane-necked hoe – which he had forged in various sizes. This was just one of the topics about which he waxed lyrical in his letters to Loudon. These letters, published in The Gardener's Magazine, *provide an insight into the working life of Barnes of Bicton.*

Improving the soil, contents of the tool shed and skills levels of his staff were only prerequisites, for Barnes also insisted the soil be properly prepared for the sowing or transplanting of each crop. And, as his hygiene programme within the glasshouses helped prevent pest infestations, so Barnes was convinced that working the soil aided plant growth and prevented problems. Forking the soil 'on every frosty morning' not only 'sweetened and mellowed it', but also killed slugs and other insects. Likewise, once the plants were in and growing, Barnes' rule was 'hoe, fork, and stir the surface, at every opportunity, when it is in a proper state for performing these operations'. Hoeing increased water penetration of the soil, eradicated weeds and vermin, and by keeping the 'surface of the earth clean, open, and healthy ... vegetables profit in every way; they are clean, healthy, and of a finer flavour'. From this approach, he was convinced 'by long and close practice' there was more benefit to be derived 'by crops from keeping them well hoed, than there is from the manure applied'.[32]

CONCLUSION

After visiting Barnes in August 1843, a previously sceptical James Cruickshank, head gardener to Right Honourable the Earl of Lonsdale at Lowther Castle (Cumbria), was also unstinting in his praise. Having read Barnes' earlier articles he had to confess that his 'description of the plants, and his mode of treating them, seemed to some of us in the North not a little marvellous; or, at least, we put them down, as we do some of the advertisements of dahlias, as not to be depended on'. But having seen the gardens and plants at Bicton, Cruickshank had to confess 'in justice to Mr Barnes, that I never was so surprised and pleased in my life. There are not many places that a gardener can visit but what he may find fault with, or have reason to do so on careful examination; but I must say I carefully inspected the gardens at Bicton, and found every department in the highest state of cultivation, both as regards the crops, and the keeping and general management of the gardens and plants, which are such as, in my humble opinion, do Mr Barnes great credit.'

But let us leave the last words on this subject to the master himself: 'To sum up all in a few words, trench the ground and throw it into rough ridges immediately after any crop is done with; choose good and proper seasons for every crop, that is, the right season for putting it into the ground. Hoe and fork the ground at every opportunity; but never get trampling on it when in a very wet state, or it will soon become soured and unkind. By following the above method you will never be troubled much with slugs, snails, or any other sort of vermin, but have all vegetables sweet, clean, and wholesome.'[33]

EPILOGUE

The years of the twentieth century before the First World War are often viewed through rose-tinted spectacles. This was the last period of great wealth accumulation by the few, of great house and garden building, and weekend parties in the country. Yet between 1880 and 1900 there had been an agricultural depression and many landowners had been forced to sell; but simultaneously those involved with business were making fortunes in newspapers, tobacco, gold, shipping and other ventures in the City. By 1900 the *nouveaux riches* were gaining their peerages and entering the exclusive world of country house owner.[1]

Despite the relatively large number of country houses on the market as a result of the slump in land prices, demand from the new wealthy exceeded the supply, and many new country houses were built. In *The Last Country Houses* (1982) Clive Aslet includes 'A Catalogue of The Last Country Houses'. Of the 178 entries, ninety-six (that is, 54 per cent) were built or altered between 1900 and 1918.[2]

The garden and head gardener remained central to the rural idyll of the country house lifestyle, but by 1900 there was a debate raging about the future direction of garden design. This ill-tempered 'Battle of Styles' was fought out primarily between the architect Sir Reginald Blomfield (1856–1942), and the horticulturist William Robinson (1838–1935). The former championed the formal garden designed by the architect, the latter, an informal garden designed by the horticulturist. Neither gave ground, but both detested the High Victorian style epitomised by excessive formality and expansive bedding schemes, citing Paxton's garden for the Crystal Palace at Sydenham as the apogee of what was wrong with garden design. But from the fire of debate arose a new garden form which came to dominate – the Arts and Crafts vernacular based on a return to Englishness. This style was epitomised by the partnership between architect *and* gardener – (later Sir) Edwin Lutyens (1869–1944) and Gertrude Jekyll (1843–1932). Together they 'created a new English garden: inventively geometrical, using local materials in local ways, and filled with planting which was simultaneously disciplined and profuse ... Always it consulted the genius of the place and the character of the owners.'[3]

Yet, even for those who could not acquire the services of Lutyens and/ or Miss Jekyll, a garden and head gardener was considered an essential accoutrement during this period. In 1907, the Hon W.M. and Mrs Jervis had the services of Mr R. Northwood at Quarndon Hall near Derby. Here the gardens were 'not large' and nothing Northwood did was 'done on a large scale', but the head gardener emphasised in an interview with *Garden Life* in early 1907 that 'even if in small quantities' great store was laid on growing the 'newest varieties of plant, fruit and vegetables'. The ornamental gardens boasted four herbaceous borders, a collection of hybrid perpetuals and tea roses, a shrubbery, and some bedding – wallflower and *Arabis*, *Myosotis*, and double white *Arabis* and Cottage Maid Tulips in spring; various pelargoniums, fuchsias, white Marguerites and *Calceolaria* 'Golden Gem' in the summer. The conservatory, in which the flowers were changed twice a week, was filled with a fine show of camellias together with callas, cinerarias including the new Veitch variety 'Antique', crocus, daffodils, freesias primulas, tulips, *Euphorbia jacquiniæfolia*, *Genista fragrans* and *Salvia splendens*, hanging baskets of *Asparagus sprengeri* and *A. deflexus*. Many of the inhabitants of the conservatory, and the two hundred 'Roman Hyacinths' used to fill the bowls in the drawing room – the cut flower arrangements in the house being freshened daily, were forced in the single stove, also home to forced vegetables including tomatoes, sea kale, chicory, mustard and cress. The kitchen garden boasted violets raised in frames, an herbaceous border dedicated to cutting flowers, a peach house for nectarines and peaches and a vinery. In addition to the expected vegetables grown outdoors, there were wall and bush fruit – apples, cherries, currants, gooseberries, loganberries, pears, plums and raspberries.[4]

This was a typical example of what were often called 'lesser country houses', which could be rural, or as in this case, a large house on the very periphery of suburbia. Larger country houses were built, but one of the grandest expenditures on a garden – over £65,000 – was made by King Edward VII (1841–1910) who spent a decade devising not an elaborate ornamental garden, but revamping the walled vegetable gardens at Frogmore.

Then, on 4 August 1914, Britain declared war on Germany, and many gardeners laid down their spades to answer their country's call to arms.

Many were numbered amongst the 750,000 men killed in the ensuing fifty-one months until the armistice of 11 November 1918. Gardens need peace and stability to develop, and although victorious, Britain emerged from the war a very different country to the prosperous one that had entered it. The reverberations were felt hardest by the Edwardian wealthy, whose affluent and agreeable life had been shaken to the ground. Not only was there the psychological shock of the many casualties, but agricultural land prices slumped and taxes rose. A rich man paid 8 per cent income tax before the war, 33 per cent after, while death duties were introduced in 1919 at 40 per cent on estates over £2 million. Much private land was sold immediately post-war, with the largest disposal being the Duke of Rutland's sale of half his Belvoir estate, some 28,000 acres (11,331.6ha), for £1.5 million in 1920. By the end of 1921 the *Estates Gazette* estimated one quarter of England had changed hands since the end of the Great War.[5]

The country house garden was also irredeemably changed by the war. Not only had so much horticultural talent perished in the trenches, but this tragic loss was compounded by the privations of the inter-war years. The gardens' plight was highlighted by *Gardening Illustrated* in 1922 which lamented the fact that 'the most famous gardens of England, which were a national asset and a nation's pride, are more or less under eclipse owing to the abnormal economic conditions arising out of the war'. More specifically, 'the continued lack of labour and fuel had sounded the death knell for hot house gardening'. The most dramatic example of this was the Great Conservatory at Chatsworth, which was demolished in 1920, rising coal prices having forced the decision to allow the boilers to go cold in the winter of 1916. Ironically the demolition was supervised by Paxton's grandson, Charles Markham, and in his *The Covered Garden* (1962) Kenneth Lemon quotes a contemporary writer describing the sad end: 'I stood in the rain today, in a tree-girt enclosure, looking long and sadly at a dismal expanse of debris stretching away from my feet to where tall trees swayed down as if to hide the spectacle. Great iron pillars snapped in several places littered the ground. Thick baulks of timber, split and shivered, sprawled about. Over the turf was spread a glittering carpet of broken glass. . . Out of the litter two withered palm trees raised their forlorn heads. My companion, an old retainer, exclaimed, "A national calamity!" I agreed, for this vast heap of broken glass and metal was all that remained of the proud conservatory of Chatsworth.'[6]

Despite the hardships, some new country houses were built – the aforementioned catalogue lists thirty (17 per cent) built, restored or changed during the inter-war period. New gardens were also made – the Jekyll/Lutyens partnership undertook fourteen commissions between 1919 and 1928; but the First World War marked the end of the era of the head gardener.[7] There simply was not the manpower, money, nor the will to garden in the extravagant ways enjoyed by a world that had disappeared forever. Gone were the extensive, expensive and labour-intensive bedding displays, replaced by low-maintenance shrubberies filled with so many attractive flowering shrubs brought back from the Far East by plant hunters such as George Forrest, Frank Kingdon-Ward and Ernest Wilson. Mechanisation also reduced labour requirements, with the motorised lawn mower replacing its horse-pulled predecessor, and electrically powered hedge trimmers usurping shears as the tool with which to trim endless yew hedges. And most significantly, there was an unstoppable decline in the kitchen garden. Those at Frogmore continued to produce a minimal output, while the great range of glass at Waddesdon was demolished in the early 1970s. Today fourteen staff work in the gardens where just over a century ago more than 100 toiled.

Today's head gardener may not command the large workforce enjoyed by his or her predecessor, but then neither does he or she have to endure the privations of a long apprenticeship. Yet head gardeners do still suffer from relatively low pay – about £20,000 compared with an average national gross income of £32,600. Fortunately, though, this sum is considerably more than their counterparts received 150 years ago, for a £100 salary from 1850 was worth just £7,900 at 2006 values. The role of the head gardener has also changed, with the focus now on the ornamental grounds rather than the productive ones. It is far less expensive and less bother to buy orchids flown in from Thailand, carnations from Colombia, cucumbers from Kenya and pineapples from Hawai'i, than to grow them. But we all – professional gardeners and amateurs alike – owe the head gardeners of a previous era a debt of gratitude. For it was their work that gave physical form to the greatest age of garden development that Britain has ever enjoyed, and as such we continue to enjoy many fruits of their labours, be it visiting an historic garden made by them, growing plants bred by them, or reading the books and magazine articles written by them and wondering just how they achieved so much and so expertly.

Head gardeners of today, and those who served of old,
We duly salute you; may all our tribe flourish.

APPENDIX A

———◆◆◆◆———

James Barnes' tips on the cultivation of vegetables

ASPARAGUS

To Barnes asparagus was one of the 'most wholesome and delicious vegetables grown, but wonderfully abused'. Both asparagus and sea-kale needed
the ground to be well-prepared in autumn 'broken up to a considerable
depth' and well-manured, but in their case with the addition of some sea-
weed or salt worked into the ground, and the ground 'trenched . . . and laid
in rough ridges so that the air, sun, and frost can penetrate through it'.
Common salt, which in high concentrations is harmful to plants, was used
as a fertiliser in small quantities. His golden rule was 'never put in your
asparagus plants until April; when the young plants are grown or shot 2 or
3in [5.08 to 7.62cm] they always do best' or if sowing seed 'do so a month
earlier in drills 2ft. [0.61m] apart; which should also be the distance at
which to plant them; thinning out the plants sown from 12 in. to 18 in.
[30.48 to 45.72cm] apart in the drills; never putting more than two rows
of plants in each bed of 4 ft. [1.22m]; and leaving from 2 ½ft. to 3ft. [0.76
to 0.91m] alley, which is essential'. Barnes did not agree with the commercial practice of earthing up the beds in order to produce 'long, tough, hard
stalks' for market. Rather, he always found that 'noblemen and gentlemen's
families are most fond of asparagus in its natural beautiful green colour,
and just long enough for the cook to tie into a bunch'.[1]

BEANS

To produce early crops of beans, 'which every practical man knows, like a
good holding loam', Barnes sowed in 'pans, frames, vineries, peach-houses,
&c., and then planted out into rows a minimum of 3 feet [0.91m] apart in

a warm border or on the sides of ridges or sloping banks'. His favoured early bean was Mazagan, succeeded by Wonder Long Pod and Windsor Broad Bean. To improve the crop quality, and succession, Barnes cut off every alternate row just as they came into bloom, and to deal with the 'black dolphin' (black bean aphid) which he considered the worst enemy of beans, he sprayed using a 'garden engine and soap-suds'.[2]

CABBAGE

The 'most useful of all vegetables . . . both for man and beast' was the cabbage, of which Barnes had grown 'every new sort I have ever heard of'. His favourites 'for quickness, beauty, and good flavour, growing close to the ground, and having no waste loose leaves to encumber them' were Matchless, Nonpareil and East Ham Cabbage. Nonpareil is the earliest by two to three weeks, East Ham is the largest, and Matchless is the smallest, but of a very fine dark green colour for cooking.

Beginning around 25 July, seed was sown once a month throughout the summer on soil where onions had been previously raised, and which had been manured, trenched and 'laid up in ridges, as rough as possible; and at about every 12 or 14 feet [3.66 to 4.27m] a sloping bank is cast up, by throwing two trenches into one, which breaks the cold winds from the cabbages, and supplies fine places for winter endive, brown Cos lettuce, cabbage lettuce, cauliflower, late cabbage plants for spring planting, and many other things'. The seedlings were pricked out to 3in and then 6in (7.62 to 15.24cm) spacings 'which makes them strong and short-legged'. 'It is my usual practice to grow them on the piece of ground the onions have been raised in. As soon as possible after these have been cleared off, the lying dry and healthy, and, when carefully done, having a very neat appearance'. Spring cabbage Barnes pricked out on to his cucumber ridge which was 100ft (30.48m) in length, and 'when forked down about 8 ft. (2.44m) wide, all of good fresh earth from the frames, and waste soil from the potting-shed, which I always save'. He made two sowings of Winter broccoli, the first in the middle of April, and the second a month later. The seedlings he pricked out early, to 'get them strong' and then transplanted them in rows either side of each row of peas.[3]

CARROTS

After a long discussion about the unwillingness of Devon farmers to change, and berating them for not growing carrots as a field crop on what Barnes recognised as the best soil he had ever seen for carrot cultivation – a beautiful sandy loam – he briefly stated that the 'best sort of carrot for colour, length, and general crop is the Surrey and the Horn for forming and all early purposes'. For a general crop he never sowed before the end of March, in drills a foot (30.48cm) apart.[4]

CAULIFLOWER

Barnes never sowed cauliflowers before 18 to 25 September, and then 'sowing the seed in boxes, frames, or pans, close to the glass. The last of my late cauliflowers I sow about the 15th October, in pans in a little bottom heat'. Pricked out into thumb pots, which earlier in the year were used for the tender annuals for the flower garden, the young plants were then 'shifted on in some old melon mould until February, when the plants are become very strong'. As a rule Barnes transplanted cauliflowers into the first-cleared celery ground, which was trenched ridged, and manured 'for the purpose of placing hand-glasses for the first crop'. If the soil was wet and cold, Barnes aided his cauliflowers along by digging a shallow trench where the glasses were to go and placing 'a small quantity of dry dusty mould, old dry mushroom bed, or such like' where each plant was to be transplanted. With four plants under each glass 'keeping them well aired at all suitable times' his cauliflowers grew 'remarkably free, let the weather be what it may'. Dry weather in March meant an application of manure water 'which well repays the trouble, for they will grow through the cold March winds like as in May' and 'fine Cauliflowers' he always had by early April.

Cauliflowers could also be forced by early March if grown in pots in a vinery 'that is just put to work, or a peach house' a technique that was particularly useful for the gardener, the crop ripening 'before the spring vegetation begins to do much, and the winter stock is getting exhausted'. By sowing 'a pinch' of cauliflower seed every 20 days from the first week in January until 15 October, and using a combination of outdoor and protected cropping techniques, Barnes was able to harvest cauliflowers every day between 15 April and 21 November 1842.[5]

CELERY

That 'most wholesome' celery was 'subject to mismanagement to a great degree' particularly because it was 'generally sown too early'. However, the thirteen rows of celery grown at Bicton was child's play compared with the '13 acres [5.26 ha] . . . I have cultivated in one garden during one season' with up to three crops on the same piece of land. Nonetheless, to achieve a top-quality crop, Barnes asserted that main crops should never 'by any means be sown sooner than the first or second week in April, and then on a very slight hotbed, covering a part of the bed with a light or hand-glasses, by which means you get plants of two different ages; taking care to sprinkle your beds and plants, when up, with water a little warmed'.

At the two-leaf stage, Barnes recommended some seedlings be pricked out 'very carefully on another slight hotbed' and if 'extra large' celery were required, then two more pricking-outs were required at 16 or 18 day intervals, all the time keeping the plants well watered and hoed. Not leaving more than '10 days or a fortnight' after the third pricking out, the seedlings were to be transplanted into the 2ft (0.61m) wide manured trenches and at 10 to 12in (25.40 to 30.48cm) for between the seedlings spacing normal-sized celery and 12 to 15in (30.48 to 38.10cm) for 'extra large'. But transplanting had to be done carefully, 'with great care, with a trowel, with all the earth which will adhere to the plants' and so that the plants were not 'thrust . . . down into the cold gravelly or sandy subsoil beneath', and that 'the collar and seed leaves' were always left above ground level 'for I would sooner see half of the roots exposed, than the eighth part of an inch of the heart buried'.

Earthing up too early was another common mistake in Barnes' eyes, and to avoid damaging the plants he recommended that instead of 'muddling it about with earth ten or twelve times, once or twice, or at most three times, earthing is quite sufficient to bring it to proper perfection'. Water, of which 'every body knows that celery is fond' was to be applied plentifully, 'likewise of manure liquid: but in hot weather never water it over-head with a rose on your watering-pot; but pour abundance about the roots out of the spout, with a brushy stick put into the spout . . . so as to cause the water to come out more gently, and not wash out the roots'. For insect and rust control Barnes had the highest opinion of 'soot dusted all over the plants when the leaves are moist, so that it will adhere'.[6]

CUCUMBERS

Barnes' early career had clearly left a lasting impression on him, for he remained 'particularly fond of growing' cucumbers, but added that 'I believe there is no one thing in the whole practice of gardening that has caused more contention amongst gardeners of all classes than cucumber-growing; neither do I believe there is anyone thing that has had more treatises written on it'. On this latter point he was, for once, somewhat misinformed. As a market gardener Barnes had harvested cucumbers in January, but this was no innovation. The interest in raising early cucumbers had grown throughout the eighteenth century. Samuel Collins' *Paradise retriev'd* (1717) contains 'A treatise of melons and cucumbers' which provides instructions for those 'whose pardonable ambition it is to have their fruits earlier than their neighbours'. A year later Richard Bradley in the third part of his *New improvements of planting and gardening*, offered recommendation for producing cucumbers 'about Christmas', and the skilled Thomas Fowler, head gardener at Stoke-Newington (Middlesex) was able, on New Year's Day 1722, to present his employer Sir Nathaniel Gould with 'a brace of cucumbers well grown'. One of the great eighteenth-century innovators in the field of cucumber culture as well as pit design was James MacPhail (see page 43). Yet, in spite of the cucumber's popularity – it was mentioned by all the influential writers of the century – no book entirely devoted to its culture appeared during the eighteenth century.[7]

John Rogers' *Vegetable Cultivator* appeared in 1839 and relied for much of its information on MacPhail, so given Barnes' success as a cucumber cultivator and breeder, his account, which appeared four years later, must have generated much interest. Barnes produced cucumbers year round using a combination of forcing and greenhouse-growing. In both cases, though, seeds of 'some good variety' were sown in charcoal dust or 'light, purified, sweet earth', plunging the pot in which they are sown 'in a kind, wholesome, sweet, heat'. As soon as the seedlings emerged he transplanted them singly into 'small 60-sized pots, taking care to use wholesome sweet earth, and place them as near the glass as possible'. There followed a process of stopping (pinching out) and potting on. Pinching first happened once the seedlings were forming their second 'rough leaf', when they were potted on into '48-sized pots, leaving one third of the pot not filled with earth, to fill up as the plants advance'. Then, when the plants had made 'another joint' they were stopped again and potted into '24-sized pots'. Autumn-grown cucumbers were now left to grow to 'three joints before stopping them again'. For their third potting-on, planning was the key. Barnes brought compost into the greenhouse a few days before transplanting so that the plants' roots would not be shocked by being inserted into cold compost. Grown in large pots or tubs, the cucumbers were trained 'up a neat wire trellising, or painted string trellis, which I prefer myself . . . and were stopped the plants at every joint after turning them out, as long as they are kept growing'.

Barnes' hotbeds

To force early cucumbers, Barnes preferred a 'good frame to any pit except it be a pit on a good construction, worked with hot water, with a nice light trellis to train the plants on, and to keep the fruit from the earth.' The depth of his ideal frame was 2½ to 3ft (0.76 to 0.91m) at the back and sloping to 6in (15.24cm) shallower at the front, noting that such a frame could always be elevated 'to any degree one could wish for, according to the season of the year'. The hotbed which the frame was to cover was built to Barnes' own specifications. Made from 'dung or other fermenting material well prepared and sweetened' and utilising 'faggots prunings, or some kind of refuse' to provide good drainage from the base, Barnes' hotbeds were never 'more than 2 ft. 6 in. [0.76m] in height (2 ft. is about my measure)'. He considered those gardeners who made hotbeds of 'strong hot stable dung' up to 5½ft (1.68m) high, were simply putting themselves and their employers to what he considered unnecessary trouble and unnecessary expense. As soon as the heat began to rise off the hotbed Barnes decontaminated it by watering with boiling water in order to kill 'every living insect therein'. A few days later the hotbed was covered with 'well-prepared pulverised soil' – ideally a mixture of 'the top spit from an old pasture that is loamy and full of fibre laid together for one year . . . some sweet, mellow, well-prepared rotten dung, and a little charcoal dust'. Barnes always put 'a good ridge through the centre of the frame at once' to the depth of 18 or 20in (45.72 to 50.80cm) taking care to make use of it in as rough a state as possible', and planted one cucumber per light – every 4ft (1.22m) or so. Barnes also 'lined' the outside of the frame to 'the very top' with the same fermenting material, covering it with some dried hay or similar and encasing it within boards for tidiness-sake. Barnes was adamant that this side heat 'penetrating through the frame' was crucial to his successful cultivation, and using this technique his hotbeds worked 'regularly and kindly for a long time', and the frames were never 'troubled with foul steam, damps or burning, which the old strong-bed system is always subject to'.

Within the frame, the aim was to maintain the temperature at between 65°F and 72°F (18–22°C) in the 'first part of their growth, and for swelling the fruit kindly' to raise the temperature to between 72°F and 80°F (22–26°C). Watering was done with slightly warmed water which was poured onto the rough soil 'never . . . over-head', supplemented with the occasional application of manure water. This was a mix of ¼lb (0.11kg) of sodium nitrate dissolved in a hogshead barrel (52½ gallons or 238.66 litres) of tolerably strong cow-dung water – Barnes always took the precaution when using manure water in the glasshouses that he added a few gallons of hot water to make it a little warm.

The frames and lights were kept clean, the cucumbers given 'air freely every day', and in the afternoons when Barnes closed the lights, he also poured warm water around the frames in order to raise 'a nice genial steam and is the means of keeping down wood-lice and other vermin, which delight in drought, foul smells, burned, fusty, bad-worked, fermenting materials'. Using this method, Barnes was adamant that cucumbers would produce 'good fruit in abundance for many months'; and he had no time for those gardeners who complained about failures, for he stated unequivocally that 'no man can produce good cucumbers at an early season without some attention. Merely keeping his hands in his pockets, or boasting over a pot of ale, will not produce them. I have never yet seen an indolent man that could grow them.' When Fish visited in 1858 Barnes was still using this technique, which he enthusiastically noted he had himself used 'many years ago and could get Melons, &c., as easily by it as with a hot-water apparatus.' Perhaps wanting to gild his own reputation a mite Fish added 'I was rather proud to find, that, without previously knowing it, our practice at that time coincided with that now, and I suppose then, adopted at Bicton.'[8]

MUSHROOMS

Behind both the Heath and New Holland houses (and thus facing north) were the mushroom houses. From experience Barnes could claim that there was no vegetable 'so sought after in a nobleman's or gentleman's kitchen as the mushroom; as I once heard a French man-cook say, "de mushroom is de very life and soul of de kitchen"'. Barnes stated that the principle behind growing the fungus was straightforward, and so, from his description it appeared. However, the expert always makes the difficult appear easy, and even were Barnes' instructions followed to the letter, to produce a crop of mushrooms was no mean feat.

To achieve success with mushrooms, as with all his gardening operations, Barnes emphasised proper preparation and planning, and a high standard of hygiene. The best mushroom spawn Barnes asserted was to be collected from the wild, for preference an 'old pasture or mill-track' for 'nature produces the greatest abundance of mushrooms . . . where the ground has not been disturbed for some time'. Making a mushroom bed could be done all year round, but preparing the spawn was an autumn job. This was done by mixing well together four parts of an equal mix of horse and cow manure to one part 'good maiden loam'. This was to be chopped and beaten and trodden 'just as a potter does his clay for making pots', wetted to a consistence of mortar, laid out 3in (7.62cm) thick over a flat surface in a spot sheltered from the rain, and after two days of drying, cut into blocks the size of a brick. Taken into the mushroom house, the bricks were staked with some wild-gathered spawn laid 'between every alternate row'. The pile was covered with 'litter' – a mix of hay and straw, and taking care to ensure the pile did not get too hot, it was left for thirty-five or forty days to allow the fungal hyphae to grow through the bricks to form the mycelium. If kept in a dry place and 'without a draught' the bricks had a long shelf-life – the oldest Barnes had used to achieve a successful crop were bricks eight-and-a-half-years-old.

A mushroom bed was made by mixing together 'dung fresh from the stable, litter and all together' and 'good heavy loam . . . enough to keep the dung from heating or fermenting to any extent, and so that it may be altogether of one congenial warmth and moisture'. The mix was left to stand in the mushroom house for about a fortnight and then inoculated using the bricks, which were placed 'in the bed shallow, just covered' and the bed was left for a further week to ten days before it was 'cased'. This involved covering the bed with 'about three inches of good stiff holding loam' which was beaten 'as firmly as possible down on the bed'. Left for another week, the bed was again beaten 'well . . . with the back of a spade' then lightly covered 'with hay, litter, and straw mixed together'. This covering was removed after twenty or twenty-five days, and the bed examined. If dry, a 'stake or broom-handle' was to be used to make a row 'of good-sized holes, all up the centre of the bed' into each of which was poured 'two or three quarts' of boiling water, 'stopping the heat and steam in immediately with a whisk of mulching dung to retain the evaporation'. This technique moistened the bed and caused 'nice congenial warmth'. Barnes also made it a rule to water the casing of the bed with boiling water from a can with a rose on it, repeating both the watering processes two or three times 'allowing three days to intervene between each time, according to the state of the bed'. This, he assured not only provided warmth and destroyed 'every slug, wood-louse, or any other kind of insect whatever that is about', but also sweetened the bed 'to such a degree that mushrooms thrust themselves up through it of a firm good quality all over the bed'. Barnes cautioned never to water once the mushrooms were growing, and stated that using this technique he had made beds that 'produced mushrooms of the first quality in great abundance for four, five, or six months, picking them constantly two or three times a week'.[9]

ONION

To Barnes, the onion was 'one of the most wholesome and useful of all vegetables'. For an early sowing Barnes knew no better than Two-Bladed, for pickling he recommended Silver-Skinned and for 'general purposes throughout the year, than the Deptford, Reading, New White Globe, and Old Brown Globe, or James's Keeping'. Seed was sown in the drills a foot (30.48cm) apart on soil well-prepared the previous winter with 'manure, charcoal dust, bone-dust, or well-pulverised night-soil', and subsequently knocked down into a seed bed 'choosing a fine day to level down'. Dismissing the old wives tale that onions must be sown 'on Valentine's day, because you heard your grandfather say that he had always done so, let the wind blow whichever way it might' Barnes recommends 'any time between the 1st and 20th of March' and being wholly pragmatic and practical, adds 'and even then, if your ground is not in thoroughly good condition, defer it for another week'.[10]

PEAS

Barnes sowed his first crop of peas – he favoured Warwick – in the bottom of 'sloping banks the first week in December'. This crop he sowed in soil which was deliberately left 'rather poor', a technique that he discovered made them 'quicker'. Another technique, 'stopping them just as they begin to come into bloom', he used in order to cause them to set 'all together and quickly'. All other crops were sown in soil well trenched and manured the previous winter, and for succession he sowed 'the Frame pea, and a few Charlton; and for general summer crops the Scimitar Blue, New Green Marrow, Milford's Marrow, which is a fine pea, and Knight's Tall Marrow, the best-flavoured and most useful of all peas'.[11]

The seed was sown or panned 3in (7.62cm) apart, which caused the seedlings to 'grow up very weak, and continue so for some time; but as the season advances they gain strength wonderfully'. In order to get the peas to branch out – he managed to grow Knight's Tall Marrow to 16ft (4.88m) 'kept up with poles and ropes' – Barnes stopped the peas when 2ft (0.61m) tall, again when 4 or 5ft (1.22 to 1.52m) high, and up to twice more 'according to their strength'. This way he achieved rows with a thickness of 3 to 4ft (0.91 to 1.22m). To hold back a crop he would simply disbud it. In this way he could harvest peas 'to serve the table every day' from July to September, and produce a crop of a quality that 'I have never heard a single person say but that they were the best-flavoured of all peas'.

POTATOES

To grow good potatoes outdoors (Barnes also forced them in a variety of ways indoors) he stated that in autumn the ground should be 'well broken up ... and laid as rough as it can possibly be made, for the sun, wind, and frost to penetrate through it. Any good stable-dung, cow-dung, dung from the pigsties, or any other good manure, will grow potatoes well, if the ground is only properly prepared, and thoroughly sweetened with the atmosphere'.

Hand-in-glove with proper soil preparation was to use good stock, in this case seed potatoes. These he insisted be of 'middling-size, from the size of a pigeon's egg to that of a bantam's', and most importantly they had to be 'ripe'. To ensure their potency, Barnes had them 'exposed to the sun and air to harden' as soon as they had been lifted and sorted and then stored 'in lofts or on shelves, or in places where they will neither grow nor get heated'. Lastly, they had to be planted at the right time, 'all in between the middle of March and the last week in April'.[12]

BIBLIOGRAPHY

Contemporary sources

PERIODICALS

The Cottage Gardener continued as *The Journal of Horticulture*
The Florist
The Floricultural Cabinet continued as *Gardener's Weekly Magazine*
The Gardener's Magazine
The Gardeners' Chronicle
The Horticultural Directory
Paxton's Magazine of Botany

BOOKS

Abercrombie, J. *The Gardener's Pocket Dictionary, &c.* (1786)

Barron, W. *The British Winter Garden* (1852)

Burbidge, F. W. *Domestic Floriculture* (1874)

Fleming, J. *Spring and Winter Gardening* (1864)

Hill, T. *The Gardeners Labyrinth* (1608)

Keane, W. *The Young Gardener's Educator* (1861)

Kemp, E. *How to Lay Out a Small Garden* (1850)

London, G. & Wise H., *The Retir'd Gard'ner* (2nd edn, 1717)

Loudon, J. C. *Encyclopædia of Gardening* (2nd edn, 1824)

Loudon, J. C. *Self-instruction for Young Gardeners* (1845)

MacPhail, J. *A treatise on the culture of the cucumber* (1794)

Mawe, T. & Abercrombie, J. *Every Man his own Gardener* (1767)

McIntosh, C. *The Practical Gardener and Modern Horticulturist* (2 vols, 1827–28)

McIntosh, C. *The Flower Garden* (1838)

McIntosh, C. *The Greenhouse, Hot House and Stove* (1838)

McIntosh, C. *The Orchard and Fruit Garden* (1839)

McIntosh, C. *The Book of the Garden* (2 vols, 1853 & 1855)

Meagre, L. *The Compleat English Gardner* (11th edn, 1710)

Miller, P. *The gardener's dictionary* (1731, 1756, 1768)

Parkinson, J *Paradisi in Sole Paradisus Terrestris* (1629, reprint 1904)

Rogers, J. *Vegetable Cultivator* (1839)

Stevenson, H. *The Gentleman Gard'ner's Director* (1744)

Sweet, R. *The Hothouse & Greenhouse Manual* (1825)

Switzer, S. *The Nobleman, Gentleman, and Gardener's Recreation* (1715)

Thompson, R. *The Gardener's Assistant* (1859)

Thomson, D. *Handy Book of the Flower Garden* (1868)

Thomson, D. *Fruit Culture under Glass* (1881)

Williams, B.S. *The Orchid-Growers Manual* (1852 & 6th edn, 1885)

Williams, B.S. *Select Ferns and Lycopods* (1868 & 2nd edn, 1873)

Williams, B S. *Choice Stove and Greenhouse Plants* (1873, 1876 & 3rd edn, 1883)

Modern historical sources

Anthony, J. *Joseph Paxton*, Shire Books, Princes Risborough, reprint 1992.

Bisgrove, R. *The National Trust Book of the English Garden,* Viking Books, London, 1990.

Blacker, M.R. *Flora Domestica. A History of Flower Arranging 1500–1930,* National Trust, 2000.

Briggs, A. *A Social History of England,* Book Club Associates, London, 1984.

Campbell, S. *Charleston Kedding, A History of Kitchen Gardening,* Ebury Press, London, 1996.

Campbell-Culver, M. *The Origin of Plants,* Headline, London, 2001.

Elliott, B. *Victorian Garden,* B T Batsford, London, 1986.

Hadfield, M. *A History of British Gardening,* Spring Books, 1969.

Harvey, J. *Mediæval Gardens,* B T Batsford, London, 1981.

Henrey, B. *British Botanical and Horticultural Literature before 1800,* Oxford University Press. Vols I–III, 1975.

Hobhouse, P. *The Story of Gardening,* Dorling Kindersley, London, 2002.

Jacques, D & van der Hotst, A.J. *The Gardens of William and Mary,* Christopher Helm, Bromley, 1988.

Jellicoe, G. et al. *The Oxford Companion to Gardens,* Oxford University Press, 1986.

le Rougetel, H. *The Chelsea Gardener Philip Miller 1691–1771,* The British Museum (Natural History), London, 1990.

Leith-Ross, P. *John Tradescants,* Peter Owen, London, 1984.

Lyte, C. *The Kitchen Garden,* The Oxford Illustrated Press, Sparkford, 1984.

Morgan, J. & Richards, A. *A Paradise out of a Common Field,* Century, London, 1990.

Musgrave. T. *Innovation and the Development of the British Garden 1919–39,* unpublished PhD thesis.

Musgrave, T., Gardner, C. & Musgrave, W. *The Plant Hunters,* Ward Lock, London, 1998.

Paston-Williams, S. *The Art of Dining,* National Trust, London, 1995.

Potter, J. *Strange Blooms: The Curious Lives and Adventures of John Tradescants,* Atlantic Books, London, 2006.

Roach, F.A. *Cultivated Fruits of Britain,* Basil Blackwell, Oxford, 1985.

Roberts, J. *A Royal Landscape,* Yale University Press, London, 1997.

Strong, R. *The Renaissance Garden in England,* Thames & Hudson, London, 1979.

Stroud, D. *Capability Brown,* Faber & Faber, London, 1984.

Stuart, D. *The Garden Triumphant,* Harper & Row, New York, 1988.

Turner, R. *Capability Brown and the Eighteenth Century English Landscape,* Phillimore, Chichester, 1999, 2nd edn.

Wilson, C.A. (ed.) *The Country House Kitchen Garden 1600–1950,* Sutton Publishing, Stroud, 2003.

Woods, M. & Warren, A. *Glasshouses,* Aurum Press, London, reprint 1990.

NOTES

INTRODUCTION

1. Harvey, J. *Early Nurserymen*, Phillimore, London, 1974, p.1
2. Barnes, M. *Root and Branch: the History of the Worshipful Company of Gardeners,* The Worshipful Company of Gardeners, London, 1994, pp.30–1
3. Harvey, p.1

CHAPTER I

1. Henrey, B. *British Botanical and Horticultural Literature before 1800*, Oxford University Press, 1975, vol I, p.71
2. Henrey, vol I, p.57
3. Hill, T. *The Gardeners Labyrinth,* H Bynneman, London, 4th ed 1608, p.1.
4. Lyte, C. *The Kitchen Garden*, Oxford Illustrated Press, Oxford, 1984, p.30
5. Harvey, J. *Early Nurserymen*, Phillimore, London, 1974, p.27
6. Roach, F.A. *Cultivated Fruits of Britain,*. Basil Blackwell, Oxford, 1985, p.29
7. Harvey, p.28
8. Welch, C. *The History of the Gardeners Company,* London, 2nd ed, 1900, p.21
9. Campbell-Culver, M. *The Origin of Plants*, Headline, London, 2001, pp.117–119 & 145–47
10 Henrey, vol I, p.200
11. Henrey, vol I, p.144
12. Harvey, p.54
13. Henrey, vol I, p.181
14 Henrey, vol I, p.189

CHAPTER 2

1. Turner, R. *Capability Brown and the Eighteenth Century English Landscape*, Phillimore, Chichester, 1999, 2nd ed, p.15
2. London, G. & Wise, H. *The Retir'd Gard'ner*, Joseph Carpenter, London 2nd ed, 1717, pp.8–9

3. Stevenson, H. *The Gentleman Gard'ner's Director,* S Austen, London, 2nd ed, 1744, pp.115–17
4. Stevenson, pp.115–16
5. London & Wise, pp.48–51
6. Stevenson, pp.118–19
7. www.apothecaries.org.uk
8. le Rougetel, H. *The Chelsea Gardener Philip Miller 1691–1771,* The British Museum (Natural History), London, 1990, pp.156–60
9. Woods, M & Warren, A. *Glasshouses,* Aurum Press, London, 1990, p.17
10. Woods & Warren, p.36
11. Woods & Warren, p.64
12. Woods & Warren. pp.66–7
13. Stroud, D. *Capability Brown,* Faber & Faber, London, 1975, p.37
14. Stroud, p.38
15. (Royal Archive) RA/GEO 16834
16. Henrey, vol I, p.57
17. Henrey, vol II, p.88.
    Rodgers, J. *Vegetable Cultivator.* Longman, Orme, Brown, Green & Longmans, London, 1839, p.82
    Campbell, S. *Charleston Kedding, A History of Kitchen Gardening,* Ebury Press, London, 1996, pp.116 & 134
18. Henrey, vol II, pp.350–1
19. Solman, D. *Loddiges of Hackney.* The Hackney Society, London, 1995, p.22
20. Henrey, vol II, p.363
21. Henrey, vol II, p.369
22. *The Gardener's Magazine,* 1826, vol I, pp.24–5

CHAPTER 3

1. Briggs, A. *A Social History of England,* Book Club Associates, London, 1984, pp.235, 263 & 272–3
2. McIntosh, C. *Practical Gardener,* Thomas Kelly, London, 1828, p.vi
3. McIntosh, p.iv
4. *The Gardener's Magazine,* 1827, vol II, pp.109–110
5. Loudon on-line *Dictionary of National Biography* entry
6. Colquhoun, K. *A Thing in Disguise – The Visionary Life of Joseph Paxton,* Fourth Estate, London, 2003, p.19
7. Glenny on-line *Dictionary of National Biography* entry
8. *The Gardener's Magazine,* 1826, vol I, pp.8–9
9. McIntosh, p.iv
10. *The Gardener's Magazine,* 1827, vol II, p.109
11. *The Gardeners' Chronicle,* 10 April 1875, pp.465–6

12. *The Gardener's Magazine*, 1827, vol II, pp.109–110
13. *The Gardeners' Chronicle*, 7 January 1865, pp.7–8
14. *The Gardener*, 1881, p.225. Quoted from Morgan, J. & Richards, A. *A Paradise out of a Common Field*, Century, London, 1990, pp.206–07
15. *The Gardener's Magazine*, 1836, vol XII, pp.613–14
16. *The Gardeners' Chronicle*, 2 June 1860, p.504
17. *The Gardeners' Chronicle*, 9 June 1860, pp.526–7
18. *The Gardeners' Chronicle*, 21 July 1860, pp.672–3
19. *The Gardeners' Chronicle*, 30 June 1860, p.601
20. *The Gardeners' Chronicle*, 9 December 1865, p.1154
21. *The Gardeners' Chronicle*, 30 June 1860, p.601

CHAPTER 4

1. *Journal of Horticulture*, 1879, vol XXXVI, p.3. Quoted from Morgan, J. & Richards, A. *A Paradise out of a Common Field*, Century, London, 1990, pp.202
2. *The Gardener's Magazine*, 1842, vol XVIII, pp.445–6
3. *The Gardeners' Chronicle*, 10 October 1874, p.463
4. *The Gardeners' Chronicle*, 24 April 1875, p.528
5. *The Gardeners' Chronicle*, 7 November 1874, pp.582–4
6. *The Gardeners' Chronicle*, 22 May 1875, p.655
7. *Ibid.*
8. *The Gardeners' Chronicle*, 10 April 1875, pp.465–6
9. *The Gardeners' Chronicle*, 19 December 1874, p.783
10. *The Gardeners' Chronicle*, 22 May 1875, vol III, N° 73, pp.655–6
11. *The Gardener's Magazine*, 1830, vol VI, p.19
12. *The Gardener's Magazine*, 1832, vol VIII, pp.166–71
13. *The Gardener's Magazine*, 1830, vol VI, p.19
14. *The Gardeners' Chronicle*, 12 January 1850, pp.19–20
15. *The Gardeners' Chronicle*, 7 July 1860, p.625
    The Gardeners' Chronicle, 14 July 1860, p.648
16. *The Gardeners' Chronicle*, 20 February 1875, p.239
17. *The Gardener's Magazine*, 1827, vol II, p.627
18. *The Gardener's Magazine*, 1826, vol I, pp.141–2
19. *The Gardeners' Chronicle*, 10 April 1875, pp.465–6
20. *The Gardeners' Chronicle*, 12 September 1874, p.329
21. *The Gardener's Magazine*, 1826, vol I, pp.141–2
22. *The Gardener's Magazine*, 1826, vol I, p.411
23. *The Gardener's Magazine*, 1828, vol IV, pp.33–4
24. *The Gardeners' Chronicle*, 20 October 1860, p.934
25. *The Gardeners' Chronicle*, 30 December 1880, p.1228
26. *The Gardeners' Chronicle*, 10 April 1875, pp.465–6

27. *The Gardener's Magazine,* 1834, vol IX, p.171
28. *The Gardeners' Chronicle,* 7 November 1874, pp. 582–3
29. Quoted from Stuart, D. *The Garden Triumphant,* Harper & Row, Publishers, New York, 1988, p.225
30. *The Gardener's Magazine,* 1834, vol X, p.171
31. National Trust Oral Archive, Penrhyn Castle

CHAPTER 5

1. *The Gardeners' Chronicle,* 26 September 1874, p.399
2. *The Gardeners' Chronicle,* 20 February 1875, p.239
3. *The Gardeners' Chronicle,* 10 April 1875, pp.465–6
4. *The Gardeners' Chronicle,* 23 January 1875, p.117
5. *The Gardener's Magazine,* 1828, vol IV, pp.156–7
6. *The Gardeners' Chronicle,* 8 May 1875, p.601
7. *The Gardeners' Chronicle,* 11 August 1860, p.734
8. *The Gardener's Chronicle,* 28 July 1860, p.694
9. *The Gardeners' Chronicle,* 24 April 1875, p.528
10. *The Journal of Horticulture,* 1879, vol XXXVI, p.301
11. Colquhoun, K. *A Thing in Disguise – The Visionary Life of Joseph Paxton,* Fourth Estate, London, 2003, p.100
12. Elliott, B. *Victorian Garden,* B T Batsford, London, 1986, p.15
13. Musgrave, T. with Calnan, M. *Seven Deadly Sins of Gardening,* The National Trust, London, 2006, p.101
14. *The Gardener's Magazine,* 1842, vol XVII, pp.556 & 558
15. *The Gardener's Magazine,* 1842, vol XVIII, pp.560–2
16. *The Cottage Gardener and Country Gentleman,* 1858, vol XXI, p.68
17. *The Gardeners' Chronicle,* 27 May 1843, p.355
18. Morgan, J. & Richards, A. *A Paradise out of a Common Field,* Century, London, 1990, pp.209–10
19. *The Gardener's Magazine,* 1826, vol I, p.142
20. *The Gardener's Magazine,* vol I, pp.135–6
21. *The Gardener's Magazine,* 1833, vol IX, pp.551–4
22. *The Gardener's Magazine,* 1828, vol IV, p.32
    The Gardener's Magazine, 1826, vol I, p.142
    The Gardeners' Chronicle, 27 May 1843, p.355
    The Gardener's Chronicle, 10 May 1870, p.220
23. *The Gardener's Magazine,* 1826, vol I, p.9
24. *The Gardeners' Chronicle,* 11 September 1841, p.601
25. *The Gardeners' Chronicle,* 22 May 1875, p.655
26. *The Gardener's Magazine,* 1828, vol IV, p. 241
27. *The Gardeners' Chronicle,* 28 January 1885, p.284

28. *The Gardener's Magazine.* 1828, vol IV, p.33
29. *The Gardeners' Chronicle,* 17 March 1866, p.245
30. *The Gardeners' Chronicle,* 17 September 1910, p.216
    Elliott, p.14
    Morgan & Richards, p.221
31. *The Gardener's Magazine,* 1826, vol I, pp.141–4
32. *The Gardeners' Chronicle,* 23 January 1875, p.117
    The Gardeners' Chronicle, 21 May 1910, p.333
    Morgan & Richards, p.221
    Musgrave, p.30
33. www.perennial.org.uk
    www.londonancestor.com/charity/pensions/royal-gardeners.htm

CHAPTER 6

1. Elliott, B. *Victorian Garden,* B T Batsford, London, 1986, p.56
2. Bisgrove, R. *The National Trust Book of the English Garden,* Viking Books, London, 1990, p.180
3. *The Cottage Gardener and Country Gentlemen,* 10 November 1857, p.80
4. RA/VIC/Add Q 1446
5. *Journal of Horticulture and Cottage Gardener,* 1863, vol XXX, p.328
   The Florist, 1854, pp.100–01
6. *The Gardeners' Chronicle,* 21 July 1877, p.70
7. *The Gardeners' Chronicle,* 10 April 1875, p.466
8. National Trust Oral Archive, Penrhyn Castle
9. *The Florist,* 1854, p.100
10. Blacker, M. R. *Flora Domestica,* The National Trust, London, 2000, pp.176–8
    The Gardeners' Chronicle, 3 November 1888
11. *The Florist,* 1854, p.101
    The Gardeners' Chronicle, 10 April 1875, p.466
12. Sales, J. 'High Victorian Horticulture: the Garden at Waddesdon', *National Trust Studies,* 1979, pp.77–89
    Elliott. B. *Waddesdon Manor, The Garden,* National Trust Guide Book, 1994, p.25–6
    The Gardeners' Chronicle, 13 July 1889, p.39
13. *The Gardeners' Chronicle,* 17 March 1866, p.245
14. Morgan, J. & Richards, A. *A Paradise out of a Common Field,* Century, London, 1990, p.201
15. *The Florist,* 1854, p.2
16. *The Gardener's Magazine,* 1837, vol XIII, pp.50–5
17. Elliott, 1986, pp.12–13
    The Gardener's Chronicle, 1 January 1910, pp.10–11

18. *The Gardeners' Chronicle*, 26 September 1874, p.399
    The Gardeners' Chronicle, 7 November 1874, p.584
19. *The Gardeners' Chronicle*, 23 January 1875, p.117
    Elliott, pp.44, 51 & 87–9
20. Stuart, D. *The Garden Triumphant*, Harper & Row, Publishers, New York, 1988, pp.17–18 & 20–21
21. *The Gardeners' Magazine*, May 1875, p.655
    Stuart, p.120
22. Elliott, pp.90–92
23. *The Gardeners' Chronicle*, 13 March 1875, p.336
24. Elliott, pp.153–5
25. Colquhoun, pp.84 & 87–8
    Roberts, J. *Royal Landscape: The Gardens and Parks of Windsor*, Yale University Press, London, 1997, pp.241–4
26. Morgan & Richards, p.218
    The Gardeners' Chronicle, 12 September 1874, p.329
27. *The Gardeners' Chronicle*, 8 May 1875, p.601
28. Elliott, p.185
    Morgan & Richards, pp.52 & 222
29. *The Gardeners' Chronicle*, 22 May 1875, pp.655–6
    The Gardeners' Chronicle, 13 March 1875, p.336
30. *The Gardeners' Chronicle*, 10 April 1875, pp.465–6
    The Gardeners' Chronicle, 7 November 1874, pp.582–4
    The Gardeners' Chronicle, 20 February 1875, p.239
31. *The Gardeners' Chronicle*, 20 February 1875, p.239
    The Gardeners' Chronicle, 10 April 1875, pp.465–6
32. *The Gardeners' Chronicle*, 24 April 1875, vol III, n 69, p.528
33. *The Gardeners' Chronicle*, 13 March 1875, p.336
    The Gardeners' Chronicle, 8 May 1875, p.601
    The Gardeners' Chronicle, 20 February 1875, p.239
34. *The Gardeners' Chronicle*, 26 May 1866, pp.482–6
    The Gardeners' Chronicle, 2 June 1866, pp.512–13
35. *The Gardner's Magazine*, vol XIX, 1843 pp.45–6
36. *The Gardeners' Chronicle*, 5 June 1875, pp.718–19
37. *The Gardeners' Chronicle*, 27 March 1875, p.401
    The Gardeners' Chronicle, 10 October 1874, p.463
38. *The Gardeners' Chronicle*, 7 November 1874, p.584
    The Gardeners' Chronicle, 20 February 1875, p.239
39. *The Gardeners' Chronicle*, 3 May 1851, p.275
40. *The Gardeners' Chronicle*, 16 February 1850, p.100
41. *The Gardeners' Chronicle*, 9 February 1850, p.84

CHAPTER 7

1. *The Cottage Gardener and Country Gentleman's Companion,* 1857, vol XVIII, p.427
2. *The Gardener's Magazine,* 1835, vol XI, pp.385–91
   Colquhoun, K. *A Thing in Disguise – The Visionary Life of Joseph Paxton,* Fourth Estate, London, 2003, p.51
3. The Duchess of Devonshire, *Chatsworth Garden,* Derbyshire Countryside Ltd, Derby, 1996, p.22
   DNB on-line entry
   The Gardener's Magazine, 1839, vol XV, p.451
   The Gardener's Magazine, 1840, vol XVI, p.572
   The Gardeners' Chronicle, 2 January 1841, p.2
4. Anthony, J. *Joseph Paxton,* Shire Books Ltd, Princes Risborough, 1992, p.8
   Colquhoun, p.105
   The Gardeners' Chronicle, 4 March 1876, pp.300–1
5. Supplement to *The Gardeners' Chronicle,* 26 June 1875, p.4
   Colquhoun, pp.105–6
6. Quoted from The Duchess of Devonshire, p.48. 'A day at Chatsworth' by Mrs. S. C. Hall, *The Art-Journal,* 1851
7. Supplement to *The Gardeners' Chronicle,* pp.5–6
8. The Duchess of Devonshire, p.19
   Supplement to *The Gardeners' Chronicle,* p.3
9. The Duchess of Devonshire, p.19
   Elliott, pp.79–83
   Colquhoun, pp.99 & 111–12
   Supplement to *The Gardeners' Chronicle,* p.3
   Quoted from The Duchess of Devonshire, p.48. 'A day at Chatsworth' by Mrs. S. C. Hall, *The Art-Journal,* 1851
   Supplement to *The Gardeners' Chronicle,* p.3
10. Colquhoun, p.51 & pp.124–6
11. Supplement to *The Gardeners' Chronicle,* p.6
    The Duchess of Devonshire, p.35
    Colquhoun, pp.130–1
12. Supplement to *The Gardeners' Chronicle,* p.7
    The Duchess of Devonshire, p.47
    The Gardener's Magazine, 1839, vol XV, p.452
    The Gardeners' Chronicle, 26 June 1875, pp.816–17
    Colquhoun, p.74
    www.users.globalnet.co.uk/~drc/mcavendishii.htm
13. *The Gardener's Magazine,* 1831, vol VII, pp.396–7
    The Gardener's Magazine, 1840, vol XVI, p.578
    The Gardener's Magazine, 1839, vol XV, p.452
    The Cottage Gardener and Country Gentleman's Companion, 1857, vol 18, p.25
    Colquhoun, p.56

14. Colquhoun, p.62
    Supplement to *The Gardeners' Chronicle*, p.7
    The Cottage Gardener and Country Gentleman's Companion, 1857, vol 18, p.25
    Supplement to *The Gardeners' Chronicle*,. pp.2–3
15. Coats, A.M. *The Quest for Plants*, Studio Vista, London, 1969, pp.154–5
    Colquhoun, pp.62–65, 68–70, 74, 77–8
16. Supplement to *The Gardeners' Chronicle*, p.7
    Colquhoun, p.79
17. *The Gardener's Magazine*, 1840, vol XVI, p.572
    Colquhoun, p.56
18. Colquhoun, pp.84–5, 99
19. *The Gardener's Magazine*, 1840, vol XVI, p.572
    www.victoria-adventure.org/victoria/mike/gardeners_chronicle_pm.html
    The Gardeners' Chronicle, 2 February 1850, p.70
    The Cottage Gardener and Country Gentleman's Companion, 1857, vol18, p.6
    Colquhoun, p.156
20. http://en.wikipedia.org/wiki/The_Gardeners'_Chronicle
    online Dictionary of National Biography entry
    Elliott, p.53
    Colquhoun, pp.160 & 203–4
    www.worldwideschool.org/library/books/lit/charlesdickens/SpeechesLiteraryand
    Social/chap55.html

CHAPTER 8

1. *The Florist*, 1857, vol X, p.144
2. *The Gardeners' Chronicle*, 24 November 1874, p.655
3. www.ideal-homes.org.uk/lambeth/norwood/norwood-from-common-
   to-suburb.htm
4. *The Gardeners' Chronicle*, 24 November 1874, p.655
5. *The Gardener's Magazine*, 1842, vol XVIII, pp.554–5
   The Cottage Gardener and Country Gentleman, 1858, vol XXI, p.68
6. *Journal of Horticulture and Cottage Gardener*, 1871, pp.202 & 221
7. *The Gardener's Magazine*, 1843, vol XIX, pp.24–5, 30
8. *Ibid*, pp.20–1
9. *The Gardener's Magazine*, 1842, vol XVIII, pp. 563–4 & 618–19
10. *The Gardener's Magazine*, 1842, vol XVIII, p.555
11. *Ibid*, pp.617–21
    The Gardener's Magazine,1843, vol XIX, p.304
    Ibid, pp. 547 & 607
12. *Ibid*, pp.30–33
    The Florist, 1857, vol X, p.146

13. Woods, M. & Warren, A. *Glasshouses*. Aurum Press, London, 1990, p.112
     The Gardener's Magazine, 1843, vol XIX, p.607
     The Gardener's Magazine,1842, vol XVIII, pp.564–5
14. *The Gardener's Magazine*,1843, vol XIX, pp.47–9
     The Cottage Gardener and Country Gentleman, 1858, vol XXI, p.67
     The Gardener's Magazine, 1843, vol XIX, pp.47–9
     The Florist, 1857, p.144
15. *The Cottage Gardener and Country Gentleman*, 1858, vol XXI, p.67
     The Gardener's Magazine, 1843, vol XIX, pp.111–12
     The Gardener's Magazine, 1843, vol XIX, p.138
16. *The Gardener's Magazine*, 1842, vol XVIII, p.552
     The Gardener's Magazine, 1843, vol XIX, p.113
17. *The Gardener's Magazine*, 1842, vol XVIII, p.553–4
     The Cottage Gardener and Country Gentleman, 1858, vol XXI, p.51
     Journal of Horticulture and Cottage Gardener, 1871, p.202
     The Florist, 1857, vol X, p.145
18. *The Gardener's Magazine*, 1843, vol XIX, p.607
     The Gardener's Magazine, 1843, vol XIX, pp.138–9
19. *The Gardener's Magazine*, 1843, vol XIX, pp.26–8
     The Gardener's Magazine, 1842, vol XVIII, pp.563–4
     The Gardener's Magazine, 1843, vol XIX, pp.33–4
     The Gardener's Magazine, 1843, vol XIX, p.28
20. *The Cottage Gardener and Country Gentleman*, 1858, vol XXI, p.68
21. Bodleian Library (Oxford) MS Eng. Hist. C.11
22. *The Gardener's Magazine*, 1843, vol XIX, pp.26–8
     The Gardener's Magazine, 1843, vol XIX, p.607
23. *The Florist*, 1857, vol X, pp.146–7
24. *The Gardener's Magazine*, 1843, vol XIX, p.27
     The Gardener's Magazine, 1843, vol XIX, p.607
     The Florist, 1857, vol X, p.173
     The Cottage Gardener and Country Gentleman, 1858, vol XXI, p.68
25. *The Gardener's Magazine*, 1843, vol XIX, pp.29, 49–51
     Ibid, p.302
26. *The Florist*, 1857, vol X, p.174
     The Gardener's Magazine, 1843, vol XIX, p.434
27. *The Florist*, 1857, vol X, pp.173–4
     The Cottage Gardener and Country Gentleman, 1858, vol XXI, p.67
28. *The Gardener's Magazine*, 1843, vol XIX, pp.428–9
     The Cottage Gardener and Country Gentleman, 1858, vol XXI, p.68
29. *The Gardener's Magazine*, 1843, vol XIX, pp.138–9
     The Gardener's Magazine, 1843, vol XIX, p.427
     The Cottage Gardener and Country Gentleman, 1858, vol XXI. p.67
30. *The Gardener's Magazine*, p.427
31. *The Gardener's Magazine*, pp.46–7

32. *The Gardener's Magazine*, p.496
33. *The Gardener's Magazine*, p.546–7

EPILOGUE

1. Girouard, M. *Life in the English Country House*, Yale University Press, London, 1979, pp.300–1
2. Aslet, C. *The Last Country Houses*, Yale University Press, London, 1982, pp.309–32
3. Bisgrove, R. *The National Trust Book of the English Garden,* Viking Books, London, 1990, p.224
4. *Garden Life,* vol XI, 9 March 1907, pp.379–80
5. Stevenson, J. *British Society 1914–45,* Penguin Books, London, 1990, pp.104–05, 322, 333 & 335
    Taylor, A. J. P. *English History 1914–1945*, Pelican Books, London, 1970, pp.229 & 231
6. *Gardening Illustrated,* vol 44, 28 October 1922, p.723
    Quoted from Duchess of Devonshire, 1996, p.49
7. Brown, J. *Gardens of a Golden Afternoon,* Penguin Books, London, 1988, pp.173–6

APPENDIX A

1. *The Gardener's Magazine*, 1843, pp.429–30
2. *Ibid,* pp.543–4
3. *Ibid,* pp.540–1, 543
4. *Ibid,* pp.544–6
5. *Ibid,* pp.433–4
6. *Ibid,* pp.431–2
7. Henrey, vol II, pp.487–8
8. *The Gardener's Magazine*, 1843, vol XIX, pp.653–7
    The Cottage Gardener and Country Gentleman, 1858, vol XXI, p.68
9. *The Gardener's Magazine*, 1843, vol XIX, pp.234–7
10. *Ibid,* pp.544–6
11. *The Gardener's Magazine*, 1843, pp.543–4
12. *Ibid,* pp.419 & 422
13. *Ibid,* p.430

INDEX

Abbey Park, 150

Abercrombie, John, 3, 48–9

Aiton, William, 33

American Garden, Bicton, 199

'apprentice fees', 78–81

apprentices, 69–75, 78–81

arboretums, 158, 200

Arts and Crafts, 216

Ashmolean Museum, 13

asparagus, 220

Baillie, William, 125

Baines, Thomas, 145–6

Bakewell, Robert, 23

Banks, Sir Joseph, 33

Barbrook, 100

Barnes, James, 184–215; American Garden, 199; arboretum, 200; arrives at Bicton, 98; background, 184; Bicton, life at, 187–90; early days of 187–90; on exhibiting, 144; Flower Garden, 197–8; glasshouses, 192–3; kitchen garden, 201; market gardening, 185–7; New Holland House, 193; orchids, 196; organised methods of, 97–8; Palm House, 197; pest control, 207–8; pineapples, 203–6; pinetum, 200; potting shed, 202–3; publications, 190–1; tools, 211–14; vegetables, 220–30

Barron, William, xiv, 147–9

Barry, Sir Charles, 109, 111, 130

Bateman, James, 173–4

beans, 220–1

Beaton, Donald, 83, 123, 128–9, 130

Bective, Earl of, 114

Beddington Park, 9, 34

bell jars, 42

Belvoir Castle, 77, 218

Bicton, 184–215; American Garden, 199; arboretum, 200, Barnes arrives, 98; Flower Garden, 197–8; glasshouses, 192–3; kitchen garden, 201; New Holland House, 193; orchids, 196; Palm House, 197; pinetum, 200

Birkenhead Park, 181

Blomfield, Sir Reginald, 216

Botanic Garden, Oxford, 13

Botanical Magazine, The (William Curtis), 56

bothies, 71, 84–6

Bowood House, 104, 111

Bretby, 15, 27

Bridgeman, Charles, 25

British Winter Garden, The (William Barron), 148

Brompton Park Nursery, 18, 20

Brown, Lancelot 'Capability', xii, 20, 24, 37–41, 99

Burton, Decimus, 159

Busch, Johann, 47

cabbage, 221

Caie, John, 125–6, 128

Carême, Antonin, 25

Carew, Sir Frances, 9, 34

carrots, 222

Cato the Elder, 4

cauliflowers, 222

Cavendish, Georgiana, 154

Cavendish, William George Spencer, sixth Duke of Devonshire, 154–60, 163–9, 172–5; death, 93, 182; salary paid to Paxton, 103, 152

Cecil, Sir Robert, 12–13

celery, 223

Chance, Lucas, 146

charcoal, 194–5

Chatsworth, 151–83; arboretum, 158; Barbrook, 100; Emperor Fountain, 167–8; Gibson at, 133; glasshouses, 170–1; Great Conservatory, 167, 218; Great Stove, 158–62, 166, 180; harmony of, xiv, 111; kitchen garden, 168–70; orchid houses, 172–3; ornamental gardens, 154–6; Paxton leaves, 93; Paxton's house at, 100; Paxton's salary, 103, 152; pinetum, 156–7; rockeries, 163–7; Speed appointed, 120; Victoria House, 179–80; Wellington Rock, 165

Chaucer, Geoffrey, 6

Chelsea Physic Garden, 30, 33, 36, 92, 192

Cliveden, 109, 112, 116, 131, 133

cloches, 42

Cobham, Lord, 37–9

Company of Gardeners, xi

Compton, Henry, Bishop of London, 17, 19
conservatories, 114–19
Cook, Thomas, 166
crafte of graftynge & plantynge of trees, The (anon), 1
Cruickshank, James, 214
Crystal Palace, 151, 181, 182, 216
Cubitt, Thomas, 90
cucumbers, 185–6, 224–6
Curtis, William, 56

Darwin, Charles, 161
de Caus, Salomon, 11
de La Quintinie, Jean-Baptiste, 20, 27
de Serres, Olivier, 35
Devonshire, Duke of *see* Cavendish, William George Spencer, sixth
Duke of Devonshire
Dickens, Charles, 182
diseases, 207–8
Dodds, James, 74–5
Douglas, David, 74, 156–7, 175

Edmund the Gardener, xi, 7
education, 57–68
Elements of Agricultural Chemistry (Sir Humphry Davy), 139
Emperor Fountain, Chatsworth, 167–8
Enclosure Acts, 23
Encyclopædia of Gardening (John Claudius Loudon), 47, 56, 59, 108
Evelyn, John, 7, 15, 21, 35, 42, 43
Every Man his own Gardener (John Abercrombie), 48
examinations, 63

fees for apprentices, 78–80
fertilisers, 139
finances, 99
Fish, David Taylor, 74–5, 77–8, 103
Fish, Robert, 74, 77, 98, 111, 120, 122, 189
Five hundred pointes of good husbandrie (Thomas Tusser), 5
Fleming, John: bedding innovations, xiv, 129–31, 133–4; Cliveden, 112; house designed by, 100; publication by, 124; Trentham, 122, 147; William Miller and, 90–1
Flower Garden, Bicton, 197–8
Fortune, Robert, 191

Foster, Thomas, 134, 141
Fowler, Archibald, 74, 78–9, 84, 90, 124, 141, 147
frames, 42
Frogmore, 100, 112, 135–7, 219
Frost, Philip, 92, 106, 125
fruit, 6, 8, 37, 87–9, 208–10

Garden, The, 122
Gardeners' Benevolent Institution, The, 106
Gardeners' Chronicle, The (Joseph Paxton), 90, 181
gardener's dictionary, The (Philip Miller), 6
Gardener's Gazette (George Glenny), 56–7
gardeners labyrinth, The (Thomas Hill), 1, 2, 4, 41
Gardener's Magazine, The (John Claudius Loudon), 56, 57, 120, 181, 191
Gardenesque, 108
Gibson, John, xiv, 73, 132–3, 173–5
glasshouses, 56, 116–19, 170–1, 192–3, 206–7
    see also greenhouses
glazing bars, 56
Glenny, George, 56–7, 106
Gordon, James, xii, 45–6
Gordon Castle, 95
Grand Tour, 22
Great Conservatory, Chatsworth, 167, 218
Great Exhibition, 151, 182, 183
Great Stove, Chatsworth, 158–62, 166, 180
Grecian Valley, 38
greenhouses, 34–7, 86, 87–8 *see also* glasshouses

Hampton Court Palace, 9, 14, 17, 20
Hatfield House, 12
Harvey, John, 5
Henry VIII, 7–9
herbs, 7, 29 *see also* vegetables
Hill, Thomas, 1, 2, 4, 41
History of English Gardening (George W Johnson), 108
Hooker, Sir Joseph, 59
Hooker, Sir William, 74, 178
Horticultural Directory, The, 53
Horticultural Register and General Magazine (Joseph Paxton), 180
Horticultural Shows, 141–2
Hortus Kewensis (William Aiton), 33
Hospital of St Mary of Roncesvalles, 5
hotbeds, 6–7, 41, 43
hothouses, 36–7

How to Layout a Garden (Edward Kemp), xiv
Hudson, Henry, 94, 96–7
hybridisation, xiv, 134

Ibn Bassal, 5
Ichnographia Rustica (Stephen Switzer), 25
Improvement Societies, 61–2
Ingram, Thomas, 100, 135, 136
Ingram, William, 77, 131–2, 140, 142
International Horticultural Exhibition, 143
Italianate style, 109–10

James I, 10–11
Jekyll, Gertrude, 53, 216–17, 219
Johnson, George W, 108
Johnston, George, xiv, 80, 142
journeymen, 58, 75–8, 81–2

Keane, William, 61
Kemp, Edward, xiv, 181
Kennedy, Lewis, 44–5
Kent, William, 25, 38
Kew Gardens, 33, 159, 178
kitchen gardens, 3, 25–9, 37, 69, 111–14, 168–70,
   201

Langdon, Philip, 100
Lawes, Sir John Bennett, 139
Le Nôtre, André, 14, 16, 110, 197
Lee, James, 44–5
Leighton, James, 104
Linager, 63–4
Lindley Medal, 146
Linnæus, 30, 46, 72
Linton Park, 99
Loddiges, Joachim Conrad, 46–7, 48
London and Wise, 18–21, 24, 25, 27, 29
Longleat, 95
Loraine, Sir William, 38
Lord Emsworth and Others (P G Wodehouse), 96
Loudon, John Claudius, 54–61; on Bicton, 200;
   at Chatsworth, 155,
169; Gardenesque, 108; *Encyclopædia*, 108;
   Gardener's Magazine, The, 120, 181; on
   Loddiges, 47; on wages, 82
Lovell, John, 8
Lupus, Hugh, first Duke of Westminster, 112
Lutyens, Edwin, 216–17, 219

MacPhail, James, 43
Marot, Daniel, 20
Mawe, Thomas, 48–9
McIntosh, Charles, 53, 54, 57–9, 110, 123
Mediæval Gardens (John Harvey), 5
Miller, Philip, xii, 6, 30–3, 36, 42
Miller, William, 59, 82, 90–1, 141, 142
Mollet, André, 14, 15, 110
Molyneux, Edwin, xiv
mushrooms, 226–8

Nesfield, William Andrews, 110
New Holland House, Bicton, 193
Normans, xi
nurserymen, 44–7, 75

onions, 229–30
orangeries, 34
orchids, 119, 172–3, 196
Owen, Thomas, 112

Palm House, Bicton, 197
Palm House, Kew Gardens, 159
Parkinson, John, 42
Parsons, Anthony, 93, 138, 142
parterres de broderie, 14, 15, 20
Paxton, Joseph, 151–83; arboretum, 158;
   background and character, 151–4; Barbrook,
   100; builds house at Chatsworth, 100;
   Crystal Palace, 216; Emperor Fountain,
   167–8; garden design, 181; Gibson
   apprenticed to, 133; glasshouses, 170–1;
   Great Conservatory, 167, 218; Great
   Exhibition, 182–3; Great Stove, 158–62,
   166; harmony created by, xiv; kitchen
   garden, 168–70; leaves Chatsworth, 93;
   orchid houses, 172–3; ornamental gardens,
   154–6; pinetum, 156–7; publications, 180–1;
   remembered, xii; in retirement, 104;
   rockeries, 163–7; salary, 103, 152; Victoria
   House, 179–80; Wellington Rock, 165
peas, 228–9
Penrhyn Castle, 85
pensions, 106
Perennial, 106
periodicals, 120, 122
pests, 207–8
pineapples, 203–6

pinetums, 156–7, 200
Pipe Rolls, xi
pits, 42–4
plant breeding, 134–8
plant nutrition, 139–40
pleasure grounds, 111
Plukenet, Dr Leonard, 17
potatoes, 229
potting, 194
potting sheds, 202–3
Practical Gardener and Modern Horticulturalist,
    The (Charles McIntosh), 53
productive gardens, 3, 25–9 *see also* kitchen
    gardens
profitable arte of gardening, The (Thomas Hill), 1
publications, 123–4, 180–1, 190–1
publishing, 48–50

Repton, Humphry, 107, 164
Roaldus of Preston, 94, 95
Robinson, William, 216
Robson, John, 99, 104, 106
rockeries, 163–7
Rolle, Lady, 188–9
Romans, xi
Rose, John, 15–16, 18
Royal Horticultural Society, 62, 65, 110, 145
Rutland, Duke of, 218

Sander, Frederick, 119
Scotland, 74
Self-instruction for young gardeners (John
    Claudius Loudon), 60
Shrubland Park, 109, 123, 128, 130
Sloane, Sir Hans, 12, 30
soil science, 140
South Lambeth garden, 13
Speed, Thomas, 77, 120
Spencer, John, 104
Spring and Winter Gardening (John Fleming),
    131
spring bedding, 131–2
Stevens, Zadok, 104
Stevenson, Henry, 27, 28, 48
Stowe, 37–41, 99
Strozzi, Filippo, 5
subtropical bedding, 132–3
Swanley Horticultural College, 8

Switzer Stephen, 19, 24–5
syllabuses, 64

tanners' bark, 43–4
taxonomies, 5
Taylor, William, 95, 97, 124
terraces, 107
Theobalds, 12
Thomas, Norman, 85
Tillery, William, 72–3
tools, 81–2, 211–14
Tradescant, John the Elder, 3, 12–13, 102
Tradescant, John the Younger, 13
trainees, *see apprentices*
Trentham: Barry designs, 109, 111; conservatory,
    116; Fleming at, 122, 147; Fleming's house
    at, 100; glasshouses, 117; innovations at,
    130; kitchen garden, 112; paths at, 147;
    William Miller at, 91;
Tuileries, 16
Turnbull, Andrew, 76–7, 82, 83, 90, 137
Tusser, Thomas, 5

Underley Hall, 114

Vaux-le-Vicomte, 14
vegetables, 5, 7, 28–9, 42, 220–30
Versailles, 14, 34, 124
Victoria, Princess, 167
Victoria House, Chatsworth, 179–80
Villa d'Este, 9
Vineyard Nursery, 45

wages, 81–3, 86, 102–5
Webster, John, 73, 95, 142
Welbeck Abbey, 73, 164
Wellington Rock, Chatsworth, 165
Williams, Benjamin S, 124
Wills, John, xiv, 138
winter gardens, 114–16
Wodehouse, P G, 96
Wolf, John, 8–9
Worshipful Company of Gardeners of London,
    The, 10
Worshipful Society of Apothecaries of London, 30

Young Gardener's Educator, The (William Keane),
    61